# LANDSCAPING

# EN ARS

Cover and text design by Nancy Freeborn
Illustrations by Mary Ballachino

**Library of Congress Cataloging-in-Publication Data**

Foster, Ruth S.
  Landscaping that saves energy and dollars / by Ruth S. Foster. — Rev. ed.
     p. cm.
  Includes bibliographical references and index.
  ISBN 1-56440-358-0
  1. Landscape architecture and energy conservation. 2. Landscape gardening. I. Title.
SB475.9.E53F67 1994
712'.2—dc20                              93-40916
                                          CIP

Manufactured in the United States of America
First Globe Pequot Edition/First Printing

# Contents

## Chapter 14 *Buying New Plants and Trees 162*

## Chapter 15 *Priorities, What to Buy First 174*

## PART III  PLANT LISTS FOR SPECIAL PURPOSES  183

## Trees

## Shrubs

## Ground Covers

## Plants for Special Situations

# Introduction

**P**eople create gardens for beauty and enjoyment, to enhance our lives. Thoughtful planning and careful design give form and practicality to these landscapes and enable us to save energy and money in our private gardens as well as in the city parks and preserves that serve as our public ones. There are many ways.

*Designing for energy efficiency* produces the greatest savings. The techniques are not difficult to understand, but they may seem difficult at first because so many factors are involved in each decision. Each section of the country has a different climate, each with its own particular environmental conditions. Because of these variations, each has to use different techniques for saving energy. Saving energy translates into saving money. An added benefit is that energy-efficient designs make spaces more pleasant and comfortable.

*Using water wisely* can save money. With water rates along with their codependent sewer rates ever increasing, simple steps can make a difference.

*Choosing the correct plants* for each location is very important. It can lower initial purchasing expense, as well as long-term costs. Over time, because the right plant in the right place needs much less maintenance and lives longer, the savings multiply. Correctly planted landscapes thrive and grow old gracefully and increase in beauty. As inappropriate plants age, however, they become unattractive maintenance burdens. Extensive lists for correct plant use are included in the last section, part III.

*Functional and aesthetic planning and design* go along with choosing correct plants. A well-thought-out landscape that is practical and functional and has good basic form, will serve well, while a haphazard unfolding of disparate items will require constant and costly tinkering. Developing a sense of design is not difficult, it just takes a particular way of looking at things.

*Maintenance* costs can be lowered by understanding the needs of each plant and developing sensible maintenance practices. As tasks are managed more scientifically, not only are actual dollars saved, but human energy as well. Correct tools and techniques save time and prevent a sore back.

*Fertilizers and chemicals* are another area where expenses can be lowered by sensible maintenance. Savings can result from using less, using the right products for the right reasons, and using them at the right time.

*Saving soil* is an area often overlooked. Even if there is no monetary reward, over the long run healthy soil amply rewards those who can be patient with nature's slow pace.

*Quality of life* also needs to be saved. The air we breathe, the livability of our cities, the purity of our water, our forests, this very earth. We need to enhance its beauty and our enjoyment of it. Good landscaping, most particularly the use of trees, improves all these aspects of our quality of life.

# LANDSCAPING THAT SAVES ENERGY

If one plans and plants to save energy (such as electricity, gas, and oil), savings can be significant. These are some examples of the energy and money you can save.

## Use trees to save 10 percent to 50 percent on air-conditioning costs

- One large tree has the same cooling effect as fifteen room-size air conditioners.
- Just three trees can reduce air-conditioning costs for a single house by 10 to 50 percent.
- Shading the air conditioner can increase its efficiency by 10 percent.

## Save on heating and cooling costs

- Heating and cooling consumes 11 percent of all U.S. energy use.
- In U.S. cities, if every two homes had three trees (100 million trees total), thirty billion kilowatt hours per year and $2 billion could be saved.
- In Lake Charles, Louisiana, just three mature, properly placed trees could save 23 percent of the electricity for air conditioning, about $150 per year.
- In Madison, Wisconsin, an energy-efficient planting design could reduce a single home heating-and-cooling bill by 13 percent, or about $100 per year.

## Urban areas with trees are cooler and more comfortable

- Because of the "heat island effect," cities are 10 degrees warmer than the country.
- Areas with mature tree canopies are 3 to 6 degrees cooler than newer areas with no trees.

## Windbreaks

- A proper windbreak can reduce wind velocity by 85 percent.
- Windbreaks can reduce winter heating costs 10 percent to 25 percent.

## Surface colors

- In sunshine, light-colored surfaces average 15 degrees cooler than dark-colored ones.
- Trees and light-colored surfaces can lower home air-conditioning bills by $200.
- In a test conducted in Oak Ridge, Tennessee, dark-colored roofs reached 160 degrees on summer days, white flat-paint roofs were 135 degrees, and white glossy-paint roofs only reached 120 degrees.

## Air quality

- One mature tree gives off enough oxygen for a family of four.
- Trees are pollution sponges. They remove many pollutants from the air, including ozone, carbon monoxide, and sulphur dioxide.
- One mature tree can clean up the pollution created by a car driven 11,000 miles.
- One mature tree absorbs twenty-six pounds of carbon dioxide from the air each year. One acre of trees removes five tons of carbon dioxide from the air each year.
- Trees in cities absorb and tie up 800 million tons of carbon dioxide; forests even more. Tree planting is a cost-effective way to slow carbon dioxide buildup and global warming.
- A mature tree can intercept fifty pounds of particulate ash (dusty soot). In Tucson, for example, planting 500,000 trees could reduce this ash by 6,500 tons a year.
- In Los Angeles, pine trees remove about 8 percent of the ozone from the air and decrease the concentration of ozone around their leaves by 49 percent.

## Noise

- A shelter belt of trees and shrubs can reduce noise by 50 percent.

## Water

- On a hot, sunny day, a tree-shaded lawn uses up to 95 percent less water than one in full sun. The combined water requirement of a tree plus shaded lawn is less than the lawn alone.
- Xeriscaping is landscaping that uses drought-resistant plants and less lawn area. It uses 50 percent less water than traditional landscaping.
- In Dayton, Ohio, the tree canopy reduced potential water runoff by 7 percent. Just a modest increase in trees could reduce runoff by 12 percent.

## Property values

- Property values are 5 to 20 percent higher when a house has trees around it. Value is highest in tree-shaded communities.

*Gardening techniques and maintenance*

- Massachusetts apple growers have reduced their pesticide use by 50 percent by using Integrated Pest Management programs.

- New understanding of natural cycles, new biological insecticides, and concern about the safety of our environment have resulted in growers using fewer chemicals, particularly toxic chemicals. This saves not only money but, more important, our own health.

This book is about how to effect these savings and why the various techniques work. It *is* possible to design beautiful, satisfying gardens that conserve this earth and save energy, soil, water, money, and time. In today's busy world, we all need more time to smell the roses.

FIGURE 1: **A GARDEN IS A PLACE TO SMELL THE ROSES**

# Part I

# THE
# THEORY

# CHAPTER 1

# Energy, Climate, and Human Comfort

Sometimes it seems that environmentalists want us all to freeze in the dark, while oil producers would prefer to suspend us, coughing, in air-conditioned skyscrapers above polluted cities. Somewhere between the two is a rational compromise where we all can live

Ever since the first caveman moved indoors and lit a fire in the darkness, man has used his ingenuity and whatever was at hand to make himself more comfortable. The land around us provides many opportunities for energy saving. If we understand how our environment functions, then we can change it to suit our needs. To change our surroundings in an aesthetically pleasing way is called landscaping, the art of sculpting the land and what grows on it to serve us.

This does not mean ruining the planet but, instead, using it thoughtfully and healing it from previous devastation.

Man has long raped the land, unmindful of the consequences. What was once the biblical land of milk and honey is now the desert of the Middle East. The people have yet to restore the sod where shepherds overgrazed, causing most of the vegetation to disappear. Today, that desert absorbs sunlight during the day and becomes unbearably hot; then, because it has no green canopy to protect it from the black night sky, it becomes cold and windy. Good healing plants can't get a foothold.

The deserts, however, can be made to bloom again. The most successful reclamation projects are in Israel. As the trees and forests become reestablished, the nearby houses become pleasant places during the day and cozy at night. A house in the woods is more comfortable than one on the romantic, but uncomfortable, desert sands.

Centuries ago in the southwest United States, Indians made use of their desert land for climate control. Their pueblos were built under cliff overhangs, which protected the dwellings from the high sun in summer, yet admitted the lower winter sun. Built into the hillsides, these houses had thick walls with small openings, which conserved heat at night and preserved coolness during the day. In parts of the Sahara and Turkey, people still live in houses built into cliffs and caves to escape the uncomfortable climate extremes outside. So do modern Australian opal miners.

FIGURE 2: **MONTEZUMA'S CASTLE**

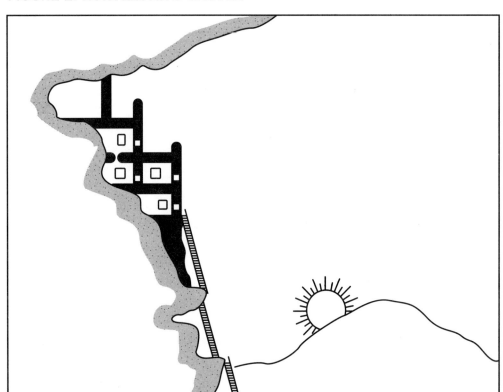

*A pueblo cliff dwelling in Arizona*

You may not have a cliff or a cave on your lot, but the same principles still apply.

In cold New England, the early settlers learned how to use the sun. For them, a window facing the south meant less time chopping wood. The barns and outbuildings were usually to the north side of the house, against the wind, while the orchards were on sheltered hillsides, protected from wind and cold.

In New England, trees and shrubs were not used near the house because Indian attackers could hide behind them. They would, though, have provided additional winter wind protection. Settlers on the prairies did use trees and shrubs for windbreaks, which provided protection from the cold winds that sweep across the flat landscape. These windbreaks are still a necessary, significant feature of the midwestern plains.

# CLIMATE

Landscaping to save energy dollars involves changing the climate around a building in order to reduce the cost of cooling, heating, and irrigating. Climate is shaped by many factors, including sun, wind, temperature, humidity, solar radiation, evaporation, precipitation, and thermal differentials. These factors are then influenced by land and bodies of water, ocean temperature, wind direction, mountains, cities, cloud patterns, atmospheric dust, snow, thunderstorm frequency, gravity, air pressure, and global temperature trends.

Climate is a geographic term. Some regional climates affect large areas, such as the Southwest or the Great Plains. Such regional climates, however, are modified by different local conditions, so that in reality, any particular climate is local. The old Maine farmer may be part of the northeast region, but he knows it's always colder in Maine.

Some local climates may affect only a single town, a particular valley, or an individual mountain. The climate on one side of a mountain or valley can be quite different from that on the other, depending on the sun exposure and the wind direction. In the Rocky Mountains, the aspens and juniper grow on the warmer, sunny, south-facing slopes where spring comes early, while the north-facing forests, shrouded with fir trees, are still snow covered and dank.

Smaller still are microclimates, so limited that they affect only one street, one side of a lake, or even one side of a building. The lot on which your house is built (or will be built) has its own microclimate. By adjusting that small place, you can significantly reduce your energy costs. The more urban buildings your area has, the more the regional climate is modified. Also, the more buildings there are, the more different microclimates there will be. A group of microclimates is sometimes called a microenvironment.

The sensation of comfort (warmth in winter, coolness in summer) depends on the interaction of all climatic factors. A careful analysis of the local climatic elements identifies those you can use or control. Start by asking some questions. What are the most unpleasant aspects of your particular microclimate? What are the most troublesome? What features are most comfortable? The ultimate aim of climate control is to improve human comfort.

To create a sense of comfort indoors, we use energy in furnaces, air conditioners, dehumidifiers, and fans. Cutting down your use of these mechanical appliances saves energy—and dollars. It can be done to a surprising extent through thoughtful landscaping.

The most useful landscape elements used for controlling climate are trees, which shade, cool, and shelter. Once trees are growing, they cost much less than the electricity or fuel oil they save. And the savings can be significant. One mature tree, for instance, provides as much cooling as fifteen room-size air conditioners. Consider Richmond, Virginia: A survey found that without its 200,000 public shade trees, the city would spend more than a million dollars a day for equivalent air conditioning.

# MICROCLIMATES

Microclimates (or microenvironments) are small areas in which conditions and temperatures vary one from the other. One microclimate, such as a sunny, paved corner between two buildings, may be hot. Another, downwind from a small lake, may be breezy and cool, even while the lake's upwind side will feel hotter and be drier.

The microclimate under a grove of trees is quite different from that along a paved city street. A blacktop street will feel up to 25 degrees warmer and may actually measure up to 15 degrees warmer. In summer that heat calls for more air conditioning in adjacent houses. In winter, however, warm paved streets can help save heating costs by absorbing sunshine and heating up. A windy mountain canyon presents yet a different set of characteristics. An ocean-front house would have others.

Each microclimate around a house requires a certain amount of energy to make the house and yard comfortable. Chances are that your house's microclimate uses excess energy and costs

FIGURE 3: **THE ELEMENTS THAT MAKE YOUR MICROCLIMATE**

| | |
|---|---|
| *Temperature* | winter and summer<br>duration of hot and cold weather |
| *Sun* | direction in winter and summer<br>height in summer and winter<br>angle of sunset and sunrise in winter and summer |
| *Wind* | direction of prevailing wind in winter and summer<br>direction of frequent storm winds<br>direction of hurricane winds |
| *Frequency of storms* | types, winter and summer |
| *Rainfall* | amount in winter and summer<br>direction of water runoff<br>location of wet and dry spots |
| *Snowfall* | amount in winter<br>direction of snow drifts |
| *Humidity* | winter and summer |
| *Radiation of heat from ground to sky* | at night from buildings, water and land |
| *Absorption of heat from sky to ground* | during day by buildings, water, and land |
| *Topographical features* | mountains, lakes, valleys, plains, woods |
| *Site* | rolling, sloping, level, dry, wet |
| *Ground surfaces* | concrete, blacktop, grass, other |
| *Building surfaces* | stone, brick, concrete, wood, aluminum, other |
| *Roof* | color, slope |

you more money than it should. Before planting, determine the energy potentials of your microclimate and then analyze your area for maintenance, aesthetics, and horticultural requirements. In cold climates, for instance, a hot paved corner will warm the side of the building adjacent and extend the comfortable outdoor season. In hot climates, winds in a canyon can be channeled to cool in summer. Each location, with its particular microclimate, has certain plants that will grow and thrive. For example, the planting of cactus in Maine or azaleas on the exposed North Dakota plains requires horticultural gymnastics for survival. Matching plant material and microenvironments is more sensible. The best cost-benefit ratios, growth rates, and lowest maintenance always accompany plants that are genetically adapted to their microenvironments.

# THE HUMAN COMFORT FACTOR

If energy—from sunlight, for instance—strikes a person or a building, the surface molecules in that object move around faster, causing a sensation of warmth. If energy moves away from the body by evaporation or contact with cold air, for example, there is a decrease of molecular movement, and a sensation of cold is experienced.

Human comfort is not determined only by air temperature. Humidity, evaporation, and wind chill are also involved in the sensation of a pleasant climate. When it's both hot and

FIGURE 4A: **HUMAN COMFORT ZONE**

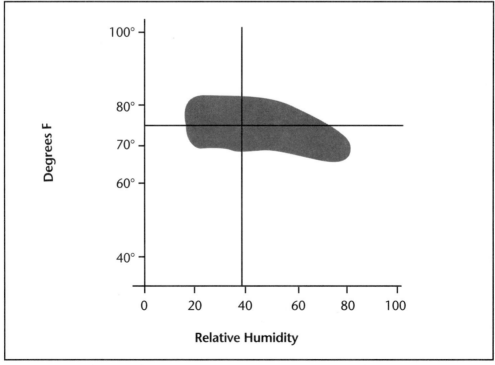

humid, it's uncomfortable. But the same temperature may be quite pleasant when the humidity is low or a breeze is blowing. This is referred to as the *human comfort zone.*

The variables that affect the human comfort zone are temperature, humidity, air movement, and heat radiation. They may be adjusted independently or simultaneously to provide the most pleasant atmosphere closest to the comfort zone.

**FIGURE 4B: HUMAN COMFORT ZONE**

**In order to feel comfortable:**

*A person sitting in the sun needs cooler, drier air.*

*A person running in the sun needs cooler, drier air.*

*A person sitting in the shade in a cool breeze needs warmer air.*

# RELATIVE HUMIDITY

Relative humidity at a specific temperature is the ratio of the actual amount of moisture in the air to the amount it potentially could hold. The relationship, expressed as a percentage, is crucial to the sensation of comfort. Evaporation from the skin makes us feel cooler. At low temperatures, relative humidity is less important than the actual thermometer reading. But when it's warm, the relative humidity is important. For instance, when a relative humidity of 60 percent or more coincides with an air temperature above 65° F, it feels uncomfortable and muggy. In a dry climate, the same temperature would be very comfortable.

When it's hot and humid, breezes that evaporate moisture from the skin remove heat from the body. This makes it feel more comfortable. In hot-humid climates, air flow indoors and outdoors is as important to human comfort as the actual air temperature. Outdoor breezes can be harnessed, using the wind velocity and channeling its direction. Summer winds properly directed by site topography or vegetation, or both, can reduce the need for air conditioning.

# MECHANISMS OF HEAT LOSS AND GAIN

Controlling the variables to produce conditions closer to the human comfort zone is what this book is about. By modifying the shrubs, trees, terraces, walks, walls, fences, and land forms around your house, you can modify temperatures indoors as well as outdoors. As a result, less fossil fuel is then needed for heating and cooling. And when less energy is used, dollars can be saved.

In order to use plants and land forms effectively for energy savings, one must first understand how heat energy is transferred and how the transfer affects us. Each mode of energy exchange responds to specific techniques. For instance, if a hot wall is wet down, evaporation while it dries will cool the wall. The reason is that when water changes by evaporation from a liquid state to a gaseous state, each molecule of water absorbs an enormous amount of energy. This is perceived as a heat loss or cooling effect. On the other hand, it is useless to spray water into the prevailing wind to cool a house if the spray is downwind from the building. It will just increase the water bill.

Heat loss and gain in buildings follow four main routes: (1) conduction, (2) convection, (3) radiation, and (4) evaporation.

*Conduction* heat loss is through walls, floors, foundations, ceilings, and directly from surfaces themselves.

*Convection* heat loss is through leaks where air can escape, such as loose doors and windows. The stronger the wind blows, the more heat is lost by convection. (Proper windbreaks can reduce wind by up to 85 percent.)

*Radiation* heat exchange takes place through glass. During the day, sun warms the inside of the house. Black night skies draw heat from interiors to the outside.

*Evaporation* of water vapor uses energy to produce its cooling effect. Evaporation heat exchange is why trees and plants have so much cooling effect. (About 75 percent of the cooling effect of trees is from evaporation; 25 percent is from shade.)

# BUILDING MATERIALS

Heat is absorbed differently by different building materials and by plants. Terraces, walls, driveways, and pools are made of building materials but are also part of the landscaping. Also, the material of which the house is made has considerable effect on the heat absorption and radiation patterns of the yard.

Because heat is absorbed differently by the different substances, small pockets of widely differing temperatures are created in the yard. These microclimates often vary from one side of the building to another.

Some materials, generally those with light-colored surfaces, reflect heat. Some materials (such as a white wall on a house) reflect and send heat back into the air, while keeping the space behind them cool. But one has to use this device thoughtfully. In the desert, white walls and terraces may reflect so much sunlight onto outdoor living areas as to make them too bright and too hot. In that situation, shade is needed during the heat of day, or a medium color should be used.

Although pale buildings have long been common in hot areas, more careful scientific measurements are suggesting ways to increase efficiency. The use of light-colored surfaces to reduce air-conditioning costs (called albedo) is being strongly recommended by the United States Environmental Protection Agency (EPA). The EPA has estimated that old houses using albedo in the following cities would benefit greatly in air-conditioning energy use and cost savings. In Phoenix, using lighter colors could result in an energy savings of 13 percent; in Miami, 19 percent; in Sacramento, 22 percent; in Minneapolis, 11 percent; in Pittsburgh, 19 percent; in Chicago, 16 percent; and in Washington, 15 percent.

Some materials absorb energy from the sunlight and yet remain cool. A tree is a good example. Leaves absorb energy in the blue and red spectrum of light. They do not use green light as much, but they reflect that part of the spectrum. That's why they appear green.

There is practically always a pleasant breeze under trees. As their leaves evaporate water vapor, air currents are produced, creating the breeze and a mild wind chill factor, which makes the air feel cooler. The energy used in the evaporation process is taken out of the air and reduces the need for air conditioning in adjacent buildings. That pleasant breeze is why one always heads for a big tree on a hot day.

Grass is more cooling than any paving, or even bare dirt. The reason is again the energy used for photosynthesis and evaporation of water vapor. In hot climates, any vegetative surface is preferable to paving; however, considerations of use, maintenance, and design usually necessitate some paving and stepping stones.

## FIGURE 5: **DIFFERENT ABSORPTION OF HEAT BY DIFFERENT SURFACE MATERIALS**

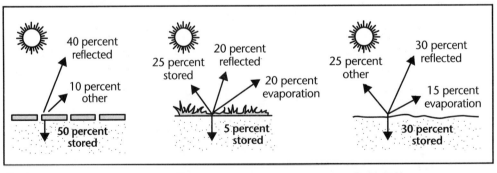

**Paving**
*Hot surface*
*Hot air*
*Hot soil*

**Grass**
*Cool surface*
*Air cooled by high evaporation*

**Bare soil**
*Hot surface*
*Some evaporation*

Certain materials absorb energy and get hot. A blacktop driveway becomes hot in the sun. It absorbs all of the sun's light but doesn't use any of this energy for evaporation or metabolic processes like photosynthesis. Blacktop is preferred in areas that have snow because snow melts and evaporates faster on blacktop than on concrete. In hot climates, it's a different story; adjacent driveways and parking lots coated in blacktop can really increase air-conditioning costs in both cars and buildings (not to mention a decrease in human comfort). Yet more energy-efficient concrete is so expensive that developers continue to use blacktop.

FIGURE 6: **TEMPERATURES IN THE YARD**

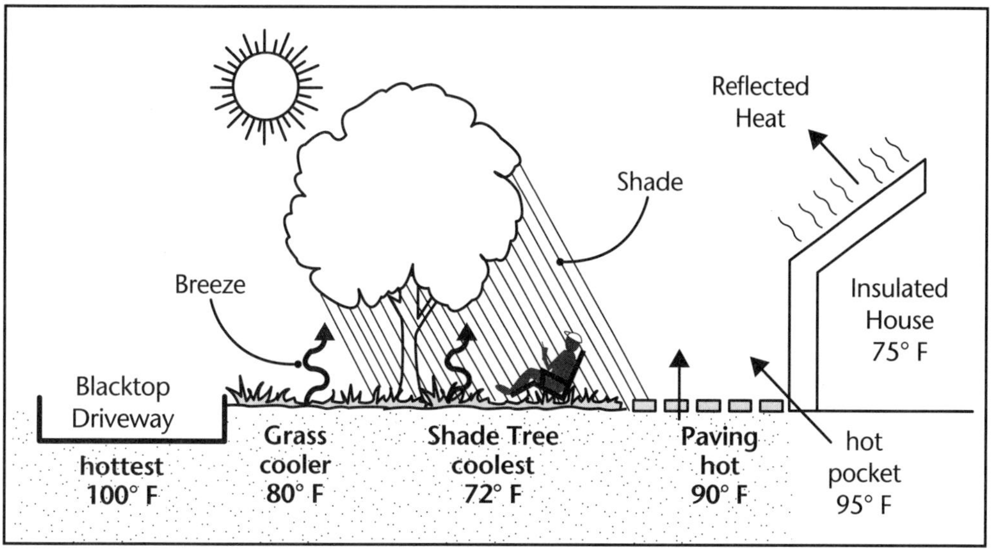

# NIGHT TEMPERATURES—
# RADIATIONAL COOLING

At night, heat energy that has been absorbed during the day by the ground, by masonry, and by buildings is radiated up into the black sky. Its direction is exactly opposite of the sunlight energy that radiates down during the day. In dry areas that have cloudless skies, there can be enormous radiational cooling at night. Though an area may have an air temperature of 95° F at noon and 75° F at sunset, by 5:00 A.M. it may fall as low as 28° F.

Buildings and masonry, which absorb heat from sunlight, cool slowly at night, keeping the area warmer. In desert areas with chill nights, it is useful to have masonry, rocks, and concrete near the house.

In cities, low overhead smog prevents nighttime radiational cooling. The heat just hangs there. This is one of the reasons cities, in both winter and summer, are warmer than their green suburbs. The city buildings, sidewalks, and streets absorb massive quantities of sunlight and heat during the day and don't lose much of it at night. This is the cause of the phenomenon known as the heat island effect. The weather, climate, and comfort of cities (and their down-wind suburbs) are affected by this heat island.

FIGURE 7: **CITY HEAT ISLAND**

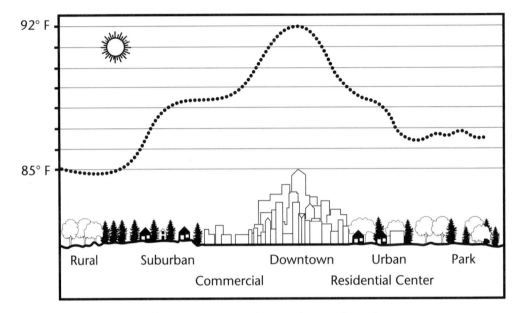

**Air temperatures above urban and rural areas**

Radiational cooling is less of a factor near large bodies of water than in the desert, because the water causes frequent fog and mists, which effectively trap the heat of the day under their blanketlike nature, much like city smog. Moisture lowers the effective night heat loss. Dry, clear air increases it.

# GLOBAL WARMING

As more energy is used on earth, it enters the global biosphere. And as more "greenhouse gases" (carbon dioxide, methane, nitrous oxides, and others) are produced, they trap more of the sun's heat, just as glass traps heat in a greenhouse. The total effect is more energy in the global climate system. This much we know.

The results are less predictable, but certain changes are anticipated. Temperatures will become more extreme, both hot and cold. The average temperature in cities in fifty years,

FIGURE 8: **RADIATIONAL COOLING**

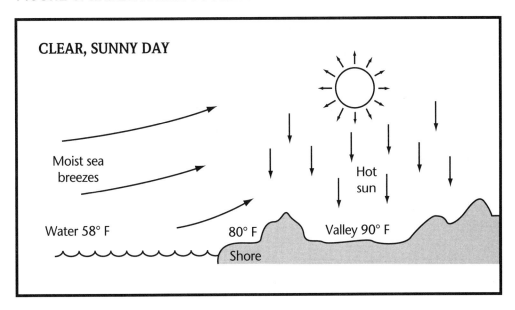

**CLEAR, SUNNY DAY**

Moist sea
breezes

Hot
sun

Water 58° F

80° F

Valley 90° F

Shore

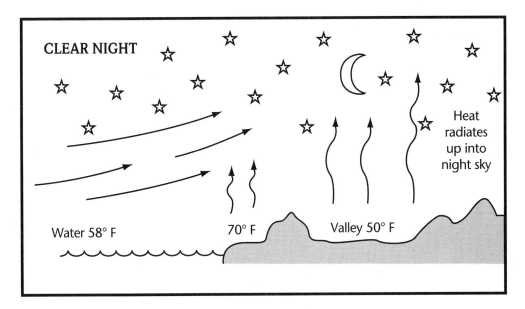

**CLEAR NIGHT**

Heat
radiates
up into
night sky

Water 58° F

70° F

Valley 50° F

*Moisture lowers the effective night heat loss. Dry clear air increases it.*

could be 10 degrees hotter. (Bear in mind that it takes thirty to fifty years for a shade tree to reach maturity.)

Storms will become more frequent and stronger. The Northeast may have more snow damage. The Gulf of Mexico may have more hurricanes. There may be more tornadoes. California may have even more droughts and floods. Present calculations anticipate that certain areas of the earth will become much warmer; others will become drier. These changes have the potential to alter social, economic, agricultural and ecological systems. Ocean water temperatures have already warmed up. There is concern that once the present global equilibrium is upset, weather changes may occur even faster than anticipated.

Urban heat islands contribute greatly to the process of global warming. Trees and forests, however, are one of the few natural systems that lower temperatures. By planting urban forests of trees, we could mitigate their climates, which would result in less energy use for cooling. Lower use of electricity would help curb the rate of global warming.

FIGURE 9A: **GLOBAL WARMING PROJECTIONS**

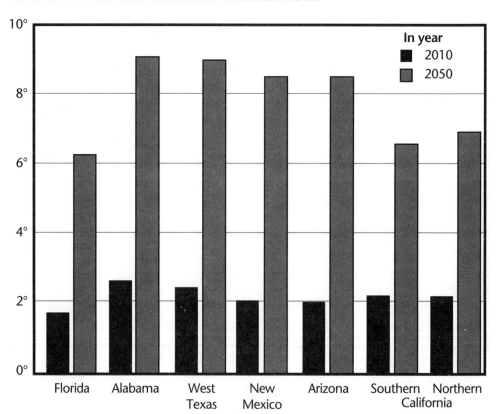

**Change in annual average temperature in degrees F for southern areas**

Experiments show that three trees per house could slow heat buildup and the city heat island effect, much as an oasis cools the barren desert. Trees are the natural solution to a more comfortable personal climate as well. Just a few properly placed trees can result in significant savings in air-conditioning costs.

FIGURE 9B: **SAVING MONEY BY USING TREES FOR COOLING**

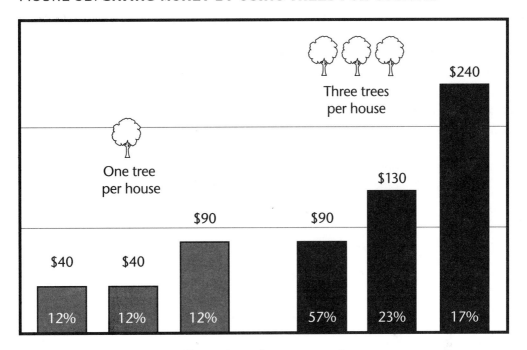

Percentage of energy saved

# CHAPTER 2

# The Sun

The sun is the source of a tremendous amount of heat energy. Therefore, the more sunlight hitting and entering a building in summer, the warmer that building will be and, therefore the cost of air conditioning will be higher. The opposite is true of winter heating costs. In winter the sun is warming and welcome.

A simple way to block summer sun and admit winter sun is to plant a carefully placed deciduous tree, one that loses its leaves in autumn. It will provide shade in summer, and yet in winter the warming sun will pass through or under its leafless branches.

## FIGURE 10: **A STRATEGICALLY PLACED DECIDUOUS TREE**

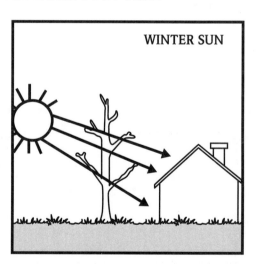

*A strategically placed deciduous tree keeps out summer sun but lets in winter sun.*

But proper placement is not so simple. The relation of earth and sun changes with the seasons. The earth revolves around the sun once each year. As it does so, first the northern, then the southern portion of the earth gets the direct rays of the sun. In summer, the northern hemisphere is toward the sun, so days are longer and the sun is higher in the sky. In winter, the converse is true.

Because of this seasonal tilt, the angle of the sun on any given day is different at each latitude and during each season. Although in the northern hemisphere, the sun is always to the south at noon, it may be high in the sky in summer or low on the horizon in winter.

# THE SEASONS

Ancient civilizations were fascinated with astronomy. High priests did secret calculations to predict where the sun would rise and how high it would be in the sky. So in awe were they at the regularity of the skies, that they fashioned religions based on sun worship. Abu-Simbel, the great temple on the Nile, is oriented to the sun in an extraordinarily sophisticated fashion. On one day of the year, the rising sun shines exactly through the small door, lighting the whole inside. The shaft of light precisely illuminates the statue of the sun god, Amun-Re, at the very back wall.

In England, there is Stonehenge. It stands as a silent memorial to a simple people who immortalized the spring equinox in granite monoliths. When their sun rose between a narrow slit in the sacred circle of stones, it was time to plant the crops—the eternal, vernal equinox. Stonehenge has other stone markers that plot the sunrise in other seasons—even moonrises, catching forever their variations during the changing seasons.

Today we have a calendar that tells the day, the month, and when to plant the tomatoes.

FIGURE 11: **SUN PATH DIAGRAM**

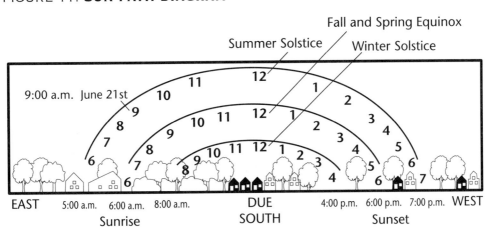

*A sun path diagram is a circular graphic map of the elevation of the sun at all hours of the day for each day of the year. (This one is for 40° North Latitude.)*

But, to ensure efficient energy savings, it's still worthwhile for the cost-conscious homeowner to figure the different angles of the sun. Planting by gosh and by golly will help some. But why waste good plant material by using it ineffectively?

The best approach is to understand the sun and shadows on your own site before adding plants. If you plan their location carefully, the same trees will allow both maximum winter sun and maximum summer shade.

Few houses are oriented exactly due north and south. If you think of your homesite as round, rather than rectangular, however, you will see which sides benefit or suffer from the sun. Then plant trees and use the other energy controlling techniques in this book to help these sides. Think of ancient Egypt and Stonehenge, and you will see the different angles of your sun at different seasons.

# DIRECTION AND ANGLE OF THE SUN

A breakdown of the changes in direction and angles of the sun during the year in your latitude is available (with some perseverance) from your weather bureau. Or you can easily plot them yourself.

FIGURE 12: **MEASURING THE SUN AND SHADOWS**

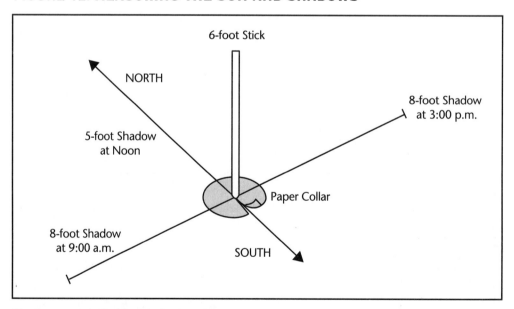

### To measure the sun and shadows:

*1. Put a small paper collar around the 6-foot stick.*

*2. On it, record the direction and length of the shadows at different times of day. Use a separate paper collar for each season.*

*3. Be sure the collar is always correctly oriented to North and South.*

To plot your own Sun Path Diagram, first place a 6-foot-tall stick in the center of an open area. Record the length and direction of the shadows during one full day in early July and one full day in December. Measure at 9:00 A.M., at noon, and at 3:00 P.M., and, in July, also at 6:00 P.M. Record the shadows on a large paper collar that's slit to fit around the stick. The marked collar will help you to situate future trees and will be a permanent record. The direction of the shortest shadow is a true North-South axis, daylight-savings time notwithstanding.

Since six feet is generally the height of a sliding glass door, the length of the shadow will tell how far the sun will reach inside the house through a glass door that it is the same height as the stick. The stick's shadow will also enable you to establish the dimensions of a trellis or overhang to keep the sun out in summer. (For instance, at a latitude of 42 degrees North, which spans Boston, Salt Lake City, and Denver, the width of an overhang should be 3 feet. This will shade out summer sun but let in winter sun.)

FIGURE 13: **TO MEASURE THE ANGLE OF THE SUN**

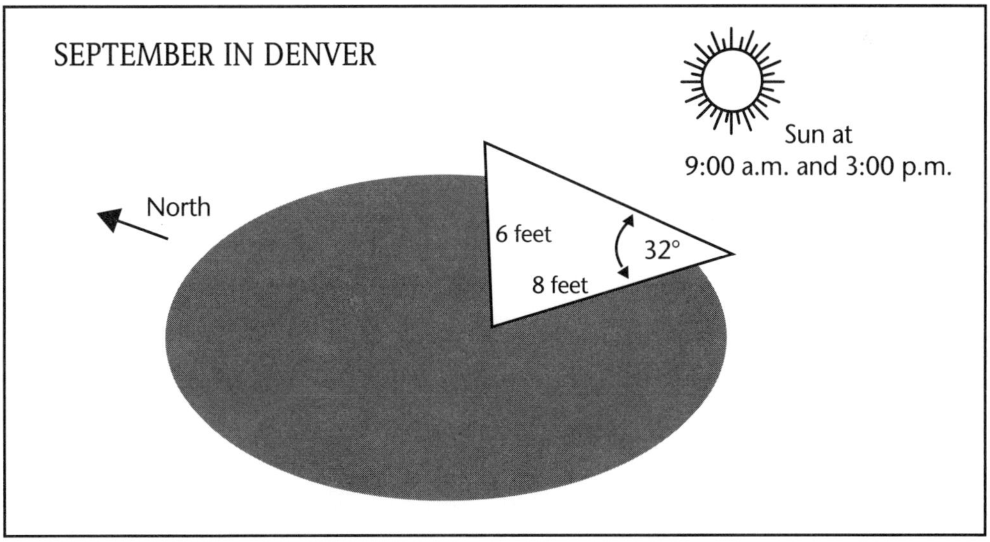

To plan for the most efficient use of winter sunlight and warmth, you must first know the direction and lowest angles of the winter sun. Heat from winter sunlight is effective only between 9:00 A.M. and 3:00 P.M. So while the winter sunrise and sunset are interesting and beautiful, the important calculations concern only midday. For the summer calculations, however, you must make an exception for the late, low-angled, western sun, which occurs during hot seasons. Buildings are at their hottest by then, and any additional heat is unwanted. The late afternoon sun in summer still generates a lot of heat.

To calculate the angle of the sun from the length of the shadow and the height of the stick just takes a little geometry. The aim is to make a right angle on paper. Using a scale of 1 inch equals 1 foot, the height of the triangle will be 6 inches, corresponding to the 6-foot stick. The base of the triangle will be the length of the shadow made by the 6-foot stick at 9:00 A.M. or 3:00 P.M. recorded on the paper in inches (using the 1 inch equals 1 foot scale). If the two lines are connected, an angle will be created at the base.

After you have drawn the triangle, measure the angle using a protractor. This measurement will tell what the angle of the sun is in your location.

# USING PLANTS FOR
# SUN CONTROL

Using these calculations, you can choose optimal planting sites and varieties. Deciduous trees are useful both for admitting rays of winter sun and for providing summer shade.

FIGURE 14: **CONTROLLING THE SUN FOR HEATING AND COOLING**

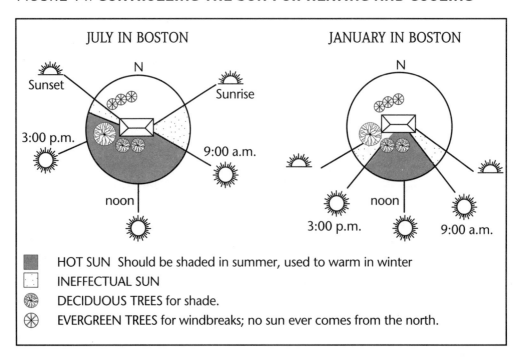

Evergreen plants may be used on the south side to screen or block a bad view, as long as they don't grow so tall that they block the low angle of the desirable winter sun. On the north side, there is never any sun, so evergreens of any height may be used.

On the southern exposure, fences may also be used, their heights determined by the distance from the building. For instance, a 6-foot evergreen rhododendron or a 5-foot fence may be placed 20 feet in front of a sliding glass door with no loss of winter sun.

**FIGURE 15: HEIGHTS OF DECIDUOS TREES AND EVERGREENS ON THE SOUTHERN SIDE FOR MAXIMUM SUN EFFICIENCY**

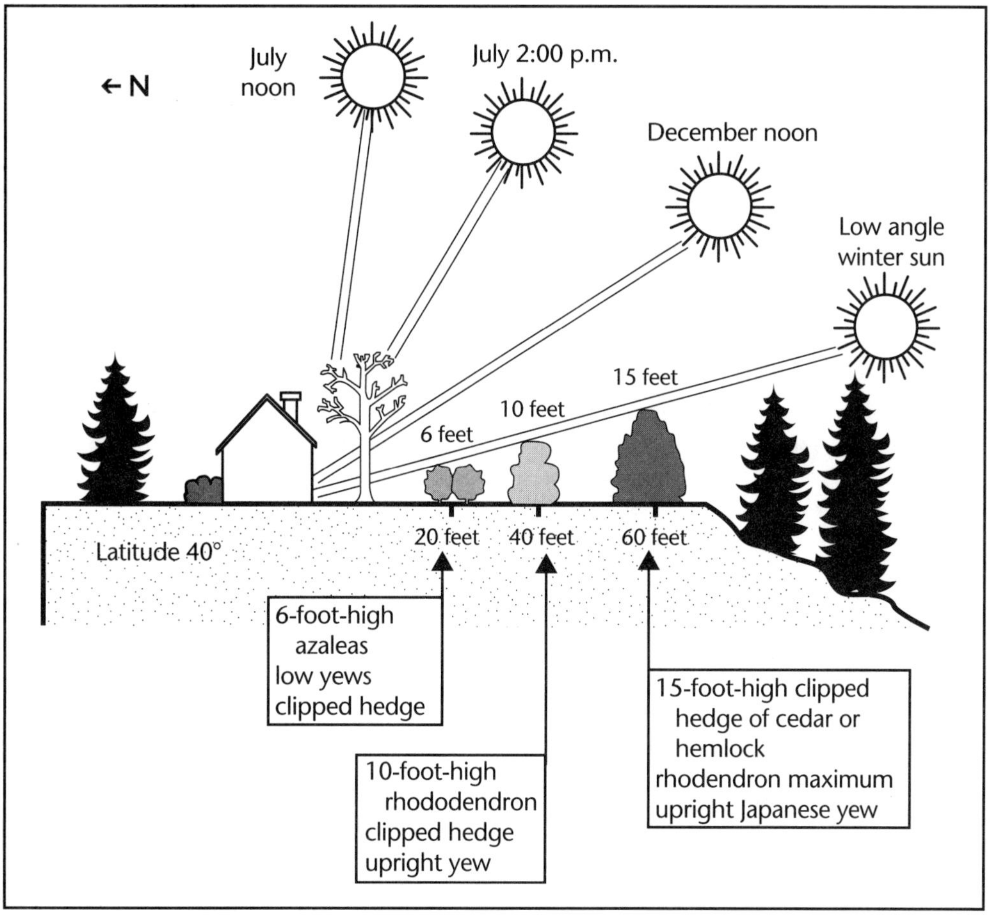

**EVERGREENS:** *On the southern exposure, maximum height is determined by the low angle of the winter sun.*
**DECIDUOUS:** *Height is determined by high summer sun. The clearance of the lowest branches should be high enough to allow the low winter sun to go beneath them. Sun goes through bare branches with about a 25 percent loss of energy.*

Obviously, the mature size of plants is a major consideration. Choosing the proper genetic variety, which will grow to the height you want, is as important as the calculations of where to place it. The more carefully you plan the planting, with attention to detail and nuance, the better it will function.

Trees on the southern exposure have to shade only a small angle of high summer sun. For that reason, fast-growing or columnar trees may be used. It is interesting to note that a tree 25 feet distant from a building must be over 50 feet tall to provide shade on the south side in summer. It takes a long time to grow a tree that tall. But if it's planted 10 feet from the building, it needs to be only 25 feet tall.

There are many trees that remain a proper size and are attractive for planting near buildings to provide shade for south-facing windows or wall. (See List of Small and Medium Trees, part III.)

In summer you'll want trees on the western exposure to protect the house from the hot afternoon sun. In winter, no effective sun comes from that quarter, so those trees can be evergreen or deciduous.

The taller the trees, the better. They will shade not only the windows, but also the roof. Not, however, too near the foundation, please. The majestic trees we think of as "shade trees" would soon interfere with water pipes, foundations, landscape plantings, and gutters. Avoid planting any trees with invasive roots near a house—it's just asking for trouble. (See List of Fast Growing Trees, part III.)

## FIGURE 16: **HEIGHT OF TREES FOR PROTECTION FROM HOT SUMMER SUN ON SOUTHERN EXPOSURE**

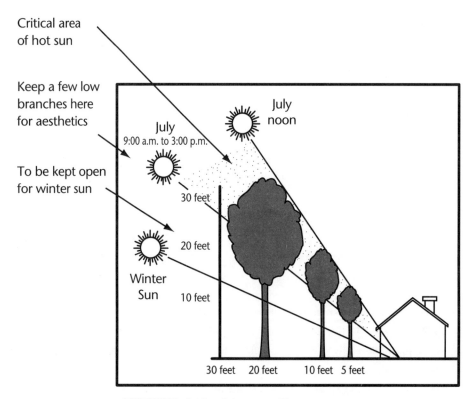

**OBJECTIVE:** *Let in winter sun and keep out summer sun.*

FIGURE 17: **HEIGHT OF TREES TO SHADE WESTERN EXPOSURE**

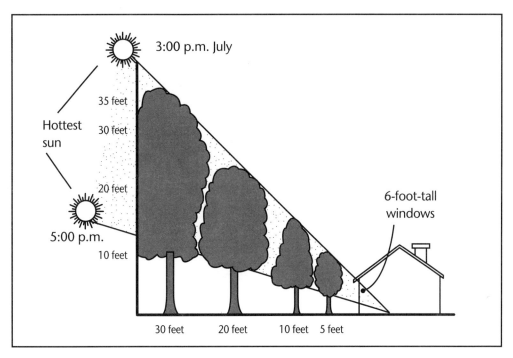

**OBJECTIVE:** *Keep out hot, low angled summer sun. Trees may be deciduous or evergreen because warm winter sun never gets this far west.*

On the southern exposure, because the summer sun is high in the sky, lower branches are not needed for shade. Trees can be trained to grow tall, with high space under them. This treatment gives a feeling of spaciousness and opens a view. It takes several years to develop a high canopy of leaves, but in the end it is worth the effort.

Columnar, upright trees function well on southern exposures because they naturally grow tall and not too wide. A clump or row of such trees, such as birch or flowering pear, is highly attractive. (See List of Columnar Trees, part III.) These narrow, upright trees are also useful in places where shade is needed but space is limited, such as courtyards or driveways. In the South, tall palm trees are successfully planted by nurseries for this purpose.

To get both summer shade and winter sun from the same tree takes a peck of planning. It also requires raising the branches to make a high canopy of leaves. In hot climates, tall evergreens may be used. In northern areas, deciduous trees should be used. (The rule of thumb is to lop off only two lower branches in any one year, until the desired 7-foot clear space is reached. It may take three or four years to achieve this.) In winter the low sun can enter windows underneath the raised canopy of branches.

Actually, leafless branches of deciduous trees can block out about 25 to 40 percent of the sun's rays. Ideally, the thickest part of the branch structure should be at the top, where it will not block low winter sunlight to windows, even though some of the roof will not receive maximum winter warming. Most energy-conscious homeowners have heavy insulation under the roof, so the roof is not as important as the windows for benefiting from winter sun. Snow on the roof is an excellent natural insulator.

# OVERHANGS AND TRELLISES

Overhangs and trellises may be used for blocking sunlight in summer. Sometimes there just is no place for a tree. A short overhang or awning will allow winter sun to enter but keep out the higher summer sun. A trellis with vines will do the same thing; plus the metabolic processes of the vines also contribute to the cooling of the area. Some vines grow fast and provide cover the first year (see Lists of Vines, part III).

One big advantage of overhangs and trellises is that they provide welcome shade fast, while you must wait longer for trees to grow. A combination of a solid overhang and a trellis is often used. In southern climates, a deep overhang allows the windows to be kept open during rainstorms, thereby cooling the interior of the house. The usual overhang for simple summer sun control is about 3 feet deep. (This is calculated for a latitude of 40 degrees, which is between Boston and Denver.) In very northern climates, it may need to be a little deeper.

FIGURE 18: **OVERHANGS AND TRELLISES**

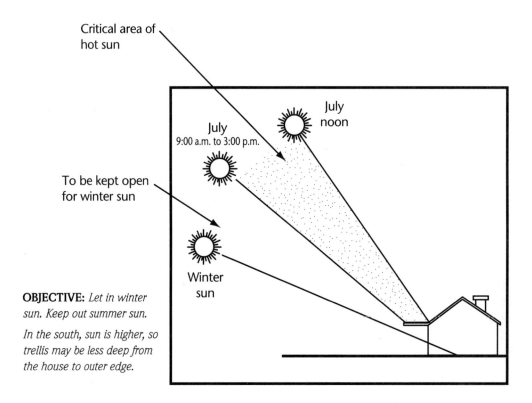

Critical area of hot sun

July noon

July 9:00 a.m. to 3:00 p.m.

To be kept open for winter sun

Winter sun

**OBJECTIVE:** *Let in winter sun. Keep out summer sun.*

*In the south, sun is higher, so trellis may be less deep from the house to outer edge.*

# PRIORITIES FOR SUN AND SHADE CONTROL

The primary passage of solar heat into a building is through the windows. Walls and roofs also significantly affect interior temperatures. In southern climates, shade is very important to control excessive heat buildup. Since one can't always afford to do everything that would be beneficial, however, one should prioritize starting with the areas that are most effective. To add shade, start with the western exposure, then do the southern side. The order of importance for shading is:

1. windows
2. air conditioners
3. uninsulated roofs
4. walls next to windows
5. other walls

# CHAPTER 3

# The Wind

The most overlooked aspect of energy saving is control of the wind, yet wind is the easiest factor to manage with landscape techniques. You can control it by using trees, shrubs, and hedges. Make use of the ground surface with hills, berms, and canyons, which form baffles against wind or channels that funnel it. Earth forms may be natural or man-made.

## WIND FUNNELS

A funnel of tall hedges that channels the prevailing wind can provide constant, natural "air conditioning." As the funnel narrows, the wind velocity increases, increasing the cooling effect. As the wind is forced into a smaller and smaller space, it has to move faster to get through. A large scoop that narrows considerably can increase prevailing winds that are light but steady and would otherwise be ineffectual. If the narrowest end of the funnel is covered by a breezeway or a high canopied tree, the cooling effect improves.

Funnels can be helpful in hot climates, but in northern areas funnels and canyons can increase winter discomfort and heating bills. High buildings in cities create "canyons" out of city streets, where the steady prevailing winds are funneled and increased. That is one of the problems in Chicago, where the winds associated with the lake are funneled between the tall buildings into cold blasts that swoop down the streets.

Wind funnels are complicated to design. Universities test designs by using expensive wind chambers with tiny buildings carefully built to scale. For home analysis, a smoky fire in a garbage can is an inexpensive way to determine where the prevailing wind comes from, how fast it travels, and how it is affected by buildings.

Wind patterns around a building can be traced in northern areas by watching the way snow blows. Make your first observation after a fresh snow, when all is white and serene. Then, wait a few days and compare where the wind has blown channels through the snow.

The prevailing winter winds will redirect the snow. Where is the ground blown bare? Where has the snow piled in drifts? These show where the winds come from in winter.

When the prevailing wind directions are known, the wind can then be redirected by trees and hedges to be deflected from the building in winter. In summer, the light breezes are enhanced by a funnel to blow directly on and around the house. Cold winter prevailing winds usually come from a somewhat different direction than cooling summer breezes, so different wind controls can be designed for each one. In hot climates, cooling wind funnels can cut air-conditioning costs. In humid climates, moving air evaporates water vapor as well, lessening mildew and fungus problems and the need for dehumidifiers.

FIGURE 19: A **WIND FUNNEL**

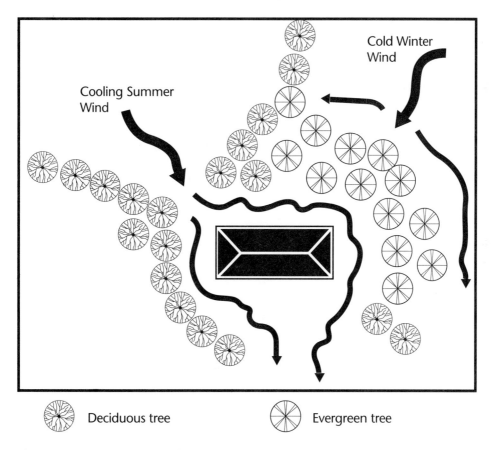

*Showing wind patterns corrected for maximum efficiency.*

# THE WINDCHILL FACTOR

Wind contributes to the "comfort zone" as much as any other factor. In hot climates, wind cools our skin through evaporation and by carrying heat directly away from the body. The amount of coolness we perceive is directly related to the speed of the wind, for the faster it passes over us, the more it can evaporate and the more heat it can blow away.

In cold weather, the dangerous "windchill factor" is well documented. At 20° F a hiker can develop a frostbitten nose if the wind speed is 40 miles per hour. But even at a chilly −10° F, his nose will be safe when the air is still.

At 70° F, an 18 mile-per-hour wind can make the air temperature feel like 58° F. Just walking creates a wind flow equal to 4 miles per hour.

Buildings suffer from windchill, too. As cold air swirls around them, the furnace must produce more heat to compensate. Winter windbreaks can reduce air-flow velocity by 85 percent. That adds up in fuel savings.

FIGURE 20: **WINDCHILL CHART**

## DANGER OF FREEZING EXPOSED SKIN

**ACTUAL AIR TEMPERATURE DEGREES F.**

| WINDSPEED IN MPH | 50 | 40 | 30 | 20 | 10 | 0 | −10 |
|---|---|---|---|---|---|---|---|
| 5 | 48 | 36 | 27 | 17 | 5 | −5 | −15 |
| 10 | 40 | 29 | 18 | 5 | −8 | −20 | −30 |
| 15 | 35 | 23 | 10 | −5 | −18 | −29 | −42 |
| 20 | 32 | 18 | 4 | −10 | −23 | −34 | −50 |
| 25 | 30 | 15 | −1 | −15 | −28 | −38 | −55 |
| 30 | 28 | 13 | −5 | −18 | −33 | −44 | −60 |
| 35 | 27 | 11 | −6 | −20 | −35 | −48 | −65 |
| 40 | 26 | 10 | −7 | −21 | −37 | −52 | −68 |
| 45 | 25 | 9 | −8 | −22 | −39 | −54 | −70 |
| 50 | 25 | 8 | −9 | −23 | −40 | −55 | −72 |

*Effective temperature that, due to the windchill effect, is equivalent to the actual temperature in still air.*

# INTERNAL AIR FLOW

Control of internal air flow is mainly an architectural consideration, which may require structural changes in a building. An outdoor wind funnel, however, can be directed to a suitable window or door to produce a cool, drying breeze indoors. A house can be cooled off at night by such wind. In areas of low wind velocity, a fan or vent can be used.

# EXTERIOR WIND CONTROL

Control of exterior air currents has more variables. Before you can use and control the wind, you must understand its nature. Air flow acts much the same way as water. Neither takes easily to detours. Air will flow over, under, around, or through them. Winds will topple anything not sturdily engineered.

Warm air rises. Cold air sinks and seeks the lowest spot. Cold air flows across the surface of the ground from higher to lower elevations. It settles in low spots and stays there. That is why there are mists in the gloaming when the cooler air settles on the warmer water. It's also why some spots are perennial frost pockets. Farmers plant the lowland fields last, for they are the coldest.

FIGURE 21: **COLD AIR FLOWS LIKE WATER**

Cold air flows around house

Cold air trapped in patio

Cold air deflected by
evergreen trees

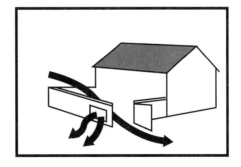

Cold air drains
from patio

# PREVAILING WINDS

In the United States, the prevailing winds are generally from the west. But wind direction in any particular spot may not coincide with the prevailing wind for the area. Wind is bent and bounced from buildings, trees, hills, and valleys. It is affected by large bodies of water and open plains. It may sweep down into a yard as a small whirlwind, or blow right over it.

To learn the direction of prevailing winds at your house, tie strips of cloth (a trailing tab) on several sticks 5 or 6 feet tall. Anchor them securely on the north, west, and south sides of the house. Add a stick and strips at any other place that seems windy. Keep a chart for several weeks, preferably for part of the winter and part of the summer.

If spring is usually windy, check that season, too, before planting windbreaks and collecting funnels, for the gales of the Ides of March can blow away energy dollars. In addition to the prevailing winds, there will be odd pockets of erratic wind in courtyards and between and around buildings. These should also be plotted on your property plan.

It takes some time to find out what the seasonal wind patterns are around your house, but landscapes are designed to last a half century or more, so it makes sense to get the needed information first.

# ON THE PRAIRIES

The prevailing wind of open flatlands is persistent, annoying, and very cold in winter. The problem is greatest on the Midwest prairies, with their ever-blowing blasts.

On flatlands in winter, the velocity of the cold air increases, unchecked by any natural impediments on the boundless space. Creating windbreaks is one important way to use landscaping for saving energy, and to make yards and gardens tolerable. Almost all farms and buildings on the plains have good, thick windbreaks on the north and west, the source of their prevailing winds. These windbreaks create a wind shadow behind them in which comfort is possible.

Because of the temperature extremes, the unrelenting persistence and velocity of the winds, and the alkaline soil, windbreaks on the plains have special horticultural requirements. These needs are discussed in the section on vegetation, and there are special plant lists in part III.

# AT THE SEASHORE

Near the coast, too much wind can be a problem, too, particularly near the Pacific Ocean. The wind can blow strong enough to be unpleasant on all but the hottest days. In the San Francisco area, for instance, two out of every three days from May through September will have winds above 20 miles per hour. In Seattle and San Diego, every summer day will have winds above 10 miles per hour. Consider the implications of the windchill chart. Even warm days can seem chilly.

Solving a seashore problem of too much wind is not easy. A well-anchored fence is the best solution. Eventually, windbreaks of trees and shrubs can be made to grow, but they may cut off the view. Glass or plastic panels can be used as fences to preserve a valuable vista.

FIGURE 22: **FENCE WITH A VIEW**

*Plexiglass or glass panels provide wind protection. They may be removable for protection during storms.*

# FENCES

There are many kinds of fences to control the wind. Each fence creates behind it an area of protection called a "wind shadow." But because air tends to flow like water, different fence designs affect the wind differently and create different wind shadows as wind passes over them. Surprisingly, the fence that gives the largest area of protection is a louvered one, even though the wind passes through it into the protected area. The reason for this is that the air flow is buffeted and fragmented as it passes through.

FIGURE 23: **FENCE DESIGNS**

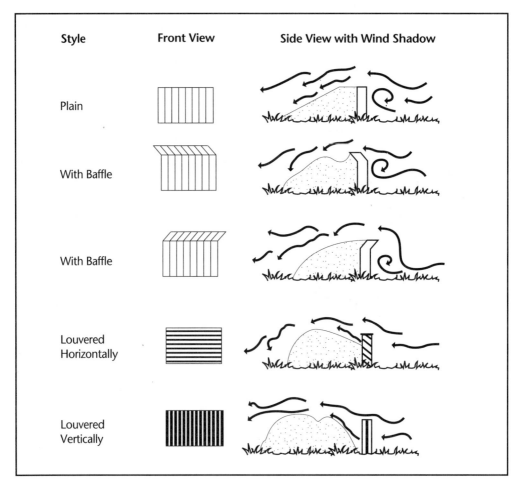

*Fence design affects the deflection of the wind and the shape of the protective wind shadow behind the fence.*

# DOWNDRAFTS

A downdraft occurs when a solid impediment directs the wind downward. They can cause unpleasant conditions in an outdoor living space and are especially troublesome near cliffs, mountains, and tall buildings. They are a constant problem in urban areas because the taller the buildings, the stronger the downdraft. They are very difficult to ameliorate, to say the least.

Ingenuity with baffles or screens or enclosures can sometimes help. In city planning, the scientific way is to make a scale model of the buildings and land contours, and then blow smoke over it with a fan, as in a wind tunnel experiment. Various structural modifications to both buildings and land can then be tried. This is not a job for an amateur, for the corrective structures are too expensive for random experimentation.

FIGURE 24: **A DOWNDRAFT**

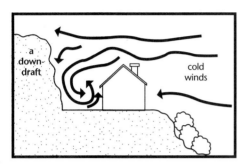 

*Protective evergreens and wind scoop make house and yard more comfortable on a cliff in Maine. The principle of a wind scoop is the same as that of a smoke shelf in a fireplace.*

# WIND SHADOWS

Wind shadows are the calm area around a protective barrier. These tranquil shadows are the main way landscaping can control energy loss from wind. Wind can be deflected or channeled by solid objects or by clusters of trees and shrubs. The wind is broken up and weakened there, so the air there is warmer, and it's better than braving the gale.

The size and shape of the wind shadow (the protected area) is determined by the height and shape of the barrier. Natural hillsides make the best natural barriers. Man-made hills, called berms, can also work well. Where no hill exists, walls or evergreen trees can be used.

Windbreaks cut the wind both in front of and behind themselves. A mass of trees can decrease air velocity for a distance of five times its height to the windward (where the wind blows from). Velocity decreases for as far away as twenty-five times the trees' height to the leeward (where the wind blows to). There is protection even in front of a barrier.

Immediately behind the mass of trees will be a space with very still air. This quiet space is where cold-weather energy savings are highest. When planning a windbreak and wind shadow for a building, one tries to get this quiet space right next to the walls.

Four times as much energy is spent in the United States to heat homes as is spent for air conditioning. Windbreaks are very effective at reducing windspeeds, which reduces cold-air convection into buildings. Research shows that a windbreak of trees can cut the windspeed by 85 percent. This translates into a 10 percent to 15 percent dollar savings in the Northeast and as much as a 15 percent to 20 percent saving in the north-central United States.

The best kinds of trees to plant are tall, dense evergreens that will fit into the space available. Where there is lots of space, fast-growing white pines and Norway spruce are good. White

FIGURE 25: A **WIND SHADOW**

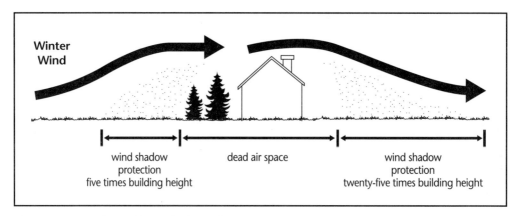

An evergreen windscreen breaks the force of the wind and creates a protective wind shadow in front and behind. Dead air space protects the house.

spruce and blue Colorado spruce are equally good windbreak trees where space is more limited. On small lots, hemlock makes a good screen and can be easily sheared. Where the space is narrow, columnar arborvitae, planted about 3 feet apart can be used. They, too, stand shearing, and when they get too tall, the tops can be cut off with no loss of form. Where evergreen trees are impractical, deciduous trees that are twiggy and dense also work well.

The more depth to a windbreak, the better it functions. The more twigs and branches and needles there are, the more the wind is broken up, so it loses velocity. An ideal windbreak is multilayered, consisting of a row of tall evergreen trees on the north and west sides, then deciduous trees outside of them to break the wind, and finally, outside of the trees a row of tough shrubs, whose twigs will break the wind even more and give some protection to the trees. As the wind tries to pass through the many layers, it is broken up, hence the name windbreak.

The distance over which windspeed is reduced is determined primarily by the height of the windbreak. The amount of wind reduction, however, is determined by the density of the windbreak. The more porous (open) the windbreak, the less dead air space, but the distance of wind shadow protection is longer. An evergreen windbreak is 60 percent more effective than a deciduous one.

The wind also increases in velocity around the edges of windbreaks. To counter this, the edges are curved to protect the quiet area or are planted on two sides to provide a sheltered interior. (See Figure 47, A Windbreak on the Plains.) In very windy areas, shrubs and low branches at ground level help, because the wind can concentrate and funnel underneath at increased velocity. In snow country, deciduous shrubs will catch and hold snow and act as a better barrier.

In very cold climates, too dense a windscreen may trap cold air behind it and become a constant cold pocket. In such cases, some air movement may be desirable. This can be a problem on driveways or other areas that tend to be icy, particularly in northern latitudes, where the winter sun is very low but helps melt the ice.

Driveways, ideally, should be higher than the surrounding land and open, so that the wind will blow off the snow. On the prairies, many highways are above grade for this reason.

# WIND DAMAGE TO PLANTS

High-velocity wind is damaging to plant material. It not only shreds tender leaves but also increases evaporation of water from leaves and twigs. Wind-stressed plants become dry and desiccated, with twig and bud dieback commonly occurring. Trees exposed to such winds become dwarfed, their shapes become contorted from wind force, and they grow away from the wind. On such trees, most healthy, green leaves grow on the protected, downwind side.

Trees subject to constant blowing need more water. The higher the wind speeds, the more water they need. Without this additional moisture, plants and trees adopt a desert habit of growth. They grow more slowly, the trunk thickens, and they have smaller leaves. They spend their limited energy producing quantities of seeds because they know they will not live to a ripe old age. They mature too soon and die too young. Hot sun and high temperatures compound the effect. City trees especially suffer from this syndrome.

Where such conditions exist, it is important to choose trees and plants that are better adapted to them. (See lists of windbreaks and drought resistant plants, part III.)

# STORM WINDS

Storms produce high winds, which sometimes cause trees to fall on buildings, doing considerable damage. Good pruning is the best way to keep trees safe and prevent undue damage.

Good pruning removes dead wood, weak wood, and unbalanced branches. (See Corrective Pruning, chapter 9.) Some tree species are more likely to break in storms, while other strong-wooded ones will survive unharmed. It is prudent to plant soft-wooded trees far enough away from the house so that weak branches will not fall on it. Generally, the faster a tree grows, the weaker and softer its wood. Especially susceptible to breakage are silver maples, poplars, willows, cottonwood, Siberian elms, and tulip trees. Oaks and plane trees break less often.

Areas downwind from major polluting cities have a higher incidence of thunderstorms, rain, high winds, and 200 percent more hailstorms. If you live in such an area, consider planting soft-wooded trees far enough away from the house to prevent trouble.

Another protective device is to plant a smaller tree between the large tree and the house. If the big tree falls, it lands on the smaller tree before it can seriously damage the roof. (And don't ever take a leaning tree down yourself, for they are more dangerous than they look. Call a forester. They don't call leaning trees "widow makers" for nothing.)

Most severe weather is from storms that come from the west-southwest exposure, or the southeast. Caution should be the watchword for plantings on this quarter. Of course, regional and local variations affect storm winds. Large bodies of water also modify storm direction. For example, New England has its northeasters; the Gulf Coast has hurricanes.

FIGURE 26: **KINDS OF STORM DAMAGE AND REGIONAL FREQUENCY**

| KINDS OF STORM DAMAGE | REGIONS MOST AT RISK |
| --- | --- |
| **Droughts** | Western states |
| **Forest fires** | California, Western forests, Eastern forests in summer |
| **Floods** | All low lying land and areas near rivers |
| **Hurricanes** | Gulf and Atlantic coasts |
| **Severe thunderstorms** | Rocky Mountains to Midwest Plains and Gulf Coast |
| **Severe freezes** | All states except southern California and Florida |

Droughts and periods of low rainfall are more common in the West but can occur anywhere, depending on upper-atmosphere jet-stream movements. Cities and urban areas are especially prone to drought damage because of the heat accumulation from buildings and pavements. With droughts come increased fires. When planning landscapes, particularly in California and the West, more attention is now being directed to designing protection from the forest fires that periodically rage through.

Too much water creates problems, just as too little does. When the atmospheric system is overcharged, floods often accompany severe storms that have heavy rainfall. Heavy snowfall, when it melts, periodically crests rivers to flood levels. Also, severe or unexpected freezes are common in most of the United States, except for southern California.

The most damage is done by high winds, however. Hurricanes are common along the Gulf and Atlantic coasts. Although thunderstorms are common, very severe thunderstorms are frequent during warm months from the crest of the Rocky Mountains in Colorado and New Mexico east to the midwestern plains, as well as along the eastern Gulf Coast and Florida.

Global warming will make all these storms more powerful. So when planning landscapes, take the storm factor into consideration and include a little risk aversion. Trees will live half a century, and we don't know exactly what the effects of global warming will be when they reach maturity. See Global Warming and Tree Damage in chapter 9 for ways to lessen storm damage to trees.

# CHAPTER 4

# *Water*

Water is the great equalizer for ameliorating climates. During summer, large bodies of water absorb and retain heat from sun and air, like giant solar storage tanks. Because water cools more slowly than air, as winter approaches, it stays warmer. Then as it slowly releases its heat, it warms the surrounding land. By spring, though, oceans and lakes are chilled enough to provide slow cooling in summer. As the seasons come and go, the cycle repeats.

## WATER AND CLIMATE

Water's absence helps explain why the midwest plains have temperature fluctuations from $-40°$ F to more than $100°$ F. Ocean areas at the same latitude are far more mild. The seashore in summer is cooler and more pleasant than inland areas, and shore winters are milder. This ameliorating effect of water on climate helps contribute to the premium value of ocean and lake properties.

In addition, water generates wind currents. During summer, hot inland air rises above the cooler air at the water's surface. Temperature differentials result in the familiar shore breezes. The larger the body of water, the more effect it has on climate patterns near it.

Even small ponds, however, can affect their local climates, from the breezes these temperature differentials generate, as well as through evaporation. The reason is that when water evaporates, it takes heat from the surrounding air. Even small ponds and fountains can affect their immediate area. The more total volume and evaporative surface a body of water has, the more influence on climate.

## EVAPORATION

The process of evaporation requires energy (or heat), as water molecules change from a liquid to a gaseous state. It takes much more energy to evaporate water than just to heat it. As evaporation takes place, energy is drawn from the surrounding air. So heat is used up, and the air becomes cooler.

This cooling also creates a movement of the air (convection heat exchange), which one can feel as a breeze or wind. At ocean or lake side, these evaporation-induced air movements augment those produced by the simple thermal differentials of the air and water.

Homeowners can use these energy-exchange phenomena (evaporation, convection air currents, and shade) to their maximum advantage by incorporating both plants and water into their garden designs. Think of the classic Spanish gardens, all of which had a fountain in the center—to cool the air, and the soul. No great classic garden or outstanding retreat is without some water. The tranquil or rippling surface, the ever-changing play of light and shadow as well as the sounds of running, bubbling water, have universal aesthetic appeal.

As evaporation takes place, the resulting energy (heat) loss makes a person, or a building, or any object feel cooler. It explains the old Bedouin desert trick that keeps water cool. Water is kept stored in a canvas bag or porous clay jug. In both instances, seepage makes the outside surface stay wet. As the water evaporates from the surface, it draws heat from the water inside. The drinking water stays cool.

Traditionally, hot courtyards always had fountains. In dry climates, an increase of humidity is especially welcome to people, plants, and good furniture. Man-made lakes, pools, and fountains can be used to advantage where no ocean or lake exists naturally. For maximum effects, they should be placed upwind, to both cool and humidify the largest area.

The amount of evaporation is directly related to the amount of surface area. A spray or fountain exposes more surface than still water. A similar cooling effect can be created by wetting or hosing down a patio, driveway, or roof. Roofs can have sprays or just running water over them for evaporative cooling. In very hot climates, a shallow water pool on the roof provides considerable energy savings. As the water cools at night, it becomes a cool blanket, which is ready when the next day heats up again. It evaporates during the day, drawing heat energy from the building.

In climates with hot sun but chilly nights, water roofs are warm and insulative, especially if the water has a chance to warm up late in the day. Sod roofs are also warm and insulative, but sometimes interiors tend to be damp.

# PLANT MATERIAL AND EVAPORATION

All plants, especially trees, are very good at harnessing the water-evaporation energy exchange cycle. In addition to cooling by shade, trees also cool by evaporation of water from their leaves. The energy required for this evaporative process is taken out of the air as heat right in among the leaves. Then, as air temperature differentials develop between the interior of the tree and the air surrounding it, convection currents are set up. These draw air through the leaves and create the breeze that is always present under large trees on warm days.

# THE TREE FACTORY—COOLING AND CLEANING THE AIR

The combination of shade, evaporation, and convection air currents can lower the temperature beneath a big tree by 25 degrees. In fact, one mature tree produces as much cooling as fifteen room-size air conditioners.

Trees are also pollution sinks. They collect pollutants and particulate ash from the air (by both absorption and adsorption). And as they photosynthesize, they remove carbon dioxide from the air and manufacture oxygen, which is especially useful in urban areas with poor air quality. Trees give back a great deal in exchange for a little loam and some water.

For the homeowner in a sultry climate, large trees are worth their weight in electric bills. A grove of trees will always provide a cooler spot. The higher the air temperature, the more leaf surface needed to produce enough cooling. Also, the higher the leaf canopy needs to be to provide maximum air movement.

If a tree is expected to cool efficiently, it must evaporate water vapor from its leaves, and so it is essential for it to have adequate water at all times. If the ground dries, trees don't have as much water in their leaves to give off, nor ground water in their roots to replace what they lose.

Desert plants don't cool as much because in order to protect themselves from drought and prevent evaporation and water loss, they expose a minimum of leaf surface. Where adequate irrigation isn't possible because of water restrictions, drought-resistant trees might have to be used. They will still provide shade, but much less evaporation of water will take place from their leaves, so they are less efficient in cooling the air.

# CONSERVING WATER

Collecting rainwater from the roof is an age-old practice. Too often these days, roof rainwater is just channeled into the ground via sewer or dry well. The old rain barrel was no joke, just commonsense conservation.

Roof water can be put to good use with just a little thought and planning. It can go from the drainpipe through a small pool or fountain. Or it can go over paved areas in hot, frost-free climates. It can be used first for these cooling purposes, and then used again for irrigation. Perforated underground "Bemco" pipes can distribute it under tree roots and shrubbery beds. Finally, the water can be directed to the vegetable garden. Clean waste water from sinks, bathtubs, washing machines, and dishwashers can be used similarly for underground irrigation. This is called "grey water" and is fine as long as it is not overly contaminated with detergents.

FIGURE 27: **IRRIGATING WITH RAINWATER**

1. *Roof runoff water*

2. *Drain pipes*

3. *Hot paved area cooled with surface runoff*

4. *Trees, grass, and shrubs irrigated with surface runoff*

5. *Overhang to shade windows from sun*

6. *Shrubs under overhang irrigated with perforated pipe placed on crushed stone for good drainage*

7. *Trees and shrubs irrigated with perforated pipe on crushed stone*

8. *Vegetables irrigated with runoff from end of pipe*

A WORD OF CAUTION: *If you plan to build a small ornamental pool or fountain, don't use ground runoff water; it usually has silt and debris in it. Roof water, however, is clean and usable after it's run through a screen. Goldfish or a thin coat of cooking oil will help control mosquito larvae.*

In Shalimar, the unbelievably beautiful Persian Garden of Love in the Kashmir, water from the Himalaya mountains runs down a series of terraces. At each level, it irrigates the flower beds, charges the fountains, and fills the wading pools. Then it falls a few feet to the next terrace to work again.

Uncomplicated irrigation systems such as this, using directed surface runoff, pipes, or crushed stone, can save water bills, produce better trees and shrubs, and possibly help with evaporative cooling. Under roof overhangs, plants normally receive no rainwater and so may suffer from drought, but using this kind of irrigation can help avoid sickly shrubs and high water bills.

# XERISCAPING

Xeriscaping is a new kind of landscaping that saves water by using only drought-tolerant plants that can survive without supplemental irrigation. In desert places like Arizona, it means using cacti, native desert flora, and other drought-resistant plants instead of the usual thirsty grass and palm trees. Ground surfaces are covered with decorative stones or sand. The effect is different but quite beautiful, like the desert itself. It has been incorporated into the central highway strips in many desert cities which were depleting their water supplies to keep the palms and grass highway dividers lush and green.

In temperate regions and in California, where water is often scarce, xeriscaping is done using native plants, ornamental grasses, and drought-tolerant plants. The effect is not so stark as in the desert and can be quite verdant with careful choices of plants. Part III has a list of drought-resistant plants, with their yearly rainfall requirements, that can be used for xeriscaping. See page 148 for further discussion of this topic.

FIGURE 28: **XERISCAPING IN ARIZONA**

# SNOW

Snowfall patterns can be useful for saving energy, too. Snow is an insulating material in cold climates. When it stays on the roof, heating costs are lower as long as the weight of the snow is not too heavy for the roof. Similarly, when snow is piled against a north or windy wall, particularly when held in place by shrubbery, it protects that wall from windchill and low temperatures.

Snow blowers can be directed to blow on exposed walls, or to create large mounds that serve as temporary windbreaks. In open areas, as in the prairie states, the use of carefully placed shrubs or snow fencing can catch and hold snow blown by winter winds. It may require a season of watching the wind and some trial and error before you find the best locations.

CHAPTER 5

# Land Forms,
# Natural and Man-made

The natural surface of the earth is wrinkled by shapes that we call hills, valleys, canyons, and ridges. These land forms affect our climate. They modify the wind and sunlight, form cold and hot spots, and determine which trees and shrubs will grow. And by so doing, they influence how much it costs us to make the microclimate of our own backyard more comfortable.

Mountains, for instance, force the wind around or over them, into erratic gusts and swirls. Rainfall patterns are affected. Hills do the same to a lesser degree. Canyons and narrow passes constrict the wind, increasing its velocity or "wind speed." The faster it blows, the cooler it feels.

## HILLSIDES AND VALLEYS

Because cold air flows much like water, from higher to lower elevations, hillsides have special climates. Cold air tends to flow down their sides into the valleys. The middle elevations of hills and mountains are more comfortable and most energy conserving, because the cold air flows right through them. The night air there is often warmer than the air in the valley, where the cold air settles. Because there usually is some breeze on hillsides, hot days are cooler. The top and side of a hill or mountain facing the prevailing winds are always colder. Orchards are planted on the middle elevations, where extremes of temperatures are less likely and cold flows right through.

Valleys may be hot if their sheltering hills are broadside to the prevailing winds. But if the valley parallels the existing wind, it acts like a wind tunnel and is usually cool. In the North, such a valley can be very uncomfortable during winter. It is worth considering the wrinkles in the earth's surface when buying a house lot or an existing home.

# MICROCLIMATES

When air flows around hills and mountains, hot pockets and cold spots are created. They are natural microclimates. It is possible to create similar pockets on almost every existing lot by using the building and carefully planned earth mounds, fences, trees, and shrubs. The theory is to capture or exclude air currents and sun.

In nature, these pockets determine which plant materials will grow in which spots. For instance, the north sides of mountains have a community of trees that withstands wind, cooler air, and less sun (in New England, spruce and birch). Different trees will colonize the warmer south face of the same mountain (maple, beech, and hemlock).

Similarly, in the home garden, different plants and trees thrive in shaded or exposed pockets. Some withstand strong winds better and are more suited for windbreaks. Spruce and pine, for example, are more wind resistant than hemlocks. Man-made earthworks, even modest hills and slopes, affect sun and shade patterns and, therefore, plant growth rates.

Choosing plants best suited for each wrinkle in the earth's crust, and suited to that particular combination of sun, shade, and exposure, will prove the most economical and successful approach in the long run. To ignore the limitations of your house lot is asking for trouble and added maintenance chores. It's wise to study the plants growing naturally on exposures similar to yours. They give clues to what will perform best for you (see plant lists for different conditions, part III).

# MAN-MADE LAND FORMS

Natural land forms have resulted from geologic action over centuries. As civilization advances, however, more and more land forms are man-made. Egyptian and Aztec pyramids and the irrigation systems of ancient Babylonia are old examples. New ones are tall buildings, broad avenues, and vast treeless spaces such as parking lots, farms, and overgrazed wastelands.

These spaces create their own weather patterns, blocking or channeling winds as natural mountains and valleys do and changing patterns of solar absorption and radiation. The more people use the earth, the more we get pockets that have extreme weather fluctuations.

# MAN-MADE WINDS

Tall buildings both funnel and fracture wind, creating turbulent downdrafts, swirls, and high velocities. When wind must squeeze between tall buildings, a canyon effect takes place. The wind speed increases dramatically.

Long, straight streets also funnel wind and increase its velocity. In hot climates, where cooling breezes are welcome, the streets should be oriented parallel to the prevailing winds to take advantage of them. In colder areas, avenues are best planned opposite to the prevailing winter winds. Otherwise, Main Street will be Cold Street when they blow, and such cold winds don't help business or pleasure. In the oldest section of Boston, there is a small colonial street actually named Cold Street, because it is oriented directly into the winter gales.

# HEAT ISLANDS

Man-made objects and land forms also change the patterns of solar heat absorption and radiation. In the forest, sunlight falls on the trees, which absorb and use most of it. Little light hits the cool floor beneath, and little is radiated back into the air in the form of heat. In cities, concrete and paving absorb and store (as heat) about half of the sun's energy. The rest is reflected back into the air. Everyone has experienced city streets that are miserably hot on a sunny day.

At night, concrete buildings and streets give off their stored heat, which could dissipate into the black, energy-absorbing night sky. In cities, however, smoke, carbon dioxide, and other air pollutants create a dome of heat-retaining particles. (Flying into Los Angeles under the dome and into the smog is quite an experience.) Since clear skies are rare in cities, they do not cool down at night as much as surrounding areas.

So cities have temperatures different from those of their suburbs and outlying farms— cities are hotter. Downtown Boston has the same temperature as a farm in southern New Jersey, 300 miles farther south. In Lexington, Massachusetts, 10 miles from Boston, the forsythia blooms two weeks later in spring, because the air is that much colder.

This heat-island effect is an important component of the urban ecosystem. It affects what grows in the city and influences the kind of weather neighboring areas experience.

What does this phenomenon mean to the homeowner? It means that calculations of heat and cold energy losses must be adjusted to compensate for the climatic effect of man-made structures and the urban heat-island. The more developed an area, the greater the effect. The greener an area, the less climatic effect. (See figure 7.)

# ALBEDO AND COLOR

The word *albedo* is used to express the reflection of solar radiation from a particular color surface. The opposite of albedo is the absorbtion of solar radiation. To save energy and cool our cities, studies have been done to show the effect of color and texture on reflection and absorption of solar energy.

For instance, studies at Oak Ridge National Laboratories in Tennessee found that the temperature of a dark-colored roof reached above 160° F on a hot day, while a flat-white surface reached only 135° F, under similar conditions, and a glossy-white surface reached only about

120° F. The color of the surface (white or black) and the reflectivity (shiny or dull) affects the amount of heat absorbed.

Similarly, on a 90-degree day, the surface temperature of asphalt can reach 140° F and increase the surrounding air temperature by 5 degrees. A light-colored surface temperature, however, would be much cooler.

Changing the color of urban buildings, roofs, roadways, and sidewalks to light colors and adding more trees, grass, and shrubs can reduce the heat-island effect. The Environmental Protection Agency is trying to effect changes in our cities to save energy, particularly in southern cities. (See EPA, *Cooling Our Communities,* in Resource File.)

Different colors absorb and reflect differently, a variable that should be considered in landscape design. Driveways and paved areas around homes should be carefully planned. In hot climates, driveways should be medium colored. Blacktop absorbs too much heat, while white glares too much, reflecting sunlight into and against buildings. Nevertheless, many driveways in hot areas are blacktop, which adds to yearly air-conditioning costs. Northern roads and driveways should be blacktop for their warming effect in winter, and because they melt ice and snow faster.

# TREE-LINED STREETS AND ALBEDO

Tree-lined streets are cooler than masonry and particularly cooler than bare blacktop. In cold climates, evergreens should not be used because the sun is needed on winter roadways. In summer, however, when shade is wanted, deciduous trees will leaf out and provide cooling.

In southern areas, streets should be lined with as many trees as possible. In Barcelona, where the summer heat is oppressive, the streets are tolerable because of masses of shade trees that create the beautiful promenades for which the city is famous. Walking down an unshaded section of road, then reaching some trees is like finding relief from Hades. The coolness and ever-present breeze under the trees is almost blessed.

For the trees to cool adequately, water is needed, and great ingenuity is used to get water to city trees. In Teheran, double rows of plane trees were planted down the centers of many roads, with depressed gullies in the middle to carry irrigation water. In India, streets are engineered so that curbs direct street rainwater runoff into pipes that go directly to the roots of their street trees. California uses irrigation on its highway trees, shrubs, and ground cover, but doesn't always have water to supply it.

Southern parking areas need lots and lots of trees, more than any other place. Unfortunately, builders are not usually interested in what they do to the total climate, only in finishing as cheaply as possible. Many cities now have ordinances that require trees in developments, on streets, and especially in parking lots. It is interesting that such cities are perceived as more desirable, and property values are higher.

# BERMS

Man-made hills, as well as natural ones, can modify sunlight and wind. This principle gives us one of the easiest and most useful tools for influencing our microclimate. It is relatively inexpensive to create a mound of earth (technically known as a berm) to block or channel wind or sun, and much faster than waiting for trees to grow tall.

A berm that's well designed and planted on top with trees and shrubs can become one of the important attractions of distinctive landscaping. A carefully located berm can provide privacy and noise control, too, reducing noise levels by as much as 80 percent.

Graceful, artistic berms are not used often enough. Most builders seem unaware of their existence. Berms form the basic artistry of Japanese gardens. Large, half-buried rocks and stone walls lend themselves beautifully in such designs. Fortunate are the few who can excavate for a new house or addition and have extra earth to work with. To truly sculpt the land, one should leave it with a graceful, undulating surface rather than flat and empty like an engineer's drawing board at five o'clock.

FIGURE 29: **A BERM USED AS A WINDBREAK**

Earth berms can be beautiful when planted with shrubbery and ground covers. They can be landscaped with interesting plants or used to grow vegetables and flowers. Berms present special growing problems, however. Because water runs off the sides, they are usually drier than the surrounding ground. If the sides are too steep, they will erode or wash away. Stone retaining walls and large rocks are useful remedies. Or railroad ties may be used to hold the soil. The roots of plant material also hold the soil, eventually. Rough wood chips make an excellent inexpensive, erosion-retardant mulch. The less steep the slope, the less problem with erosion.

When putting plants on berms, care must be taken for adequate water. The tops of berms are very dry. Water-holding plant pockets must be fashioned when you do any planting. The pockets can be depressions or terracing on the sloping sides or a shallow trench on top. Plant material that needs relatively little water does best. It is difficult to mow grass on the sides of berms, so grass should be used only if it is to be kept as an uncut meadow.

FIGURE 30: **PLANTING PROBLEMS OF A BERM**

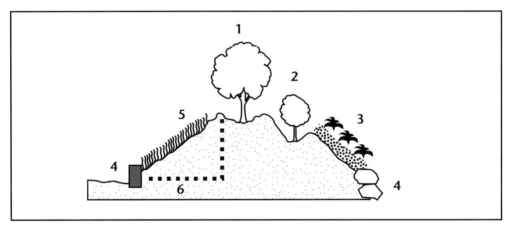

*1. Soil on top is dry, so depress center to keep water from running off.*

*2. Make water holding depressions for planting.*

*3. Mulch withan erosion-resistant material such as wood chips and plant ground covers.*

*4. Hold difficult slopes with stone retaining walls or treated wood ties.*

*5. Grass is difficult to mow on slope so use it only uncut as field grass.*

*6. Use a maximum 2–3 slope.*

# EARTH—THE ULTIMATE INSULATOR

Berms have another useful function. Because soil itself is insulating, it can be used against masonry walls as the cheapest insulating material. The soil layer just has to be very thick and very dry, since wet soil draws energy. Very good waterproofing has to be used to keep the walls dry.

Also the problem of adequate air circulation must be addressed, otherwise the interiors of earth-covered masonry walls will always be damp and moldy. The reason is that the walls are always cool, and when warm air hits them, water condenses on them. The condensation has to be removed by good air circulation. People who have built houses partially underground usually have to use air conditioning in summer to remove moisture from the cool air indoors, in order to prevent mold. Sometimes there are ways to deal with the problem by using extra insulation outside, or special barriers, but it should be carefully explored before building walls with earth insulation.

For new houses, concrete walls that are banked with earth are less expensive than conventional walls of wood and insulation. Soil, logs, or wood chips should never be used within 6 inches of structural wood because of the danger of termites. The 6-inch space should always be visible so you can check periodically for termite tunnels into the supporting beams.

# MAN-MADE PLANTING POCKETS

Man-made earthworks create areas with special microenvironments, just as natural land forms do. These can be warm spots good for chilly weather use, cool hideaways for escaping the heat, or places where the wind blows around or through (to discourage mosquitoes perhaps). Carefully planned, they can add to the comfortable use of outdoor living spaces and help warm or cool a house. Created thoughtlessly, they can make terraces uncomfortable and rob walls and roofs of energy.

The microclimates of these spots require plants adapted to their particular temperatures and conditions. For instance, in a hot sunny corner, made to capture winter sun, the plants will have to tolerate winter sun-scald. They will also have to withstand summer heat and drought.

For this kind of hot pocket in frost-free areas, desert plants can be used with rocks or driftwood, requiring little care. Or a bed of blooming aloe, natal plum, hibiscus, and Madagascar vinca will give year-round bloom and fragrance. (Natal plum has thorns and requires pruning but is vigorous and fragrant.)

In cold climates, a sunny pocket could be planted with Japanese black pine, juniper, cotoneaster, creeping thyme, and daffodils. Such a planting palette will require little maintenance.

A cool, sunless pocket requires shade-tolerant plants. In the North, these might be holly, andromeda, Baltic ivy, bulbs, dogwood, and redbud trees. Azaleas and rhododendrons grow well in the shade, but need good light to bloom well. Swamp azalea (*A. Kaempferi*), a woodland plant, is one of the few that blooms in full shade.

In the frost-free South, a shady pocket might sport the giant climbing philodendron vine called *Monstera deliciosa,* creeping fig (sometimes known by its more exotic name of Zanzibar ivy), *Brunsfelsia* (with its heavy, sweet night odor), ginger, *Agapanthus,* and caladium lily.

# CHAPTER 6

# Climate Zones

## AND HOW THEY AFFECT
## ENERGY-SAVING TECHNIQUES

There are four main climatic zones in the United States: cool, temperate, hot-arid, and hot-humid. Each zone has different needs and therefore requires different techniques for climate amelioration.

*The cool zone* has very cold winters and hot summers with a wide range of temperatures, from −30° F to over 100° F in summer. Persistent prevailing winds usually come from the northwest and southwest. In the cool zone the days are short in winter and the sun very low in the sky.

*The temperate zone* has cool and hot seasons that are about the same length. Temperatures are not as extreme as in cool regions. Seasonal winds blow from the northwest and south. Temperate zones have lots of rain and high humidity. The summers may be hot, heavy, and uncomfortable.

*The hot-arid zone* is dry, clear, and sunny. The summers are long and hot. The nights cool rapidly as heat radiates from the ground into the clear skies. Winds are generally along an east-west axis, with variations between day and night.

*The hot-humid zone* is warm and wet. Winds are variable in direction and velocity. Hurricanes are common, their winds often from the east or southeast.

By understanding the subtle differences among zones, you can use supplemental energy-saving techniques in the most effective way. In the hot-humid zone, for example, large shade trees can be used for protection from the hot western setting sun; however, they should be far enough away from the building so that a hurricane will not blow them down on the house. Also, low trees should be used on the east exposure because of the prevailing hurricane winds.

FIGURE 31: **CLIMATE ZONES**

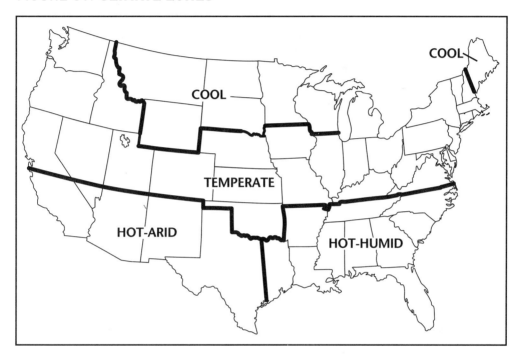

# COOL ZONE

In cold areas, keeping warm uses more energy than summer cooling and is the major thrust of energy-saving techniques. Some concern, however, should be given to relief from summer heat. Heavy insulation is mandatory.

Windows on the south should let in sunlight for warmth in winter. On the northwest, berms or evergreen windscreens, or both, should give protection from the prevailing winter wind. Land forms, walls, and fences may be used to provide sun pockets and barriers.

For longest seasonal use, outdoor living areas are best placed on the southern exposure. Deciduous trees or overhangs on the south may be needed for some protection from the summer noonday sun. In some locations, protection on the west from the hot, low summer sun may be necessary. A tree, or even a trellis with honeysuckle will work.

FIGURES 32A AND B: **COOL ZONE**

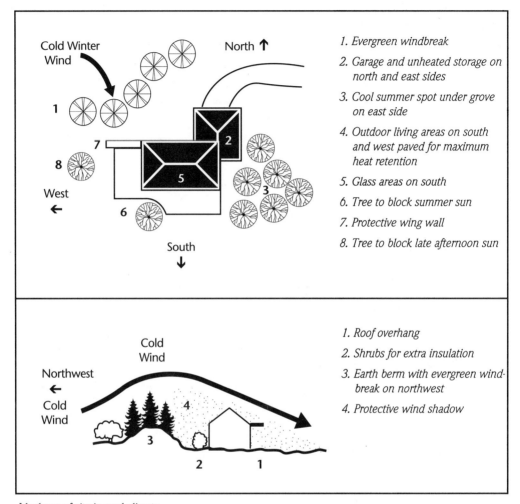

*Ideal use of site in cool climate*

# TEMPERATE ZONE

It is necessary to conserve heat in winter as well as to provide cooling and occasional dehumidifying in summer. Because of the milder climate, protected outdoor areas in the temperate zone can be used for a longer season than in cold regions. Outdoor living areas should be on the south and southwest, protected from cold north and northwest winds. Tall deciduous trees should be used on the south and west exposures to provide maximum cooling and to allow penetration of warming winter sun.

Trees, landforms, walls, and fences can provide protection from cold winter winds where they are strong. Wind shadows should be created to protect the north side of the building and, also to protect doorways from winter winds. Wall insulation is not as common here as in northern climates, so winter wind protection is most important.

Because the summers tend to be hot, outdoor areas should be designed to take advantage of prevailing summer breezes, which usually come from a slightly different direction than winter winds. Ideally, these warm-season breezes should be channeled through the house for cooling, where possible.

FIGURE 33: **TEMPERATE ZONE**

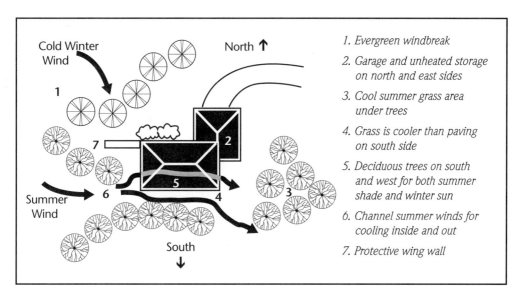

1. Evergreen windbreak
2. Garage and unheated storage on north and east sides
3. Cool summer grass area under trees
4. Grass is cooler than paving on south side
5. Deciduous trees on south and west for both summer shade and winter sun
6. Channel summer winds for cooling inside and out
7. Protective wing wall

# HOT-ARID ZONE

Keeping cool during the day and warm at night are the main goals of climate modification in hot-arid regions. Outdoor living areas should be to the east; the building will provide shade during hot afternoons.

East and west windows should be shaded. Glass walls should face north. South-facing windows need protection with a large overhang, deciduous trees, or trellises. Excessive glare from the outdoors sun area can be reduced by planting grass and shrubs near the building. Underplanting near the house should be thick to insulate and to hold humidity.

Shade roof and parking areas with overhanging trees. The roof should be light to reflect heat away from the building, and the parking areas should be surfaced with a medium-colored material that neither absorbs heat (like blacktop), nor reflects it (like white stone).

Cooling daytime breezes should be maximized by increasing their speed with wind funnels. In some desert areas, however, winds are unpleasantly strong; in such places funnels should not be considered. There should instead be protected areas for sitting. For houses that don't cool off fast enough at night, the window curtains should be left open for maximum solar heat loss after dark. When the curtains are left open, heat will quickly radiate through the glass into the cloudless, star-studded black sky.

Evaporation from lakes, pools, or fountains will provide further cooling and humidifying if they're upwind from the building.

FIGURE 34: **HOT-ARID ZONE**

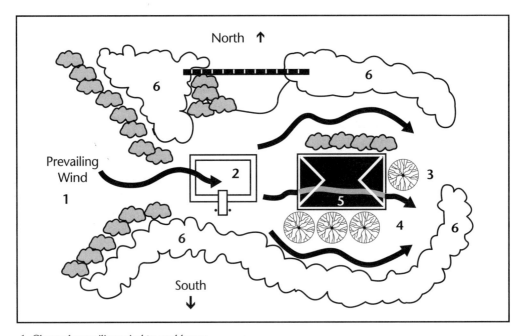

1. *Channel prevailing wind to cool house*
2. *Use pool upwind to humidify air*
3. *Outdoor living area on east*
4. *Grass near house for coolness*
5. *Southerb exposure shaded by trees*
6. *Trees for shade and humidity*
7. *Winter hot pocket against fence, facing south to catch sun*

# HOT-HUMID ZONE

Shade and movement of air through the site are the most important considerations for this zone. Outdoor living areas should be on the east or north side of the building. Plantings should shade both the structure and the outdoor living areas. East and west windows should be shaded. South windows should have overhangs or protection from trees. On old southern plantation houses, a wide wraparound porch shaded the windows, which also allowed them to be kept open for cool breezes during rainstorms.

FIGURES 35A AND B: **HOT-HUMID ZONE**

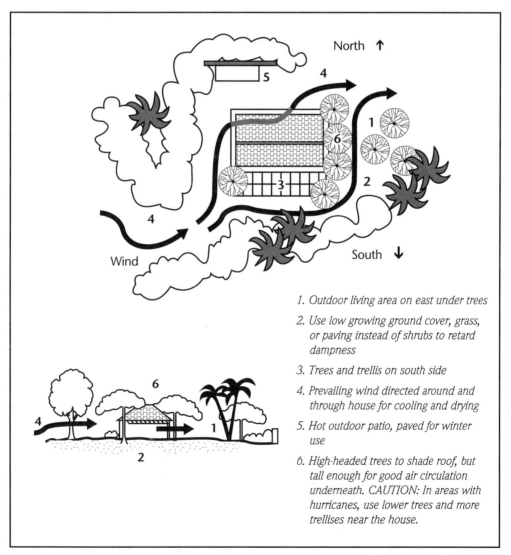

1. Outdoor living area on east under trees

2. Use low growing ground cover, grass, or paving instead of shrubs to retard dampness

3. Trees and trellis on south side

4. Prevailing wind directed around and through house for cooling and drying

5. Hot outdoor patio, paved for winter use

6. High-headed trees to shade roof, but tall enough for good air circulation underneath. CAUTION: In areas with hurricanes, use lower trees and more trellises near the house.

*Ideal use of site in hot-humid zone*

Trees should be high-headed to allow breezes beneath. Movement of air is important not only for cooling, but also for evaporation of the ever-present moisture and to lessen the resulting growth of mildew.

Wind funnels should be created with low trees, shrubs, and walls to direct breezes around the house and possibly through the house and outdoor living areas. Underplantings near the buildings should be kept very low for better air circulation and to minimize dank areas and mildew. Sunny areas should be planted with grass or low ground cover to absorb solar heat, rather than reflect it onto the walls and into the windows. Shaded areas may be paved, preferably with a medium-color paving, such as brick.

A protected winter sun pocket may be created by paving and fencing a small area to catch the winter sun and extend outdoor use.

## FIGURE 36: **DIFFERENT CLIMATE ZONES**

### COMPARISON OF DIFFERENT CLIMATE ZONES

|  | Cold | Temperate | Hot-Humid | Hot-Arid |
|---|---|---|---|---|
| Energy-Saving Objectives | Maximize heat conservation | Minimize heat conservation | Maximize shade and wind | Maximize shade and wind |
|  | Reduce winter wind | Maximize summer shade |  |  |
|  | Avoid cold pockets | Maximize summer breezes |  |  |
|  | Maximize summer shade |  |  |  |
| Trees | Deciduous near buildings | Deciduous near buildings | High canopy trees | Trees overhang roof and parking |
|  | Evergreens for winter windbreaks | Evergreen for windbreaks | Deciduous near buildings |  |
|  |  | Either on western exposure |  |  |
| Shrubs | Any kind | Any kind | Low-growing | Tall and clustered |
|  | Insulating on north |  |  |  |
| Ground Cover Paving | Paving near building | Grass and shrubs on south and west | Grass near building except in shade | Grass and shrubs near building |
|  | Medium to dark color | Paving elsewhere | Light color paving | Medium color paving to avoid reflection |
|  | Blacktop for driveway | Medium color |  |  |
| Outdoor Living Areas | South | South and Southeast | East and North | East |
| Wind Control | Protect from winter wind | Protect from winter wind | Maximize wind | Channel cooling winds |
|  |  | Channel summer winds |  | Block excessive wind |

# CHAPTER 7

# Site Analysis

S o far the general principles that apply to each type of climate have been discussed for large geographic areas. Though the same general principles apply to individual sites, they have to be modified to fit your own house in your own city or town and your own microenvironment. Each site has its own particular characteristics, which create its individual microclimate. The general principles are then applied, choosing the ones that will work on your site and adapting them to save the most energy and money. A careful site analysis is the way to begin.

First analyze your house lot and determine its orientation to the sun. New houses, thoughtfully placed on a lot, will be more energy efficient than homes automatically oriented parallel to the street. Older homes are the way they are, but energy losses may be significantly reduced, nevertheless, if you start with a careful site analysis, noting the advantages, liabilities, and possibilities.

The important features of any lot are sun, wind, contours of the land, surrounding area, existing plants and trees, soil, and precipitation patterns. Before planning improvements to the site, you should understand all these factors. The Site Analysis Chart on the next page will help you gather the neccessary information.

After collecting this information, prepare a rough plan of your site, showing these factors in relation to the existing building or the proposed one. As you analyze the energy pluses and minuses of the site, think of how you can improve them by the techniques discussed in part I of this book. Not every example will apply to your site or your geographic area, but the basic concepts will. Since this is to be a garden of beauty, the classic concerns of good landscaping design should be followed as well.

FIGURE 37A: **SITE ANALYSIS CHART**

1. Path of daily and seasonal sun (see chapter 2).
2. Daily and seasonal wind flow patterns (see chapter 3).
3. Slope of land and earth forms which block sun or wind.
4. Low areas where cold air could settle; frost pockets.
5. Which soil is good enough to support trees and plants; which areas won't (ledge, sand, concrete, etc.)?
6. Size, location, and variety of existing trees and shrubs that would assist energy conservation (by blocking wind, sun, or shade).
7. Protected areas:  a. at what times of day?
   b. at what seasons?
   c. protected by trees, etc.
   d. protected by land forms, etc.
8. Exposed areas:  a. exposed to sun—at what seasons?
   b. exposed to wind—at what seasons?
9. Rainfall:  a. water runoff patterns
   b. evaporation potential
10. Snowfall and snowdrift patterns.
11. Water-flow patterns (buildings, driveways, roads, valleys, hillsides).
12. Existing impediments and channels for airflow.

FIGURE 37B: **THE BASIC CONCEPTS**

- Allow sun to help heat in winter.
- Block sun out in hot weather.
- Block out cold winter winds.
- Channel winds for cooling.
- Use water and snow to cool or insulate.
- Use buildings and paving material for their best energy-saving potential.
- Use plant material similarly.
- Choose plants genetically adapted to perform as desired.

FIGURE 37C: **GOOD LANDSCAPE DESIGN**

- Visual beauty to nourish the soul.
- Areas for trees, shrubs, flowers, vegetables.
- Easy, attractive access for people and vehicles.
- Outdoor living areas (porches, patios).
- Recreation areas (pools, courts).
- Convenient service areas (storage, clothesline, garbage cans, wood and mulch piles).

# NEW HOUSES

Fortunate the few who are building a new house and can maximize energy efficiency. Wind channels should be carefully incorporated into the design, as well as watershed and rainfall runoff control. Simple grading and terraces can eliminate or minimize the need for supplemental irrigation of shrub borders and flower beds. With the cost of water rising rapidly, this kind of planning is very important.

Driveways and outdoor living areas should have equally careful placement to provide the most utility, enhance the microclimate, and use the materials that will do the most good.

Building into a slope is one useful technique. The side that should be protected from heat or cold is buried; the other side is mostly glass. In *cool climates* the southern side should have maximum solar exposure and as much glass as possible. Build into the southern side of a slope where feasible. The buried north side of the building is then protected from winter winds.

*In hot climates where only morning sun is welcome,* the east wall should have the glass, with the house built into the eastern side of the slope. In desert areas, with hot days and chilly nights, the morning sun would be very welcome.

*In hot climates where minimum solar radiation is wanted,* large glass areas should be confined to the north side of the building. Windows are fine on the south, if protected by a deep overhang and also protected from ground reflection. The east and west walls, where the sun is low, should be thick, protected with vegetation, and have minimal windows and openings.

Where no slope exists, it is still possible to make use of earth berms in front of (or better still, against) the exposed masonry walls. A depth of a few feet of dry dirt against walls provides good insulation. Such "below grade" areas have a tendency to be damp, so good cross ventilation is important. Air conditioning should be used for its dehumidifying effect.

Where one side of a lot has a bad view or heavy traffic, raised earth berms, carefully planted, can provide privacy and noise protection. (See chapter 5, "Berms.") A 4-foot-tall screen of evergreens would grow slowly at first but eventually give privacy. A 4-foot-high earth berm, planted with 3-foot evergreens, however, would instantly give 7 feet of protection and privacy.

# SOLAR BUILDINGS

Landscaping for solar buildings uses the same principles, except that it's complicated by the requirements of the solar collectors, most of which are wall or roof mounted and work most efficiently facing south. Large glass areas must be similarly placed for maximum passive solar heat.

Trees, even deciduous ones, must not shade the solar collectors. It's not necessary to cut down all the trees, however. Too many architects and builders do this, incurring unnecessary re-landscaping expenses. If the low angle of the winter sun is calculated, trees and shrubbery may be cut back (topped) instead of removed. Many trees can be lowered by half or two-thirds. They then serve both to screen the house and to protect the soil from erosion (a common problem on overcleared lots).

Although the practice of topping trees in this way is frowned upon by tree experts, it has a use when conflicting values (solar access versus tree aesthetics) have to be resolved. New low-growing trees can be planted, and when those mature, the older, "cut back" ones can be removed.

Another consideration is the orientation requirements of solar buildings. Because solar houses are aligned due north and south, they are subject to extremes of microclimates on either side. The south side is hot and dry; the north side is dark and cold. Each side requires different plants suited to those conditions and adapted to these extremes. It is not a problem, because many plants exist for each of these microenvironment. (See Plant Lists for Special Purposes in part III.)

Almost all new buildings have some passive solar collecting surfaces, usually in the form of large areas of glass, such as conservatories or large expanses of south-facing glass. These are areas where sunlight enters in winter and warms interior spaces. Currently, passive solar is the most cost-effective way to harness the sun's heat. If, however, energy prices rise, or technology improves, solar roof collectors may become equally economical. Solar collectors are not used where the cost of energy is low or even moderate.

Every possible energy-saving technique must be incorporated into site planning for solar buildings. The timely recovery of expensive installation costs will depend on a building that uses the least total energy. Efficiency and conservation reduce the demand, which in turn, reduces the required capital investment and the length of cost-effective recovery of solar collectors, storage capacity, and passive solar building costs.

# IMPROVING THE SITE FOR EXISTING HOMES

Chances are that you can't reorient your house. You can, however, rework the land around it, as well as the trees and shrubs. If a house needs major renovations or an addition, that's a good time to get a bulldozer to build hills and berms and wind channels. Barring a major renovation, a load or two of loam dumped in the right place can make a good berm at a small cost.

Unless you are young, strong, and accustomed to heavy labor, don't tackle earth moving with a shovel. Hire someone young, strong, and accustomed to heavy labor. It will be the best money you ever spent and may save you from having a permanently battered back.

Energy-saving techniques are compatible with creative landscape design. On some sites, excavating a sunken garden or raising a protective earth berm can change an ordinary plot into an exciting landscape. While not cheap, the final effect may be well worth the cost. While new trees and shrubs block the wind, a sunken garden area can be a protected, aesthetic bonus. The technique is particularly useful on exposed, windy sites, in urban yards, and on uninteresting flat land. The use of different levels can create private outdoor spaces that are protected, save energy, and are beautiful as well.

FIGURE 38: **A SUNKEN GARDEN**

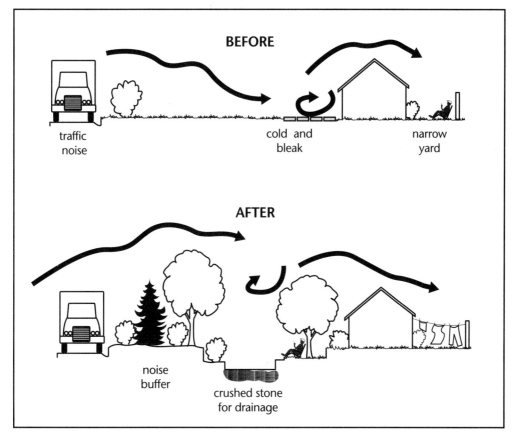

*Original backyard too small for outdoor living space. New sunken garden has patio and privacy. New plantings break force of wind and traffic noise. Backyard becomes a surface area.*

If it's unreasonably expensive to move earth around or to regrade your site, consider building walls or fences for climate control. Masonry walls are expensive, but they may be more aesthetically pleasing and durable and so provide the best value over a long period of use. Sturdy cedar or treated wood fences function as well, particularly over a shorter time span.

The style of an existing building, its location, and the land itself determine whether masonry or other materials are most suitable. In the long run, economies hastily taken without regard to aesthetic appeal and good design are often regretted at leisure. You have to look at fences and walls all year, every year. And there is nothing more irritating than an ugly wall.

## Water

Water can be used to advantage on existing sites. Small ponds or fountains will help improve the comfort level of a site while adding appreciably to its charm. They are not hard to build. Perhaps you can even do a small job yourself. The sound of moving water is most pleasurable.

Water conservation should be a consideration in all site work. Where does the rainwater run off? It should be channeled for irrigation purposes as it passes through the property. Ground-water runoff can be easily rechanneled to irrigate and sometimes even humidify an existing garden. (Most plants grow better in moist air.)

Roof water similarly should not be neglected as a source of dollar savings. Where does the roof water go now? It, too, can be used for irrigation instead of just running into a drywell. Both the increasing cost of water, and the expected effects of global warming will make this kind of planning more and more cost effective.

If you build a swimming pool on an existing lot, consider the pool's energy-saving potential as well as its recreation value. Passive solar heating, or solar collectors, should not be overlooked for supplemental heating. Evaporation from a large pool can improve a dry climate or worsen a muggy one. Prevailing summer winds should be considered in relation to evaporation. They may need to be rerouted through the property. Winds also blow debris, pollen, and leaves onto the pool surface.

While building a swimming pool is beyond the ken of most homeowners, improvements to the ground-water flow are not. They require a lot of thought, a little regrading, and a strong person with a shovel.

# HOW TO MAKE YOUR OWN
# SITE PLAN

Buy some graph paper. Lay out your yard and house to scale. For a manageable scale, 1 inch should equal 10 feet. (A scale using the number 10 makes the arithmetic much easier, too.) Any very complicated areas can be separate drawings using a scale of 1 inch equals 5 feet. Very large sites may need 20 feet or even 40 feet to the inch for a macro-site plan.

First draw the lot boundaries. Then draw in the buildings.

Then draw in all the weather and energy factors (sun, winds, cold pockets, evaporation, shadows, north-south axis, and so on).

Next draw all the landscape factors (road, good views, bad views, access, service areas, and such). Finally, plot the existing trees and shrubs.

Make about a dozen copies of this basic plan to work on. On the first one, sketch in pencil what's needed. Where should there be trees, shrubs, flowers? Don't forget patios, play areas, vegetables, maybe fruit trees. Be sure to think about maintenance! Make several different designs, with different shapes. They don't have to follow the lot line or be all square.

A good therapy for insomnia is to redesign your garden in your head when you can't sleep. It's pleasant, relaxing, and makes use of a time when the mind is at its most creative. Keep a pad nearby to write down the incredibly wonderful ideas that will come to you, because once you fall asleep again, you will forget them.

## FIGURE 39: **A SAMPLE PLAN**

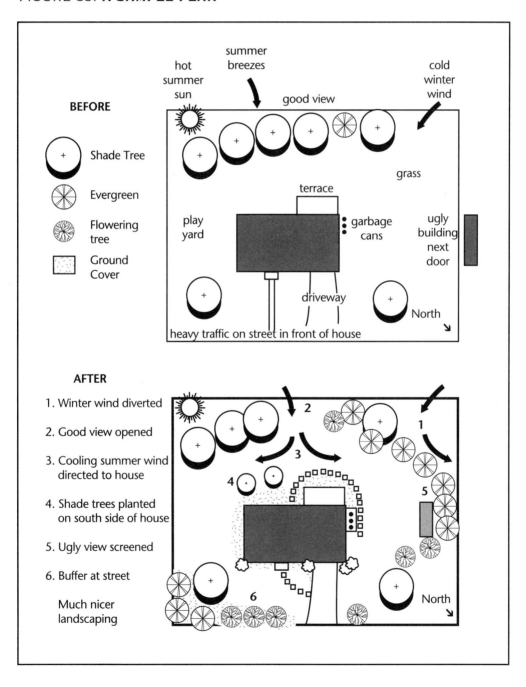

After you have a pleasing design, begin to add the specific kinds of trees and plants to be used. Visit your local parks and arboretum to see what the mature plants look like and what survives in your area. Garden-house tours are helpful. Illustrated catalogues may be also, although your plants will never look like the pictures.

Beware of magazines. Their pictures tend to present only the very latest style or sensational aspects of a garden. Potted trees and flowers are brought in just for the story. (I know. I've done it.) No mention is ever made of how many gardeners the owner employs or how much the garden cost to create. Many of the gardens are too busy, with too many different things jumbled together in them. Such presentations are fine for ideas, but must be adapted with caution and good taste.

A truly satisfactory garden is a pleasant, peaceful retreat, a cool, green oasis in an otherwise hectic world. One needs a place to smell the roses. A fussy, high-maintenance garden will be an unpleasnt burden in the end, but carefully chosen trees, shrubs, fruits, and flowers will give pleasure and soothe the soul.

# Part II

# THE
# LAND

## AND USING IT WISELY

# THE
# PLANTS

## AND USING THEM WELL

The art of landscaping is actually very scientific. One thinks that gardens are where the fairies live, which they do, but there is more to the landscape than just the flowers. Understanding plants, their growing requirements, their particular idiosyncrasies, and the science behind it all is essential. The more one understands the reasons for certain practices, the more successful the projects at hand will be.

Some of the practices are age old. Some are old wives' tales passed down through folklore. Some are old farmers' wisdom or accepted and respected agriculture practices. Today, however, many of the old ideas are being questioned and revised in light of new research and new problems.

Today, we are very concerned with preserving the environment in which we live, rather than just maximizing crops and ignoring the consequences to the planet. After World War II, chemicals seemed to offer a brave new world, where growing plants could be controlled and made to always produce bumper crops. A half century of chemical use has indeed produced the bumper crops that were expected; however, troubling hidden costs have appeared: polluted water supplies, eroded topsoil, resistant insects, and human health problems.

As our infatuation with chemicals wanes, and as their usefulness is incorporated into scientific information, we move to other theories that will fuel future decades.

# CURRENT THEORIES

The current theory is to use nature as a helper to enhance outcomes. It means manipulation of microenvironments to get the desired results. It also means choosing and adapting plants to fit available biological niches.

Biological solutions are the current rage. They may include "good" predatory wasps that destroy damaging "bad" insects. They may mean redesigning old natural pesticides to increase their potency and usefulness. They may mean using Integrated Pest Management or Plant Health Maintenance strategies and theories (see page 132).

Also, there have been incredible discoveries in plant genetics, which have advanced agriculture and plant sciences to a new, higher plateau. With these advances, complex scientific techniques have been developed for dealing with the new improved plants. The Green Revolution in Southeast Asia, which increased food supplies, developed rice plants with strong stems that wouldn't fall over. This increased productivity, but also required more fertilizer and new growing methods.

When the United States was founded in 1789, 90 percent of the population worked on the farm, just to feed the new nation. Now, with modern agriculture, it takes only 2 percent of the population to grow enough food for the whole country and have a surplus to export.

# A NEW AGE

With the advent of genetic splicing, we are on the threshold of an era of unimaginable advancement in plant growth, adaptability, and vigor. New species and new varieties with inserted genes will appear as their sales makes them profitable. The Pomato, or Potato-tomato, which produces red fruit on top and edible tubers on the roots may yet be practical. Frost resistance, insect resistance, nitrogen fixing, even sugar genes will be put into all sorts of plants.

How does this hard science mesh with the pleasant art of gardening? It means that nowadays, to fully realize the potential of the land, one must make use of these advances. There is much useful information. The amount is mind boggling and sometimes discouraging in its complexity. It is difficult to coordinate all the disparate facts in making decisions. The more one knows about plants, however, the easier and more satisfying the art of landscaping can be.

Part I dealt with the theory of saving energy by calculated plant placement. Part II deals with the ways to use plants efficiently. It describes how to plant, what to plant, how to care for plants, and how to prune to get the most out of your plant material. It deals with the needs of the plants themselves and with the many ways to save energy, to save landscape money, to save maintenance time, to save water, to save the soil, to garden sensibly, and to save your own health.

# CHAPTER 8

# *Plant Material*

## WHAT IT DOES AND
## HOW TO USE IT

Plants affect the buildings and microclimates around them in several ways. They provide shade and they channel winds. They cool by evaporation of water vapor and by actually absorbing sunlight into their leaves. The energy from the sun is used by the green chlorophyll cells to make food by photosynthesis. The energy so used is removed from the air, making the air cooler.

Bare ground with no plant material just absorbs most of the sunlight energy it receives. It feels warmer than a lawn. It is. The rest of the energy is radiated into the air. Where the ground is bare, temperature readings are much higher both underfoot and in the surrounding air. A lawn and shrubs would be cooler. Growing plant material gives shade, creates windbreaks, directs breezes, and performs in a multitude of ways to ameliorate human comfort.

The basic principles of using plants well for energy savings are:

- Grass cools.
- Trees cool and shade.
- Deciduous plants are for summer protection and winter warmth as windbreaks.
- Evergreen plants provide year-round shade and wind protection.
- Plants should provide attractive, good design with beauty at all seasons.
- Plants should be suitable for their climate zone of plant hardiness.
- Plants should be adapted to their particular location. (See Lists of Plants in part III.)

# PLANT HARDINESS ZONES

Each plant has certain geographical zones in which it will prosper. If a plant is at the extreme end of its climate zone, it may survive, but it will be stressed. Stressed plants don't thrive and grow to maximum size. Too hot a climate is as bad as too much cold. If the plant is placed outside its zone of tolerance, it will die. Some plants die quickly, such as tropical plants in a frost. Some die slowly—they just peter out, or perhaps they lose their resistance to fungus and insect attacks because they are so stressed. Most gardeners learn through experience which plants will do well, but it can be an expensive learning experience. It's better to know ahead of time what your zone of hardiness is and match the plants you buy to it.

FIGURE 40: **U.S.D.A. PLANT HARDINESS ZONE MAP**

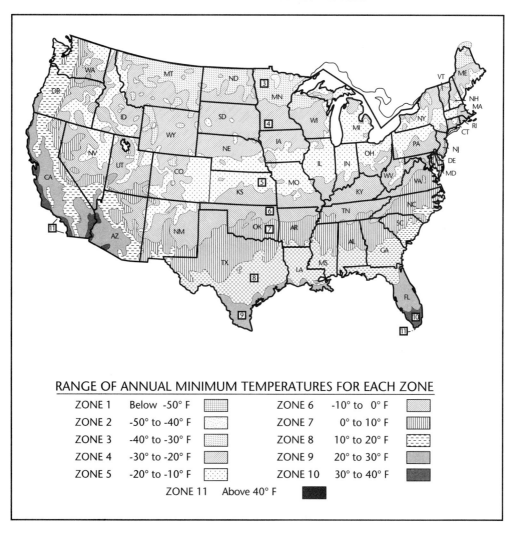

## RANGE OF ANNUAL MINIMUM TEMPERATURES FOR EACH ZONE

| | | | | |
|---|---|---|---|---|
| ZONE 1 | Below -50° F | | ZONE 6 | -10° to 0° F |
| ZONE 2 | -50° to -40° F | | ZONE 7 | 0° to 10° F |
| ZONE 3 | -40° to -30° F | | ZONE 8 | 10° to 20° F |
| ZONE 4 | -30° to -20° F | | ZONE 9 | 20° to 30° F |
| ZONE 5 | -20° to -10° F | | ZONE 10 | 30° to 40° F |
| | ZONE 11 | Above 40° F | | |

The United States Department of Agriculture has prepared a full-color Plant Hardiness Zone Map of North America. This map replaced the old Arnold Arboretum map, which had different zone numbers. Based on scientific temperature readings, this new map more accurately represents actual climate zones.

Zones are defined by the lowest expected winter temperature in each region. Each zone represents a drop of 10° F. Individual zones are subdivided into 5 degree sections, which are labeled A and B.

The microenvironment of your particular planting bed can be warmer than its zone if it's on the south side of your building and protected from cold winds. A blanket of snow will keep covered plants warmer during cold spells, which is why tender perennials often survive farther north than one would expect.

In order to understand your existing plants or what to look for when buying new ones, these hardiness zones are helpful and are included in many of the plant lists in part III.

# THE EXISTING VEGETATION

Every house has existing vegetation. Whether you buy, build, or inherit, something is growing in the soil. It may be just weeds and a tree or two. Lucky the homeowner who finds a well-designed landscape with a sequence of blooming plants and trees that herald the seasons in an ever-changing panorama of color and interest.

It's best to start with the existing vegetation, whatever it is. Plants and trees in the ground have great value. If you doubt it, price a large tree at a nursery. The cost is shocking. Making use of what's already on your site saves both the purchase price and the planting costs.

Contractors and landscapers are very quick to say, "It's a junk tree [or shrub]. No problem to cut it down and replace it." Ask for all the reasons and then think it over. They may be giving good advice, or they may be making money. Or they may be designing a garden to boost their own ego or reputation. It's easier to cut a tree in haste than to replace it at leisure.

Begin by analyzing the tree cover. Are the trees useful and attractive? Next, evaluate the shrubs. Are they worth saving? Evergreen shrubs are valuable and often can be moved. Deciduous shrubs are not expensive to replace but are very easy to move. Finally, consider the surface of the ground, whether it be weeds, grass, paving, blacktop, or ground cover.

# WHAT TO SAVE AND WHAT TO MOVE

After analyzing the total landscape, a decision has to be made. What is serving a useful purpose, either aesthetically or by saving energy? What is neither attractive nor useful? What can be salvaged at its present location? What should be moved to some other spot?

Deciduous plants are generally the easiest to move. They recover the fastest. Shrubs that have a large root system and several vigorous main stems become large plants faster. Small trees are easier to move than large ones, because small specimens recover from transplant shock faster and make up the size in faster growth. If an 8-foot tree and a 15-foot tree are transplanted side by side, in five years the 8-foot one will be taller.

It is interesting to watch an experienced nurseryman dig and replant. No quantity of words can fully explain the nuances of how he handles plant material, or even how he uses a shovel. Observe, if you can, before plunging in.

The most critical aspects of moving plants are: (1) getting a good root system, (2) keeping the plant out of the ground the shortest possible time, (3) moving during the right season, and (4) always providing enough water. (See chapters 9 and 10 for more details about transplanting.)

# MOVING PLANTS FROM THE WILD

If very many plants are to be moved, it is worth hiring a backhoe to dig holes. Then each plant is scooped up bare-rooted, with its pile of soil, and set into the pre-dug hole. This system is especially useful if you have access to a woodland and fields that have unlimited plant material.

When moving plants from the wild, however, success is not guaranteed. Plants in the wild often have long, diffuse root systems that transplant poorly. A greater percentage of loss is to be expected than with nursery-grown stock. Also the growth habit of woodland material tends to be more sparse and open. After a few years in the light, however, most plants fill out. Sometimes shearing of new growing tips will cause the plants to fill out and thicken sooner.

Deciduous shrubs can be cut back quite a bit in early spring. For convenience, many can be cut back almost to the ground, but some will recover slowly. If a plant is very overgrown, it is better to remove the oldest stems entirely, near the ground, and cut the younger stems back some to form a good shape and size; but this is very time consuming.

Trees that are to grow tall may have the side branches trimmed back but never the top leader stem. It is also a good time to do careful structural pruning of trees, because wild trees rarely have good form. How the tree is pruned when it is young will determine how attractive and how strong it will be at maturity.

Success also depends on whether the particular species of tree or shrub is easy to transplant. Some take hold with ease; some are almost never successful. (See List of Trees that are Hard to Transplant, part III.) The younger the tree or shrub, the more likely it will survive. Also try to match the microenvironment from which the plant was taken—shady location, open field, moist soil. The more the new location matches the old, the better the tree will adapt. Don't be disappointed if they don't all live. When you move plants from the wild, you must expect some of the transplants to die.

# RELATIVE PRICE–BENEFIT RATIO OF MOVING OR BUYING PLANTS

In general, it is more economical to *transplant* small material that can be easily dug and moved as well as valuable specimen plants that would be expensive to buy.

It is more economical to *buy* medium-sized evergreens and trees. Nursery-grown plants have better root balls, transplant better, and take hold sooner. They can be easily handled and planted. Also, improved varieties more suited to the home garden can be chosen.

Planting labor costs about three-fourths as much as the price of the plants themselves. The hardest part of transplanting is digging. Most homeowners are not accustomed to digging holes and don't do it efficiently. They overdo the exercise. They hurt their backs. If money is scarce, you can save a little by hiring someone to dig the holes, dig up the plants to be moved, and place the plants in the holes. Filling in the planting holes is not as strenuous and can usually be done by the homeowner.

Ground covers are the easiest things to move, particularly ivy, myrtle, mondo grass, hosta, ferns, creeping fig, gazania, sedum, ajuga, and pachysandra. They are quite expensive to buy and therefore, should be replanted or conserved in a nursery bed for future use. See page 116 and Figure 57 for how to go about moving and maintaining ground covers.

Lawns and grass add greatly to the appearance and appeal of a property and are very important in energy saving plans. Whether it is really more cost-effective to renovate an existing lawn, to reseed entirely, or to lay down new sod is not an easy decision. Renovating an established lawn with fertilizer and overseeding with new grass seed is always cheapest but requires patience and continual work before it will improve significantly.

Grass that is in very bad condition with lots of weeds may require a more radical approach in which the ground is dug up, new loam added if there is not enough, and completely reseeded or sodded. Homeowners can accomplish these tasks as long as they understand the process and have some nearly professional skills in laying sod property.

# FACTORS IN PLANT SELECTION AND USE

To use plants well, one has to choose carefully. There is a right plant for each use and place. To simplify the choice, a group of criteria is listed here. Not every one will apply to your site or problems, but the general thinking process is worth exploring and will help you make decisions.

## Economics

Do the plants conserve energy?
Do they increase real estate value?
Is maintenance cost reasonable?

## Ecology

Do the plants provide climate control?
Do they provide noise control?
Do they provide wind protection?
Do they provide moisture control?
Do they provide soil and erosion protection?

## Aesthetics

Are the plants interesting?
Do they frame a vista or screen out a bad view?
Do they frame the buildings?
Do they provide an architectural backbone for the landscape design?
Are they in harmony with the area?

## Shape

Are the shapes of the trees and shrubs appropriate?

## Color

Are the colors of the flowers and foliage (bluish, green, variegated) appealing?
Are twig, bark, and fruit colors and leaf patterns attractive?
Do the colors go together?

## Sound

Do the leaves rustle, the pine needles whisper, or the seed pods rattle?

CHAPTER 9

# How to Use Existing Trees

Trees are the most important plants for both energy conservation and design. They are expensive. They take years to grow to maturity, when they finally serve us best. There is an old farmer's saying that you plant pear trees for your sons to harvest. Any trees that are already growing on your site are a decided plus. So start with a frugal analysis of the trees.

## EVALUATING THE TREE CANOPY

Look carefully at what is growing. Some specimens may be worth saving, others not. Some will be beautiful, and you will want to retain them. Particularly worth keeping are valuable horticultural specimens or rare species.

Other trees may not be as beautiful but will serve a practical use, such as defining the lot or screening out neighbors. Shade in summer is valuable. On the other hand, there may be too much shade and too many trees, which make the house damp. Or there may not be enough air circulation. Do the existing trees channel cool air to the house in summer yet screen out the cold winter winds? (See Figure 39, A Sample Plan.)

Take your time, and look long and hard before cutting anything down. When moving into a house, it is worth going through one whole year to see how everything performs at different seasons, before starting any landscaping. Lots of lovely things come up as surprises. When trees are leafless in winter, it's easier to decide where necessary pruning and thinning should be done.

It takes a long time for a landscape to mature, so it makes sense to plan carefully. There is no rush to get everything done immediately.

# TOO MANY TREES?

*Is there a problem with too many trees?* It is always unfortunate to remove trees from a property, because they ameliorate the climate more than any other plant material. There are many ways of remedying problems without sacrificing the trees. Corrective pruning and thinning is often the answer.

# CORRECTIVE PRUNING

Trees that are poorly shaped, dangerous, or have grown willy-nilly unattended should have corrective pruning for better shape and strength.

*Trees that are too tall* can have the tops cut off. Technically this is called "topping" and is useful for trees that cause too much shade or could be dangerous in windstorms. It is highly frowned upon by professional arborists because it ruins the natural shape and promotes weak shoots, but it can be done. Topped trees often put out a tuft of new shoots on top, which grow quickly. When the topping is done to expose a solar collector to sun or to open a vista, it often has to be repeated every few years as the new spindly top shoots get too high. Eventually, topped trees become weak and don't live out their normal life span. But they may live for ten years, which may be as long as you are in that particular house.

The permanent solution for trees that are too tall is to top them for the short term and plant new lower-growing trees. When the new trees grow tall enough, the older, topped trees can be removed.

*Trees that hang too low* can be improved by having all the lower branches removed up to the desired height. A canopy starting at 8 feet is normal, but it can be as high as 15 or 20 feet on a tall tree.

Large trees that cause too much damp shade, especially evergreens, are a difficult problem. If you remove them, the property may look naked. The solution short of cutting them down is removing the lower branches, which is technically known as "raising the crown." This allows the free movement of air, especially summer breezes, which prevents dampness. Also, buildings can benefit from low winter sun beneath the trees on the south side.

In the forest, evergreens normally have tall, branchless trunks when they are old. There is no harm in pruning them the same way on home grounds. It retains the "pine grove" effect but allows good air circulation beneath.

FIGURE 41: **TOPPING AND RAISING THE CROWN**

Overgrown trees

**Raising the crown**
Crown raised; lower
branches removed

**Topping**
Top branches removed;
sun reaches solar collector

*Topping destroys the shape and form of a tree, and shortens its life; it is useful, however, for providing interim shade until new, lower growing trees mature.*

Grass under the trees absorbs moisture and feels cool and damp underfoot. So does moss or ground cover under trees where grass will not grow. When plants or grass won't grow under trees, pine needles, crushed stone, and paving stones set in sand will help an area feel warm and dry.

*Trees that are too dense* present another kind of problem. It can be corrected by having some of the inside branches removed for more light and air. This technique for increasing sunlight and air circulation is known as "thinning the crown." It can also be used to make a tree smaller overall and to make the tree more storm resistant. A very dense tree presents a full canopy of leaves to heavy winds, which acts like a sail and catches the wind. When a tree is properly thinned, however, the air can go right through the crown, and it is less likely to be blown down.

When thinning the crown, some of the branches in the top are carefully removed (hopefully artistically). The process actually improves the health of many older trees. Too often people just cut down dense trees, not realizing they can have both their tree and dappled sunlight, too.

Be careful when thinning certain old trees, especially top branches, because if they get sunburn on the interior bark they may die way back. The varieties that are very sensitive to sunburn are beech, oak, sugar maple, and red maple. They need special treatment and a very experienced arborist.

Branches that block winter sun from the house or patio should be removed first. Those needed for summer shade should be left untouched. Small interior side branches on main limbs should not be removed. The final result of proper crown thinning is an airy, well-balanced, safe tree. On large specimens, this is not a job for the amateur: It requires a registered arborist with proper aerial equipment, safety ropes, and liability insurance. Tree pruning is a dangerous business.

## FIGURE 42: **THINNING THE CROWN**

····· Remove these branches

Just because you use an expert, do not assume his aesthetic judgment is better than yours. It's usually not. Don't hesitate to suggest which branches should stay or be removed. He should be able to explain the reasons why he has chosen certain ones to go and others to stay. If he tells you to mind your own business, change firms.

When a good pruning job is finished, the tree should look attractive and natural. It should not look like as if it's had a haircut. Nor should the main branches look like lion's tails—with only a tuft of leaves at the ends of long bare limbs. Too many arborists just hack away thoughtlessly. *Proper pruning improves both appearance and longevity.*

## FIGURE 43: **PROPER PRUNING**

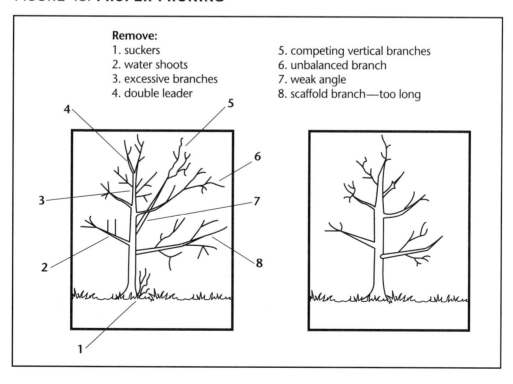

**Remove:**
1. suckers
2. water shoots
3. excessive branches
4. double leader
5. competing vertical branches
6. unbalanced branch
7. weak angle
8. scaffold branch—too long

## *Principles of Good Pruning*

- Proper pruning should provide a strong scaffold of balanced branches.

- The limbs should radiate around the trunk at well-spaced intervals for strength.

- The branches should grow from the trunk with an open angle of about 60 degrees, rather than a sharp angle of 45 degrees.

- There should be only one top central trunk. If there is a **V** split with two leaders, one of them should be cut back by about two-thirds and the other left to grow up to become a single strong central trunk.

- There should be no suckers or water sprouts left on a healthy tree.

- Overlong branches that unbalance the tree can be pruned back to about a half inch from a healthy outward-facing bud or branchlet.

- When pruning is finished, the tree should have a firm, upright center of balance to withstand strong winds and ice storms.

# GLOBAL WARMING AND TREE DAMAGE

As global warming becomes more pronounced, and the amount of energy in the atmosphere increases, the intensity of storms and velocity of winds will increase, too. Storms will be more powerful and destructive, and trees will be more at risk. In addition to high winds, trees suffer from several other kinds of storm damage. There are some preventive measures that can be taken to lessen those risks.

# SPECIAL PRUNING FOR PREVENTING STORM DAMAGE

## *Wind Damage*

High winds cause the most damage to trees. Most high-velocity storm winds come from the southwest. This exposure is also the area where most summer shade trees are needed. Special attention is necessary so that these trees are placed so they won't fall on the house.

As trees grow tall, they should be pruned for stability, strength, and general safety. Well-managed trees rarely fall. Usually, dead, dangerous, or unbalanced ones cause the damage. To prune for safety, watch for certain danger signals and correct them.

Remove all dead or diseased wood. A well-kept tree has a good center of balance, with branches well spaced all around the trunk, especially high up. Wide-angle branching is encouraged. A branch with a 60-degree angle from the trunk is much more stable than one growing at a 45-degree angle, because sharp crotches have a tendency to split in storms. Split leaders are cut back to only one because these also have a tendency to split apart. Trees can be lowered if necessary. Overlong branches are cut back, as well as all branches that hang dangerously over buildings.

With large old trees, supportive wire tree cables are often useful to keep heavy branches from splitting or pulling the whole tree down. When cabling is done all around the center, the whole tree is more likely to move as a single unit, and individual branches less apt to split away and break off.

These precautions are not necessary for all trees on a property; they are expensive. They are worthwhile, however, for certain valuable trees and for ones close to the building that might cause damage. Trees that are regularly maintained have many fewer problems in storms.

There are other ways to lessen wind damage. Avoid planting trees with brittle or soft wood, such as cottonwood, white maple, poplar, and willow. Generally, the fastest-growing trees have the wood that is most susceptible to breakage. Also, allow enough room for trees to develop adequate roots to anchor themselves securely. Trees grown in sunlight, with adequate space, generally grow wider and lower and have a lower center of gravity, which makes them less likely to blow over.

Some situations are very susceptible to "windthrow," which is when the wind blows down a tree. Tall trees, especially those at a cleared forest edge, are very susceptible to windthrow, from even minor storms. In the forest, trees sway and move as a block, holding each other up. Individual forest trees are usually too tall for their limited root systems. When the forest edge is cleared, or if a small clump of trees is preserved, the trees on the exposed edges are very susceptible to windthrow. Over a period of years, trees fall one or two at a time until there are no more or until there are so few that they are able to widen their root system for stability.

## Freezing

Unexpected extremes of cold weather or early winter storms can cause damage even when plants are in their correct zones of hardiness. Thus, planting hardy trees in appropriately protected locations is a necessary start. Understanding how plants cope with cold can help enhance winter "hardening" and resistance to cold.

Plants prepare for winter in early autumn by changing the chemical nature of their cells. The concentration of water is decreased, and the concentration of natural antifreezes such as sugar and glycerol is increased. The lower freezing point of these substances prevents the formation of ice crystals, which can puncture cell membranes. In addition, the freezing of the water in intercellular spaces changes the osmotic pressure gradients between cells. Water is drawn out of the cells, causing them to dry out and collapse. These physiological cell changes are controlled by the plant's genes, seasonal weather, and maintenance practices.

To diminish susceptibility to freezing damage, give the plant time to stop growing. This allows time to harden off and to manufacture these natural antifreezes. To do this, avoid any practices that encourage late-season growth, such as late-season irrigation, fertilization, or pruning. Give the plants lots of water during summer, but stop watering in early September. This will give the trees a chance to sense that winter is coming, and they will begin the process of preparing for cold weather.

There had been some concern that trees exposed to bright lights twenty-four hours a day, such as those planted in parking lots or trees growing at their lowest zone of frost tolerance, like London plane trees planted in northern cities, might read the seasonal change signals inaccurately and continue to grow too long. Over the years, however, this has proven not to be a problem.

## Fire

In areas subject to forest fires, particularly in California and near some of the national forest preserves, fire protection around residences should be part of the landscape planning.

The best protection is a large lawn surrounding the building, irrigated, if possible, to keep it green and moist. A clear area lawn, paving, or low plants, extending a minimum of 30 feet all around the house, is recommended. Plants should be fire-retardant, such as thick succulents or those with leathery leaves that don't burn, and irrigated, if possible, to keep from drying out.

In the clear area, as well as elsewhere, avoid "pyrophytes," which are plants high in oils or resins that ignite quickly and burn very hot. Keep all dead wood pruned off and all litter picked up.

Oakland, California provided a tragic example of what can happen. There were many Monterey pine, Monterey cypress, and bluegum eucalyptus, all of which produce volatile resins and large quantities of flammable debris. In a devastating fire in 1991, sparks ignited in a grove of drought-stressed Monterey pine. The wildfire spread quickly, and within fifteen minutes about fifty homes were engulfed. In 1993, another devastating fire, fanned by hot, dry winds, swept through southern California. Certain areas of the United States, California in particular, are prone to wildfires although they can occur anywhere during droughts.

In fire-prone areas, trees can be planted at the property line and away from the buildings, but they should be fire resistant. In Oakland, the cypress and pine were all killed, but fire-resistant native species, such as coast live oak and coast redwood, survived. These grow more slowly and are harder to establish, but reduced risk may make them the trees of choice.

Wild flower meadows and rough grass areas should be mowed where risk of fire is great.

## Floods

Another by-product of global warming is that torrential rainstorms, which cause most floods, may become more frequent. Flooding is most common in the flat Southeast but occurs in many places in the country, especially near river courses. In 1993, the Mississippi River and its tributaries overflowed their banks and broke through dikes and levees that had provided adequate protection for years.

Occasional flooding that drains away quickly does not harm trees. Flooding that remains on water-saturated soils, however, can do damage. One way is by softening or washing away the soil that supports the roots, making the trees vulnerable to falling over. Another problem is with root metabolism. In flooded soil, air and oxygen are eliminated, and organic toxins may accumulate. An early signal of root problems is chlorosis (pale green leaves that have lost chlorophyll).

Trees that are planted on raised mounds that drain quickly recover better. Or, in areas that flood often, use water-tolerant trees. Among them are swamp trees such as red maple, sycamore, bald cypress, and tupelo. Most state Agricultural Extension Services have lists of trees adapted to the soil and climate of local flood-prone areas.

## Lightning

Lightning accompanies most thunderstorms, hurricanes, and tornadoes. Tall trees are a common target, especially those that are isolated. Oaks, elms, poplars, and pines are most often struck. Damage to a tree occurs when the lightning, passing through the center of the trunk, turns the tree's moisture into explosive steam, causing the trunk to shatter. Sometimes trees are hit but not damaged. It is thought that this happens when the electric charge travels along the outside bark and into the ground. Sometimes it leaves scars on the bark.

To prevent such damage to valuable trees, some people install in each tree expensive lightning rods of copper or aluminum cable. These are so expensive though that most people live with lightning risk instead.

## Ice Storms

All states suffer from ice storms, except New Mexico, Arizona, Nevada, and southern California. These storms occur most often in an L-shaped belt extending from central Texas northward to Kansas, then eastward across the Ohio Valley and the lower lakes, to New England and the Middle Atlantic states. In these areas, one serious ice storm can be expected every three years.

The damage to trees is not from cold but from breakage caused by the sheer weight of the ice. The taller or older a tree, the more it will suffer. Trees that hold their leaves late into fall are particularly susceptible, as are wide, densely branched trees such as dogwood, crab apple, and cherry. Ice accompanied by wind makes the problem much worse.

In March 1991 a late ice storm hit Rochester, New York. The damage was similar to that caused by a hurricane, with most trees losing more than half their limbs. Since the ground had already thawed, other trees just uprooted and tipped over.

Some species are better able to withstand ice storms. They include yellow birch, American hornbeam, hophornbeam, shagbark hickory, hawthorn, northern catalpa, horse chestnut, beech, white ash, gingko, Kentucky coffeetree, butternut, oak (except pin oak), spruce, and eastern arborvitae.

One should never try to clear ice or snow from trees by hitting them or sweeping them off with a broom. The frozen trees are as brittle as crystal and break easily, especially the delicate twigs and flower buds. (In a soft snow it is possible to shake a branch free of snow gently by pulling the end up and down.) Water can be sprayed to melt ice, but only if the temperature is warm enough so that it won't freeze on the supercooled existing ice.

## Repairing the Damage

Small trees that have been knocked over can be re-rooted and staked. After re-rooting, the area should be thoroughly watered to remove air pockets in the soil. Tall, tipped-over trees should be removed, because, even if staked carefully, they can never be made safe enough.

To remove large trees, it is best to hire a certified arborist. There may be live wires. Fallen trees are often under stress and will spring violently back when sawing releases a branch. This can cause serious injury and even death. Be especially wary of trees that have partially fallen and are leaning on another tree. These are called "widow makers" and not without reason. They may look easy to clear, but they can jolt unexpectedly when someone starts cutting.

After a storm it is best to get a reputable firm to do any removal work even if it means waiting. In emergencies, the town usually will clear the road, deal with dangerous electrical wires, and may help with your driveway until proper work can be done.

# PRUNING CUTS, WOUNDS, AND HOW TREES GROW

Proper pruning cuts prevent future decay. Although tree decay progresses slowly, it eventually spreads, weakening an otherwise healthy tree. The current theory in pruning is to leave a stub so that the cut can wall off the injury properly. This stub is called a "branch bark collar" and is the area where the wounds close.

Trees do not heal as people do. A wound is never replaced with healthy new tissue. Instead, trees seal off the injury with a wall at the interface of the injury and the uninjured healthy wood. Certain chemicals, such as toluene, are produced, which fill the cells at this interface and prevent decay-producing organisms from entering the healthy tissue. It takes energy and stored carbohydrates to manufacture these protective chemicals. The healthier the tree, the better it is able to manufacture them and to withstand insults.

When woodsmen had only an axe, they always left a small stub because it's not possible to make a flush cut with an axe. The advent of power saws, however, made it quick and easy to instantly saw off anything, anywhere. For a while these nice neat cuts were in vogue.

Then arborists began to find decay spreading above and below these spots. At the University of New Hampshire, Dr. Alex Shigo spent twenty years sawing huge trees in slices to see what actually occurred inside them. No one before him had ever carefully analyzed how trees handled their wounds and how decay spread. His findings showed that trees don't repair injuries; they wall them off.

## *Tree Rings*

Each year, a new ring of cells grows just under the bark. The cells in this ring are the active growing cells for that year and can be seen as tree rings. As the tree grows, each ring records the history of that year. In good years the rings are wide. Drought or frost narrows them. Traces of past forest fires may show. In examining very old trees, one can follow the weather patterns of centuries past. The long history of California wild fires that can be read in the tree ring scars of the centuries old giant sequoias is remarkable.

Each of these new rings walls off the injuries of the years past. Columns of decayed wood may gradually extend up and down in one year's ring, but they will not move outward into the newer ones.

FIGURE 44: **TREE RINGS**

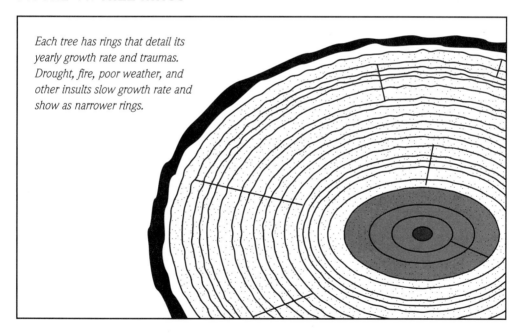

*Each tree has rings that detail its yearly growth rate and traumas. Drought, fire, poor weather, and other insults slow growth rate and show as narrower rings.*

This walling off of injuries dictates the new theory of leaving the branch bark collar stub. A pruning cut is a wound. The deeper the wound is made, the more rings of the tree are damaged and the more decay is introduced into the tree. The branch bark collar stub keeps the pruning injury out of the main trunk's cells.

## FIGURE 45: **BRANCH BARK COLLAR AND PROPER PRUNING CUT**

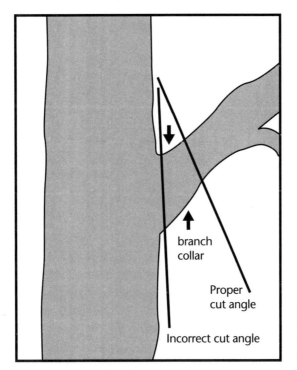

branch
collar

Proper
cut angle

Incorrect cut angle

*To preserve the protective cells in the branch bark collar, the proper angle of the cut is about 45 degrees. The collar is more easily seen on thin, light colored bark.*

As branches grow, some of the trunk tissue grows out, and the branch tissue meets it. When the branch dies or is pruned off, the tree walls off the injury at the point where the trunk and the branch meet, which shows as a seam on the top of each branch and a thickening below it. The seam on top can be easily seen on trees with thin bark such as beech or birch. The point of the trunk and branch meeting is usually at a 45-degree angle to the trunk and slants outward from the top.

When branches die naturally, they fall off at this point. Pruning cuts should be made beyond this point of meeting, which leaves the branch bark collar.

Large limbs are first cut off about a foot from the final cut. Three strokes are used. The first cut is made underneath the limb to prevent tearing the bark. The second cut removes the branch. The final cut finishes the branch bark collar.

## *Preventing Decay*

It used to be common practice to paint all wounds with tree paint or shellac. Research has conclusively shown that it does no good. It only serves to console the homeowner and cosmetically hide the raw wound with black tree paint. Creosote or oil-based paint should never be used, because they kill the growing cells and prevent proper walling off. Work is being done to find a tree paint that actually prevents decaying fungus.

Most important to prevent decay and promote healing is to leave clean wounds that drain and don't hold water. Torn or ripped bark should be carefully cut off, taking care not to damage the healthy wood. Pruning cuts should be at an angle, so water will run off them.

Sometimes a tree develops "wetwood," a condition in which a hole or pruning wound weeps and drips sap. These should be left alone because the weeping is not dangerous. Trying to open a hole can cause more damage than leaving it alone. Sometimes, when a depression holds standing water, a small tube may be inserted at the base to help it drain.

Often trees have carpenter ants or termites where there is wet or decaying wood. It is impossible to get rid of them completely, but they can be treated with pesticides for temporary control. They usually don't kill trees and generally don't attack healthy trees.

## Growth Pattern

The growth pattern of trees, followed during the course of a season, is quite interesting. Because there are not enough energy and nutrients to allow parts to grow at once, different parts (leaves, stems, and roots) grow at different times. Hormones regulate the process, switching growth from one area to another. Roots grow in spring and fall. As root growth peaks in early spring, it triggers shoot growth and leaf expansion. The leaves make carbohydrates, which then encourage stem growth. As this tapers off, new buds are set for the next year. Hormones

FIGURE 46: **TREE GROWTH PATTERN**

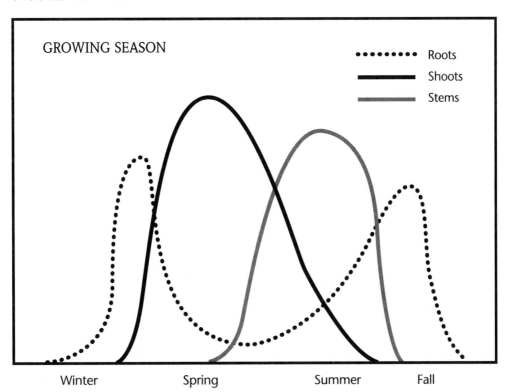

then signal the root growth to increase again in the fall. Roots actually continue to grow even when the tree is dormant in winter, as long as the ground is not frozen.

Roots initiate growth and, at season's end, they store the carbohydrates manufactured by the leaves. Anything that inhibits root growth restricts the whole seasonal growth process. Construction damage is especially traumatic. In the end, the health of the roots is basic to total plant health. (See chapter 15, Protecting Existing Trees during Construction.)

## Woodlands

The landscape effect of a grove of young trees is like a lovely woodland. It is especially beautiful when the late afternoon sun shines low under the leaves, through multiple trunks. When a clump of trees is young, a decision must be made whether to keep them as a grove or to remove all but a very few, well-spaced trees.

If someone wants to open up and clear a forested area, the best trees, such as tall or young ones, are preserved. Trees to be removed are those with basal decay or open splits, as well as dead stubs. Dead or dangerously low branches, and unsightly branch stubs are also removed. Lower branches that block the view can also be removed, so it will be possible to see through the forest.

Self-seeded trees, especially maple, oak, cherry, and poplar often grow close together on the borders of property, near stone walls, and in wild areas and so have to be thinned. When trees grow too close together, they crowd each other out and don't grow well. The way to deal with such saplings is to remove the poor ones that crowd out the more vigorous specimens. They may be pruned to a single trunk or multistemmed clumps. This thinning and shaping is usually done over a period of years.

Unfortunately, the poplars, which grow fast in any soil, are weak-wooded, short-lived trees, unsuited to residential use. The beautiful Lombardy poplar is the fastest-growing columnar tree there is. Sadly, it gets a fatal canker disease just as it reaches maturity at about twenty years. All poplars, willows, and maples have roots that clog water and sewer pipes, so don't plant them near the pipes between house and street.

# SPACING TREES

When trees have ample room, they spread more and grow into the broad giants we are accustomed to seeing along rural roadsides and in parks. Given enough room, each kind of tree matures to a certain size and a certain shape determined by its genetic makeup. Maples, for instance, often grow to be 100 feet tall. They should be spaced about 40 feet apart for optimal growth. Other large-growing trees such as oaks, beeches, and planes need similar elbow room.

Small-growing trees such as crab apple, dogwood, and cherry may be spaced 20 feet apart. They will not need more space, no matter how old they become. They are useful near buildings, where their size remains in scale with the architecture and their roots don't intrude into pipes or foundations.

Low-growing trees solve a very expensive municipal problem. Trees that grow too tall under electric wires become a safety hazard. They have to be pruned to protect the wires from damage and from breakage in storms. As often as they are pruned, new shoots appear, and they have to be pruned yet again in a few years. The pruning process is constant and very, very expensive. Herbicides that slow growth are helpful but also cost money and time. In the past, planners did not take this expense into consideration when planting street trees, so many cities are saddled with big street trees and high pruning costs.

A word of caution: Each kind of tree has many varieties. Each variety has its own genetic makeup and its own height. For instance, a sugar maple may grow to be 120 feet tall, but a Japanese maple will rarely reach above 20 feet, even when it's a hundred years old. (See List of Trees of Different Heights, part III.)

## Windbreaks

When trees grow very close together, their growth pattern changes. As they reach for light, they grow taller and faster and branch less. Their overhead canopy will be high, where it can catch the sun. Trees planted in this way function well as windbreaks. Rows of trees serving this purpose are commonly seen on farms protecting citrus groves, and on the prairies serving to break the persistent strong winds that sweep across the flat, open land.

FIGURE 47: A **WINDBREAK ON THE PLAINS**

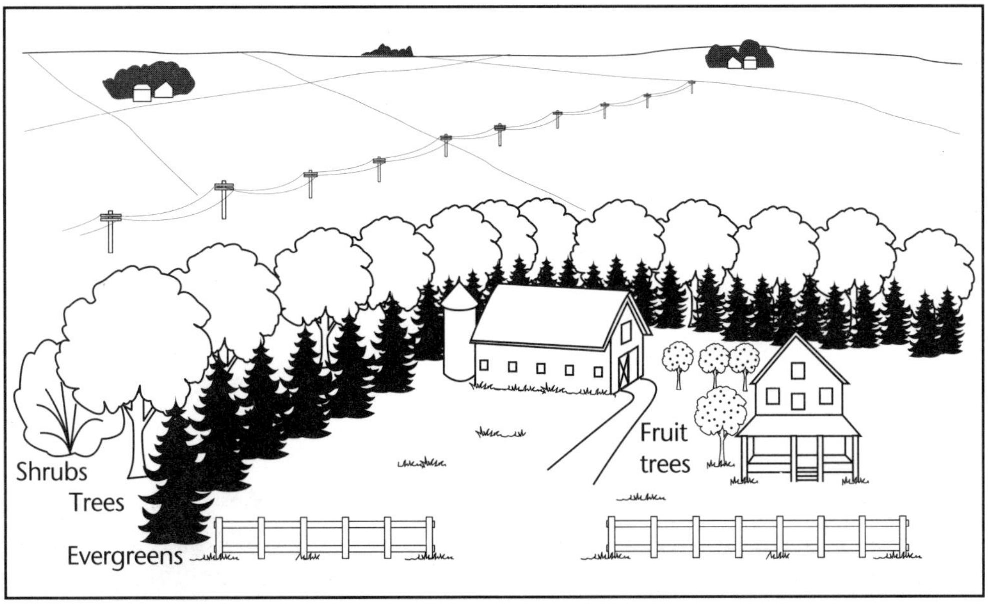

*North and west sides are protected, south is left open. There are three rows. Shrubs on the outside, deciduous trees next, finally evergreens. Fruit and flowering trees are planted inside where they are protected from the wind.*

Good windbreaks usually consist of densely branched plants that break up the force of the wind. Many small branches and twigs combined with some evergreen material do the best job. The windbreaks are placed to block the prevailing and the winter winds. In most areas this is to the north and west.

On the prairies, growing conditions are very harsh and not all trees will survive or grow fast enough to make a good windbreak. The toughest trees have to be used. (See Plant List 16 in part III.)

# TRANSPLANTING TREES

Young sapling trees transplant easily when dormant (before they leaf out) in early spring. A good size is about 6 to 8 feet tall. They may be moved bare-rooted to a prepared hole, then carefully set at the level they were growing or slightly higher.

The new theory for planting trees is to give them a wide area of loosened soil so the roots can spread out easily. The prepared soil should be several times wider than the tree crown. The reason is that most of the new tree roots spread out sideways and develop in the top 4–24 inches of soil. The roots will go where the soil is loose and soft. If the soil is hard, they will not expand but will stay close to their root ball. The planting hole is dug to the depth of the root ball, and it should be set on firm soil.

The old theory was to dig a hole 6 inches wider and deeper than the root ball; field tests, however, showed this was not the best way. In heavy soil the hole became almost a bathtub, which the tree roots grew out of very slowly. In some places the hole held enough water that the roots drowned and died. Another old custom that did not stand up to scientific scrutiny was the addition of peat moss and other additives to the backfill soil. Field tests showed that trees planted in decent soil actually grew longer roots if no additives were used. Just plain soft soil encouraged the best root growth for new trees. If the soil is low in organic material, though, some compost would be beneficial.

Trees that transplant best are those with many fibrous roots, which are the thin small feeding roots, normally near the surface. A good root ball has many of these. Some species of trees withstand the shock of transplanting better than others and may be moved during spring or fall. Tap-rooted trees, such as oaks, have long, fleshy roots, with very few fibrous feeding roots near the top. They are hard to move and should be transplanted only in the spring. (See List of Trees That Are Hard to Move, in part III.)

Trees should be dug before the buds break, not when they are in full leaf. The most sensitive time is just after the leaves or needles first expand, when the loss rate will be high. Carefully dug, well-watered trees, however, may be moved almost anytime except late spring and early summer. Trees in nurseries are actually dug when they are dormant and then put in pots or tied in burlap. These can be planted at any time. This is also true of container stock, which is grown from the beginning in big pots.

## Balled and Burlapped Trees

When planting balled and burlapped specimens, called B&B in the trade, first put the whole root ball in the hole. Then cut all the string holding the burlap together, especially the cord wrapped around the trunk at the top of the root ball. Carefully roll back the burlap, removing any nails holding it together, and tuck it under. Then add topsoil in layers and stamp in each layer to avoid air pockets.

Check the burlap! If it is the old-fashioned brown kind, it may be tucked underneath the plant and will decay in about six weeks. If it is treated green burlap, it will take about eighteen months to decay and should be removed or slashed. If it is plastic that looks like burlap, it *must* be removed from the plant and the hole. It is amazing how many professional gardeners leave the string and often the plastic wrapping on, which kills the tree in a few years.

It is easier to remove the burlap after the plant has been lowered into the hole. When the burlap is removed before planting, the root ball often cracks. Cracked root balls portend a poor take and often death. If the burlap is left in the hole, it must be completely buried. Not one bit of it can remain above the soil level, because it will act as a wick and draw water out of the root area.

## Container-Grown Trees

Container-grown trees present special problems. The planting mix in containers is usually not soil, but wood mulch and chips with additives. Container plants are constantly fed with liquid fertilizer to make them grow faster and are watered very often. It takes a long while for them to adjust, longer than for bare-root specimens moved from another part of the garden.

The roots in containers are often thick and may wrap around inside the pot. After ten or twenty years, these encircling roots will prove fatal and strangle the maturing tree. The solution is to check the root ball before planting. If encircling roots are seen around the edges, make several slices, up and down, all around the outside of the ball of earth, an inch or two deep.

The purpose of these cuts is to expose fresh-cut root edges to the new soil. Clean-cut edges are the point at which new roots are made. Use your own best judgment as to how deep to cut so as to create fresh-cut edges yet not damage the main part of the root system.

If the roots are very thick in the pot, such side slicing is also recommended. Slicing also helps at the bottom of the root ball, which will be flat from growing in the container; slice it diagonally twice to make an X. All container stock makes new roots faster if the edges are slashed or loosened.

Container stock has another problem. If the plant has been heavily fertilized in the nursery, it may suffer from fertilizer starvation after it is planted out. The leaves will begin to pale and may turn yellow. The solution is to gradually wean the plant from its rich diet by giving it half strength liquid fertilizer when it begins to pale. Do not fertilize after midsummer—just hope for the best. It can take a year or two for new roots to form and adapt to their new soil. It is not easy to diagnose fertilizer starvation because yellowing leaves can be caused by so many conditions, such as overwatering, drought, soil problems, too much sun, and too little nitrogen.

## Water

After planting, all trees should be well soaked with water, which should reach right down to the bottom of the planting hole. Enough should be given to eliminate any air pockets in the soil. Sometimes the planting area is flooded twice to make sure all the soil is settled.

To hold the water around the roots, make a saucer or a rim of earth so the water will not run off but will soak into the soil. A professional trick is to water gently directly onto the trunk, letting it run down into the soil. This prevents the force of the water from eroding the soft soil.

Most deaths of new plantings are due to incorrect watering—either too little or too much. Trees mostly die from drought, but they also can die from too much water, for the roots must be able to breathe. Check the soil. If it's soggy, wait to water. Newly transplanted tree roots take up less water than vigorously growing ones. A hosing or misting of the leaves, however, is very helpful if they appear droopy during hot or windy weather. Sometimes their few roots just can't absorb enough water to protect and hydrate the leaves.

It is sometimes difficult to tell if the soil has enough water. The easiest way is to dig down a few inches and feel the soil. Another is to buy a water meter, which is not expensive. While water meters are not completely accurate since their readings depend on dissolved salt levels in the soil, they are extremely useful. The quickest way is to look at the leaves. When under water stress, they begin to droop. It takes some experience to know what their natural look is, and what is drooping. As a rule of thumb, happy leaves are held modestly horizontal, while stressed ones have a hang-dog look.

The best way to handle watering of new trees, however, is to *give each tree 10 gallons of water each week for the first year,* rain or shine. More for larger specimens. Twice a week may be needed in desert, very hot, or windy regions. If there is one thing that will make the most difference between success and failure, it is 10 gallons of water once a week!

## Fertilizer

At planting time, the water used for the backfill may be enriched with a very weak soluble fertilizer solution, or one of the newer organic transplant enhancers or planting hormones (Rootone, Transplantone, or Roots). The hormones help the plant roots get established. Nurseries use liquid fertilizer for foliar and root feeding, but understand what you are giving, and don't overdo it. Don't incorporate granular fertilizer in the backfill soil as it will burn the new roots. Regular surface granular fertilizing should not begin until the late fall after transplanting, or the following spring. The idea is to let the transplant make new roots before pushing new leaves and stems with fertilizer. If the roots aren't there, the plant can't support the top growth.

## Mulch

A good 2-inch mulch over the entire root area helps keep the soil moist and cool, which is essential to root regeneration. The mulch should not be piled against the tree bark, nor should it be deeper than about 3 inches. Mulch that is too thick encourages undesirable anaerobic bacteria, and restricts gaseous exchange between the soil and the air.

## Staking

Trees do not need to be staked, except if they have heavy tops, or if the area is very windy. Stakes should be removed after several months when new roots have formed, and certainly in a year. Trees develop much stronger trunks if they are allowed to sway in the wind, unstaked. Any trees that become crooked or leaning, however, should be straightened immediately with appropriate tree stakes or guy wires. These should be kept on until the trees are growing upright and have very stable root systems.

## Pruning

Transplanting time is a good opportunity to prune the crown into a good, well-balanced shape (See Figure 43, Proper Pruning). It was believed at one time that at transplanting time one-third of each branch should be removed. But recent field tests showed these "haircuts" to be unnecessary. A tree puts out the same quantity of leaf surface whether on shorter or longer branches. After the tree leafs out, however, one should prune out sickly branches that aren't growing vigorously.

Almost any tree can be successfully moved if it is dug carefully, not allowed to wilt or dry out while out of the ground, planted in good soil, and watered once a week for the first year. The shorter the time a plant is out of the ground, the better the rate of success will be. If a plant cannot be immediately placed in a new hole, its roots should be kept moist and covered. Bare-rooted plants may be immersed in a slurry of water mixed with mud. This will protect the delicate root hairs for several days. Balled-and-burlapped plants, and especially container-grown ones, need to be watered frequently. Container plants need water daily, sometimes even more often. The tops should also be sprayed with water if they droop at all. And they all need protection from sun and wind, especially while being transported in cars or trucks.

FIGURE 48: **TRANSPLANTING A TREE**

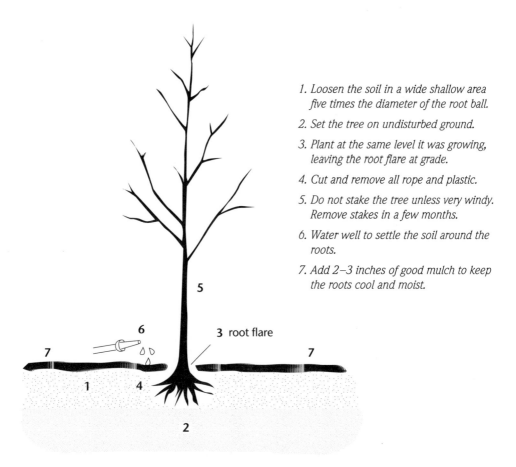

1. *Loosen the soil in a wide shallow area five times the diameter of the root ball.*

2. *Set the tree on undisturbed ground.*

3. *Plant at the same level it was growing, leaving the root flare at grade.*

4. *Cut and remove all rope and plastic.*

5. *Do not stake the tree unless very windy. Remove stakes in a few months.*

6. *Water well to settle the soil around the roots.*

7. *Add 2–3 inches of good mulch to keep the roots cool and moist.*

# ROOT TRENCHING

For plants already growing in the ground, it's helpful to condition them the year before moving them, especially large specimens or varieties that are hard to transplant (beech, oak, large evergreens, dogwood, Japanese maple). This is done by root trenching a year ahead of actually digging them up. The roots are cut all around (sometimes intermittently), leaving a root ball of appropriate size for the size of the tree. In spring—through the end of June—the soil inside the cut is fed with a high phosphorous fertilizer or watered with liquid fertilizer. The area inside the trench should be kept moist, especially during dry periods. Gradually, the tree will develop new feeding roots inside the cut edges. The following season, when the tree is dug and moved, it will have a new fibrous root system to facilitate transplant recovery.

FIGURE 49: **ROOT TRENCHING**

| **First year** | **Second year** |
| :---: | :---: |
| Cut roots | New roots grow inside cut |

# ROOT BALLS

Larger specimens and hard-to-move varieties are usually transplanted with a ball of soil to avoid breaking the roots and to protect them.

To prepare a proper root ball, dig a trench around the tree, leaving the soil around the trunk untouched. The soil should be moist, not too dry and not soaking. The size of the ball is determined by the diameter of the trunk:

| | | |
| --- | --- | --- |
| 2-inch trunk | 24-inch root ball | 300 pounds |
| 3-inch trunk | 32-inch root ball | 750 pounds |
| 4-inch trunk | 40-inch root ball | 2,000 pounds |

Obviously, moving large specimens is not a job for the weekend gardener. It requires a strong back and a good helper. And there's no guarantee the trees will survive. That's why using trees creatively where they already exist makes good sense and saves the most money. It's much easier to design around a large tree than to move it.

If large trees must be moved, consider hiring a good landscape firm with an experienced staff, cranes, and other proper equipment. Most large trees today are dug with a tree spade, a large machine that scoops them out of the ground with pincers. Wire baskets are used to keep the root ball intact. Inside the wire frames there often is burlap, especially plastic burlap. Since the burlap can't be removed from inside the wire frame, it must be completely slit in many places, up and down. The wires are usually left because it is not practical to remove them from a several-ton root ball. They can be clipped with heavy wire cutters, however. The tops of the wire baskets are usually bent down to be under the soil. Studies are being done to see whether, after a long time, the wire baskets cause problems, but since they are as yet inconclusive, clipping the wires is good insurance.

## Commercially Grown Trees

Sometimes it's just cheaper and easier to buy new trees than to try to move the older ones.

Most commercially grown trees have good root systems, carefully developed by frequent root pruning. Many small trees that are sold as balled and burlapped, however, are actually not dug with root balls. They are dug bare rooted, covered with soil and wrapped up. They survive perfectly well but should cost less. Care has to be taken to not break the root ball when planting, although this is often unavoidable.

A properly dug specimen will have a hard, firm root ball that holds its shape when kicked or replanted, even after the burlap is removed. Proper balling and burlapping is very expensive, and few experienced laborers are left who know how to do it. So it is reserved for specimen trees and interesting evergreens as well as large flowering and shade trees.

FIGURE 50: **TRANSPLANTING A BIG TREE**

# GROWTH RATE OF TRANSPLANTED TREES

The rule of thumb is: The smaller the tree, the easier the transplant and the quicker the recovery. For each inch of trunk diameter, it takes a tree about a year to recover from transplant shock. A 1-inch tree will be growing strongly and normally by the second year. A 4-inch tree will not start to grow well for about four years.

In addition, the unavoidable root pruning, done when the tree is dug for transplanting, has a dwarfing effect on future growth and eventual size. The result is that the smaller trees will be larger than big ones in five years. A 1-inch diameter maple will be taller than a 3-inch diameter specimen in a few years. Root pruning, incidentally, is how bonsai trees are kept so small.

CHAPTER 10

# *How to Use Existing Shrubs*

## DECIDUOUS SHRUBS

Almost every old house has large, often ungainly deciduous shrubs left over from pre–World War II days, when they were popular. The ubiquitous lilac is almost universally present. "Lilacs last in the dooryard bloomed..." wrote Walt Whitman in his poem about Lincoln's assassination, because they are unfailing, eternal plants. The early farmers didn't have much time to fool around with fussy plants, but they could count on the utterly neglected lilac blooming after the coldest winter. Today, most lilacs are improperly pruned or growing out of control.

Lilacs and other deciduous shrubs such as spirea, forsythia, and mock orange don't produce such spectacular flowering specimens as do azaleas and rhododendrons, with whom their blooming periods coincide. But the deciduous shrubs do reappear, reliably, year after year, to give shade, greenery, and a week or two of bloom. They also transplant easily.

Big blowsy deciduous shrubs don't belong in the front landscape border. They belong on the property lines, or against the side and back of the house. There, especially on a western exposure, they will shade house walls from hot summer sun. In winter the sun can warm the walls through the bare branches. Or the snow trapped in the bushes' shoots serves as additional wall insulation, for heat loss from an exposed foundation can be significant in winter. If fallen leaves are left under the big shrubs in autumn, they decay, returning nutrients to the soil.

## PRUNING DECIDUOUS SHRUBS

Shrubs have various natural shapes, which should be understood and respected. Pruning old-fashioned deciduous shrubs is an art in itself. They should always be pruned just after flowering. Most of them set buds for the following year shortly after they flower. Pruning should shape the bush before it sets buds.

Ideally, the oldest canes are removed at ground level, which makes space for new young, vigorous shoots to appear. Old canes crack and get insects and other problems, so they don't grow well after several years. The new shoots rejuvenate the shrubs so they can live a long time.

When removing these ground-level shoots, you must take care with grafted shrubs, especially roses. The new shoots from below the graft will be different from the ones above it. Care must be taken to leave a long stub of wood above the graft, from which new buds can come, at least 12 inches when possible. The graft is visible as a woody knob near ground level, or just under it. The shoots from the root stock below the knob are very vigorous but will be inferior in shape and bloom. These shoots below the graft should always be removed. If you fail to control them, they will eventually crowd out and kill the improved, less vigorous, grafted variety on top.

The too common practice of cutting bushes into little balls or with flat tops is not consistent with their nature or growth patterns. Such treatment destroys their natural grace and beauty. It also makes extra work. If low-growing shrubs are wanted, low-growing varieties should be planted.

## Lilacs

Lilacs are easy to grow but require special pruning to last a long time. They can be trained into small trees or kept as hedges. Each year they send up new shoots from the ground. These bloom in two or three years and will then grow for many years. As the shoots get older, they get woody, like tree trunks, and become susceptible to lilac borer larvae. The proper way to get the most mileage from lilacs is to encourage and preserve two new shoots each year and remove one of the old ones as it becomes woody and unproductive.

Standard lilacs will grow about 20 feet tall. Trying to keep them lower by cutting them down in the fall only succeeds in cutting off the blossom buds for the following spring. French and hybrid lilacs, which are often grafted varieties, grow to about 6 feet.

## Roses

Everyone loves roses, but too many people don't know how to prune them for best bloom. Roses should be pruned early in the spring. When they're grown as bushes or shrubs instead of in a rose bed, they need only trimming of the longest canes and also those that are too old. Generally, shrub roses, especially the newest ones, don't require much pruning—just enough to keep young healthy shoots coming, which bear the best flowers. The new shoots that appear in summer should not be cut off and removed, because they will make the strong new branches for the next few years, and those will bloom the most heavily.

The best time to prune is just as the buds swell and begin to break. Then it is possible to see which buds are fat and vigorous and where the stem has died during winter. Pruning is

## FIGURE 51: **PRUNING LILACS AND OTHER DECIDUOUS SHRUBS**

Overgrown lilac

Lilac after pruning

Deciduous shrub;
correct pruning

Incorrect pruning

Overgrown shrub

pruned into

a small tree

done just above a fat, outfacing bud. The cut should be at a slant so water will run off. If stem borers are a problem in your area, treat the cuts with a drop or two of Elmer's glue or push in a thumb tack to prevent the adult borer from laying eggs in the freshly cut soft stem.

On roses, the new shoots sprout from dormant buds on the stems, above the graft knob, so be sure to leave a cane at least 12 to 18 inches long. Then bend and train the vigorous new shoots as they expand to grow in the direction you want them to while they are soft and green. Remove the unproductive, old wood above the new vigorous shoots. This is especially important with climbers and ramblers. Bush and tea roses are usually cut back hard in the spring, before growth begins, to between 1 and 4 feet, depending on the kind of shape you want to produce.

You can tell the difference between shoots from the root stock and shoots from the improved rose variety by the leaves. Root stock usually has small, multiple leaves and many small thorns as do wild roses, which only bloom once, in June. Most improved varieties have large green leaves in groups of three or five, fat thorns, and most bloom more than once a season.

Unpruned roses become overgrown thorny bushes after several years, which is not necessarily bad, as long as they bloom and serve their purpose. They always seem to have dead wood inside where it's impossible to reach without getting lots of scratches. Too often, these

## FIGURE 52: **PRUNING SHRUB ROSES**

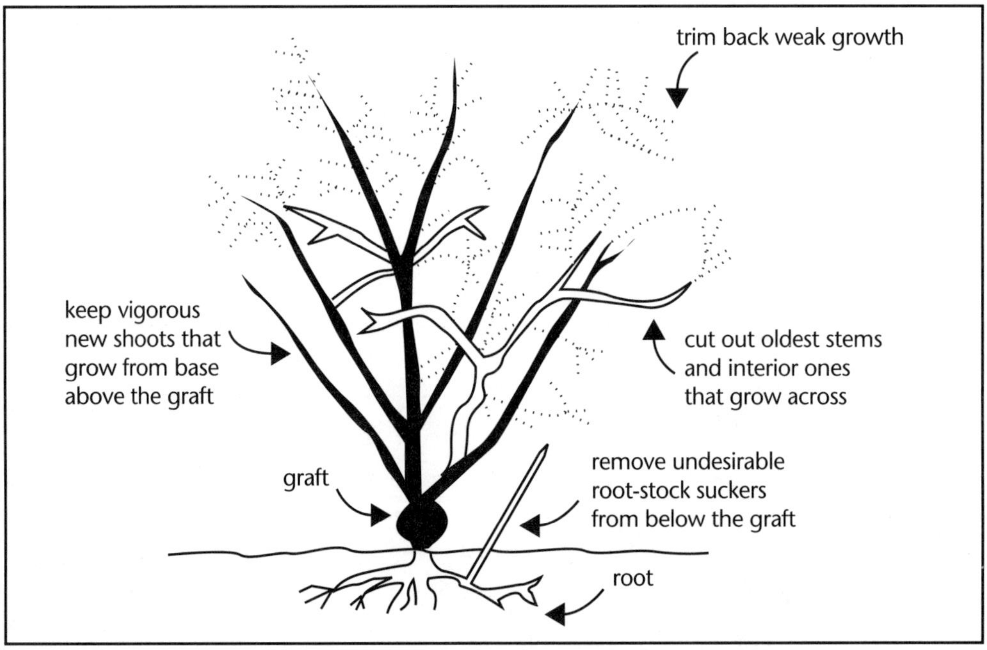

*The aim is to increase vigor by removing old unprotective wood, weak shoots, and thinning branches to avoid crowding. Vigorous growth is saved. After several years, old shoots do not bloom well. Pruning encourages new buds that will bear the best flowers.*

*On grafted plants, watch for inferior root-shoots, which usually have different leaves and thorns.*

neglected bushes are just removed, because they are messy and no one knows how to renew them. A little pruning more often would have kept them blooming well for years. If you inherit neglected roses, the thing to do is simply cut them back hard to 1 foot above the ground, fertilize them, and be patient. A nice green mound will grow the first year. The second year it should be covered with blooms.

Roses are one of the easiest and at the same time one of the hardest flowers to grow. They require sun, fertilizer, pest control, and proper pruning. There are many varieties, with different blooming dates, cold tolerances, vigor, growth habits, and use. Each has particular needs, which you must know to grow them successfully. Some survive while others die each year. But nothing is so beautiful as a freshly cut rose.

# PRUNING HEDGES

Hedges require a particular kind of pruning, which is similar for both deciduous and evergreen. Hedges are kept trimmed to the desired size by shearing all over, or by clipping out individual branches. The more vigorously the hedge grows, the more often it will need trimming. It is sensible to plant varieties whose mature size is just a little taller than the desired height of the hedge. Planting a Siberian elm and trying to keep it 6 feet high will be a constant struggle. In Europe, beech trees and other large species are often trained as tall hedges, a practice that began in royal gardens. One does, however, need a staff of royal gardeners to maintain them.

Hedges used to be more popular than they are now. One reason for their downswing is the demise of the hired hand. Trimming hedges is time consuming and costly, despite the introduction of electric hedge clipppers. Some hedge plants need cutting only once a year (tamarisk, hawthorn, saltbush, saskatoon, potentilla, winged euonymus, bush honeysuckle). Most blooming hedges should be trimmed only once a year, just after blooming. Then they should be left to grow naturally until the next year. Some examples are forsythia, spirea, spice bush, wigelia, roses, and lilacs. They are all vigorous and will grow into nice rounded mounds, about 6 to 9 feet tall.

Some trees, when used as very tall windbreaks or for noise or privacy screening, may also be trimmed only once a year (green ash, mossycup oak, coppiced willow, beech, choke cherry). Hedges that need trimming more times per year are privet, cotoneaster, alpine currant, natal plum, barberry, hibiscus, and bouginvillea.

When pruning any shrub or hedge, remember that the bottom of the bush will remain green and thick only if it has full light. Most people, even most professional gardeners, prune incorrectly. Healthy hedges should be wider at the bottom than the top. They should not be round or narrow at the bottom, because the lower leaves will not receive enough light for healthy growth. Eventually the leaves will fall, leaving bare twiggy holes.

When using hedges for windbreaks, intertwined branches break the wind better, so you really need not trim them at all. This makes planning a windbreak much easier. The secret is to choose shrubs that naturally reach the desired height. Then they can be neatened up when required, but will not require constant shearing.

Too many commercial gardeners from the old school recommend shrubs that make good hedges but ones that must be constantly pruned. They are accustomed to doing it that way, and it makes more business for them. Shrubs that withstand constant shearing, of course, must be more vigorous and often larger than the height that is wanted. It becomes a vicious cycle. You're far better off to choose plants that will serve well at their natural mature size. (See List of Shrubs in part III.)

The current fascination with European garden design prompts the use of pruned specimen plants, which are necessary to create that formal style. Round or square or pointed shrubs, usually evergreen, are one of the characteristics of royal gardens. Sometimes the plants are pruned to form animals or spirals or other interesting shapes. When the pruning passes from the purely practical to become an art form, it is called topiary. To keep plants trimmed into their desired shapes requires great skill, patience, and frequent light clipping. To those who enjoy it, it is very satisfying.

# THE EFFECTS OF PRUNING TREES AND SHRUBS AT DIFFERENT SEASONS

The traditional time to prune is in spring, just before the first flush of growth occurs. When the days lengthen and the sun warms, one gets itchy fingers, which can lead to too much unnecessary cutting. Beware the siren call of spring if you have a power saw in your hand. Before beginning, it's essential to understand what pruning at different seasons does.

Sometimes, nothing feels as good as sawing wood and clipping branches. It's pure power. And after an hour or so, there is a big pile to show for the work. Don't run amok with the saw. More damage can be done by blithe ignorant chopping than by just leaving things alone.

So what should one do to satisfy the siren call of spring? Start with corrective work. Spring pruning should be limited to: (1) training young plants and trees, (2) reshaping older plants and trees, (3) cutting back overgrown trees and shrubs to fit into their allotted space, (4) removing broken branches, and (5) sometimes renovating old overgrown shrubs.

Pruning is a complex art. It helps to understand how shrubs and trees respond to pruning cuts. In truth, you can prune at whatever season you want. It's just that pruning at different seasons produces different kinds of growth and is done for different reasons.

In the spring, each plant wants to grow a certain amount and produce a certain number of leaves. If you cut off one-third of the plant, the remaining two-thirds will produce that same leaf area. (This is why drastic pruning back of newly planted trees is no longer recommended.)

FIGURE 53: **THE CORRECT WAY TO PRUNE A HEDGE**

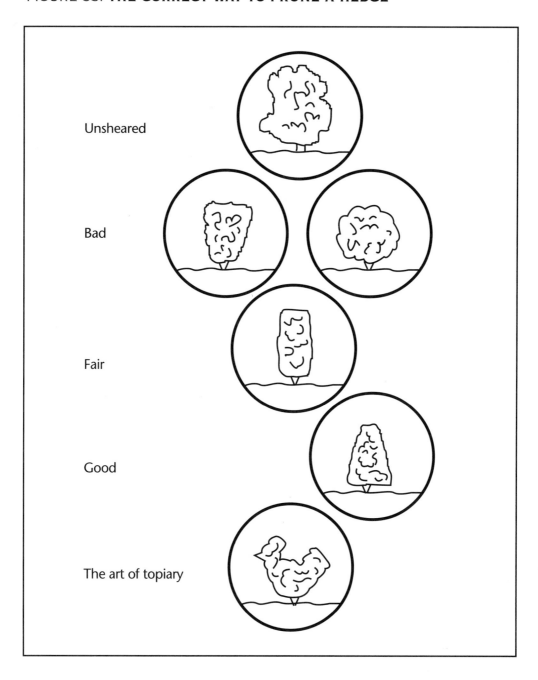

Unsheared

Bad

Fair

Good

The art of topiary

Also, wherever you cut a twig or branch, two or more new shoots will come out. The more drastically you cut back, the longer the new growth will be. (This is why tea roses are pruned back hard.) If you trim lots of twigs and branches, lots of small multiple new shoots will appear. (That is how hedges are pruned to make them thicker.)

*Spring pruning* is primarily to renovate. It encourages new vigorous shoots, which use the energy from carbohydrates stored in the roots. Many fruit trees, such as apple and peach, are kept productive by spring pruning, which encourages the new wood necessary for fruit set. This kind of renewal pruning is done just before or at bud break, so all the plant's energy can go into the remaining buds.

Newly planted trees and shrubs, as well as sickly ones, leaf out much more slowly than healthy stock. For this reason, they should not be pruned very early, because healthy wood may look dead until late June. New replacement shoots are very late, so many trees are unnecessarily removed or mutilated by not waiting. This is especially true for anthracnose blighted eastern dogwoods. (Dead branches should be marked for winter pruning when the fungus is not active, though, because June pruning will spread the disease.)

Don't prune "bleeder" trees in spring. Maples, birch, and elm, among others, drip from the cut ends, often in significant quantity. While bleeding doesn't really hurt them, they drip a lot of sap. That's where maple syrup comes from...after the sugary sap is boiled down.

*Early summer pruning* is a dwarfing procedure. Instead of leaving all the leaves alone to manufacture carbohydrates to store in the roots for the next spring, early summer pruning limits the carbohydrate production and may even trigger the plants to use extra energy to produce new summer shoots and leaves.

*Late summer and fall pruning* also restricts growth. Removing leaves limits the amount of carbohydrates that can be made for the next year. The plants, however, don't put out replacement leaves, so they don't use up any energy on new shoots. Late-season pruning is useful to limit size without stimulating new growth the way spring pruning does.

*Winter pruning* is only for repairing damage and removing dangerous trees and branches. In cold climates, the ends of cut branches and twigs can suffer from the cold, so unnecessary work is saved until early spring when the sap is running well and the tree can protect itself.

In warm areas, where the winter is mild, it is possible to prune all season as one does in early spring.

## *Flowering Shrubs*

The general rule is to prune shrubs just after they have flowered—that way you get to enjoy the flowers. After all, most plants and trees flower for only one to three weeks out of fifty-two a year. One can wait a few weeks to do the pruning.

Most plants that flower in spring bloom from buds made the year before (called second-year wood). Pruning and fertilizing these just *after* blooming directs the plant's energy into making better buds for the next year. It also prevents unsightly seed pods, by cutting off the current year's spent flowers. Examples of such plants are forsythia, spirea, magnolia, lilac, mock orange, crabapples, cherries, dogwood, rhododendron, azalea, and mountain laurel.

Other plants flower from buds made the same season (called first-year wood or new wood). Usually they bloom in midsummer, and they include buddelia, clethra, althea, hydrangea, honeysuckle, and most roses. They are pruned in early spring. Don't, however, cut back too severely or to the ground, because the growth points for the new wood are in the long woody stems. Be careful to leave many new buds on long, generous stems.

When pruning these midsummer plants, it's best to wait until the buds swell and start to sprout, which can happen quite late. When you can see which are alive, cut back to fat, vigorous shoots. The more shoots you leave, the more flowers there will be. But leaving fewer shoots produces larger flowers, particularly on roses, hydrangea, and althea. When you have the pruning shears, you have the power. The choice is yours.

## Pruning Shapes

With your trusty shears, you also have the power to turn shrubs into mounds or into trees. If many shoots are left, a mound develops. If you leave only one, two, or three shoots, a small tree will develop, because the new growth each year will be at the top. Lilacs, viburnum, rhododendrons, magnolia, and amalanchier are among those that can be trained to tree form. Overgrown yews and rhododendrons can have the lower branches removed, exposing the trunks, and they too will then become beautiful, interesting small trees.

Sometimes, when shrubs get too ratty looking, the English method is to cut them back almost to the ground, in a "kill or cure" renovation. This is done early in spring. When you cut shrubs back to the ground, a multistemmed mound will appear. The many new shoots that appear will blossom again in one, two, or three years. Spreading a ring of fertilizer around the plant at pruning time helps.

If pruning seems confusing and complicated, that's because it is. Each plant has its own growth habit, and each pruning cut has its own special effect. But gradually, if you watch each plant, you will begin to understand its growth habits.

# SIZE OF SHRUBS

The place for deciduous shrubs in the landscape is where they can grow to their full height and width. For instance, if left full and wide, spirea grows 6 feet tall and 5 feet wide. It makes an excellent barrier against cold air flowing into low spots. The charming June flowers are an added bonus. A hedge of spirea or forsythia around a low section of the property can direct cold air around the property line and away from the house. It can provide an effective cold-air barrier and windscreen around a vegetable garden, yet will never get tall enough to shade the crops.

Forsythia grows 9 feet tall and about as wide. It can protect an exposed foundation wall, while never blocking the windows above. It is useful on a windy western side, where evergreen rhododendrons would not thrive. Pines or spruce would become too tall too quickly and need constant pruning. Forsythia makes an excellent, inexpensive screen on the property border if left to grow thick and full. Yet when it gets too overgrown and ratty, it can be cut back to the ground, and it will come up fresh and new. It likes sun but will grow in the shade, even in city backyards, where few flowering shrubs will survive.

Privet is the most common material used for hedges because it grows so quickly and will sprout no matter how it's cut. That is both its blessing and its curse. To keep a privet hedge neat requires shearing three times a season. If left alone, privet becomes a very hardy but thin small tree about 20 feet tall. If cut back to about 6 inches in spring, it becomes a low, fluffy hedge that doesn't need to be cut again that year unless one wants it very neat.

Deciduous shrubs are useful as part of windbreaks. They are less expensive than pines or spruce and will outperform them for the first few years. Eventually, the evergreens will grow taller, while the shrubs continue to provide depth and color.

Shade-tolerant shrubs are tough enough to survive as understory plantings beneath tall trees, as long as they are watered. The reason is that the tree roots take up all the water, so that even though it is shady, it is very dry. Occasional fertilizing helps the understory plants, because the tree roots grab all the nutrients as well as the water.

# TRANSPLANTING DECIDUOUS SHRUBS

One of the most valuable traits of deciduous bushes is that they are so easy to transplant. Big old plants can be dug up when dormant, divided into two or three parts (each with several vigorous new shoots), and planted bare rooted. The more fibrous roots included with each plant, the more quickly it will grow.

Deciduous shrubs are not too hard for the average homeowner to handle, unlike big trees. First wet the soil and let it set a day. Moist soil is much easier to handle than dry dirt. Take a spading fork or pickaxe and loosen the soil about 2 feet all around the bush. Keep working it until the plant starts to loosen, and you can wiggle it. Then dig it free with a spade, cutting the roots if necessary.

You can usually tell if the root is big enough to divide. A 2-foot-wide root will give three good divisions or four small ones. Cut the root cleanly with a sharp spade or saw. Cut off any dead or diseased or mangled roots. Replant immediately before the roots dry out or keep the roots in a bucket of watery mud slurry between digging and planting. The shrub tops should be pruned back by at least half, and old or weak shoots should be removed at ground level. Plant-rooting hormones (such as Rootone, Transplantone, or Roots) help these and all new roots get established.

Some shrubs can be planted without big roots if given proper soil and adequate water, but it takes several years for them to become good plants. Certain plants, like pussy willow, will root from a few branches if planted in early spring when their own rooting hormones are high.

Best of all, the existing shrubs on your own property are free. When replanting, use the same care as with new trees. (See chapter 9.) Prepare and loosen the soil, carefully spread the roots, and fill the hole with soil. Flood the soil to settle it and get rid of air pockets. Or water with a starter solution (half-strength weak soluble fertilizer).

Many shrubs, especially lilacs and roses, don't like acid soil, so add a little lime at planting time.

Deciduous plants sold by nurseries are often just rooted cuttings planted in a container. It is worth paying a little more to get a good root system. Otherwise, the wait for good-sized plants may be quite long. For their size, however, deciduous plants are less expensive to buy than evergreen plants.

# EVERGREEN SHRUBS

Evergreen material is of two types:

(1) needled evergreens, such as pine, spruce, hemlock, yew, juniper, and cypress;

(2) broadleafed evergreens, such as rhododendron, holly, mahonia, camellia, and pittosporum.

Each type requires a slightly different growing environment. Almost all are more delicate than their deciduous counterparts. Some of the needled evergreens, especially pines and juniper, prefer full sun and drier locations. Rhododendron, azalea, and holly will do well if protected from winter sun and wind, and while they prefer half shade, they need some sun to bloom well.

Most broadleafed evergreens, particularly rhododendron, azalea, holly, and mountain laurel, as well as many species of pine, yew, hemlock, spruce, and fir, prefer a slightly to very acid soil. In the midwestern plains and other areas of alkaline (sweet) soil, lots of acid-producing peat moss is very helpful in the planting mix. If in doubt, have the soil tested for its degree of acidity or alkalinity (called pH) at your local Agricultural Extension Service or at a garden center. They can explain what correction is best for your area and how much to apply.

Fortunately, there is a perfect evergreen shrub for almost every location and use. Unfortunately, near most older homes, the wrong shrubs have been used in the wrong places.

Size is the primary problem. All shrubs have a mature height that is genetically determined. It affects each shrub's selling price and availability. In general, the smaller ones grow more slowly, and so they cost more to buy. The fastest-growing ones (often not shrubs at all, but baby trees) are inexpensive. Many builders and unknowing homeowners have planted, for example, delightful little blue spruces and tiny arborvitae near the house, only to discover their charming foundation plantings, true to their woodland heritage, growing through windows and removing gutters. When that happens, it is best to saw them off at ground level and leave the root in the ground. Then put more appropriate plants around the stump.

Moving such trees is often impractical. If, however, you decide to replant them and they are 8 feet tall or more, it is a job for a professional with moving machinery. Make sure the tree has branches all around and is worth moving before hiring anyone. A tree that's bare on one side or the bottom will look sparse and scrawny when moved and left to stand alone. Also make sure that digging them up won't undermine your foundation.

# PRUNING EVERGREENS

An alternative to moving large evergreens is to cut them back. Often they have grown so tall that they block sunlight from south-facing windows. Needled evergreens can have their tops cut right off, even by more than half. They will look terrible until new growth becomes full and green, but after a few years they will be covered with new shoots, which can then be kept sheared to the proper height. To go with Mother Nature's flow requires a great deal of patience. Some people prefer to avoid this ugly duckling period and just cut down old evergreens and plant new ones.

## FIGURE 54: **CUTTING DOWN OVERGROWN EVERGREENS**

Before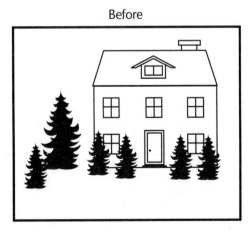

After

*New growth takes two years, and yearly trimming is needed to keep plants low. Works best with arborvitae, hemlock, and yew. Not recommended for pine, spruce, or fir. Where overgrown evergeens block windows, it's possible to cut out a branch or two and open a space, or "window," to see through the tree.*

Tall evergreens on the north or windy side of the house are another matter. They should be kept and tended carefully. These evergreens can be shaped or pruned to a desirable form but kept as tall and full as possible. To restrict growth, needled evergreens may be pruned or sheared in spring after the new growth has come, and, if necessary, again in summer. Shearing encourages new shoots and thicker growth. Unsheared plants are more open and informal looking.

Very tall evergreens can be treated as shade trees by having their lower branches removed to a height of 8 or 10 feet. They are pleasant, cool, and nice smelling underneath in summer. Leave the needles on the ground, unless there is a fire hazard. (See Figure 41, Topping and Raising the Crown, in chapter 9.)

Broadleafed evergreens are shaped by cutting off very tall and leggy branches, at the ground or just above a strong bud or leaf axil. When the newly exposed branches get enough light, they will grow and put out new buds.

With the exception of holly, never shear a broadleaf shrub like a deciduous hedge. And don't cut any evergreen below green needles, leaves, or buds. New shoots return very, very slowly, not like deciduous plants, which easily sprout from almost any stem. Some evergreens, if cut too low, may never sprout again from the old wood.

### FIGURE 55: **PRUNING BROADLEAF EVERGREENS**

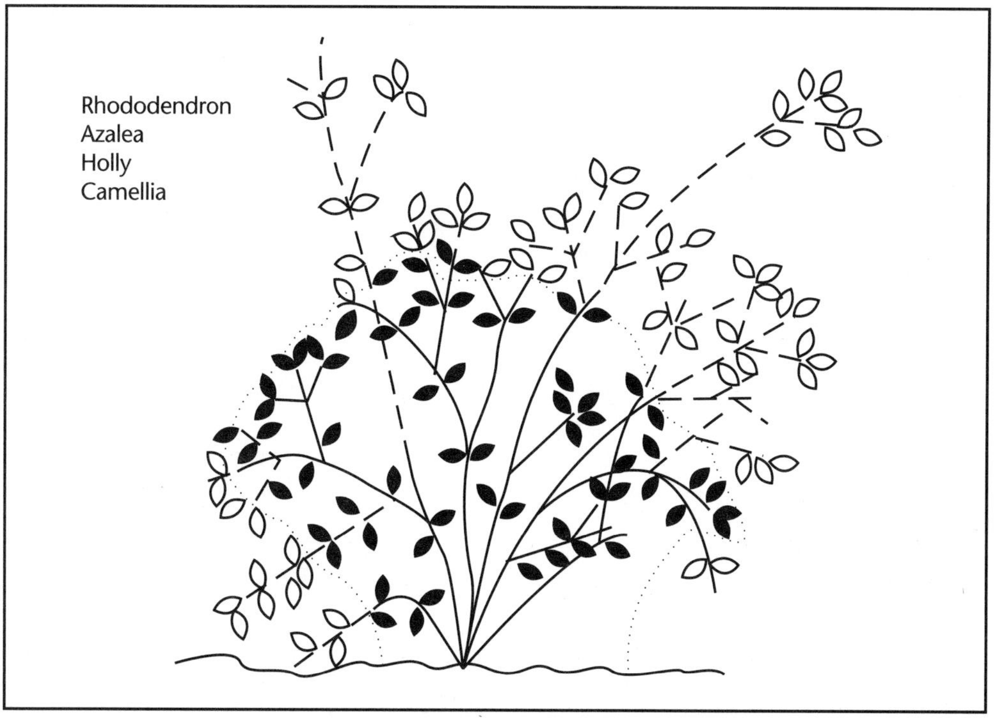

Rhododendron
Azalea
Holly
Camellia

*To lower height or improve shape of plant, trim off unbalanced growth at leaf nodes.*

# GLORIOUS RHODODENDRONS

Henry Thoreau wrote, "The splendid rhodora now sets the swamps afire with its masses of rich color." It's no wonder rhododendrons have always been one of our most popular shrubs. Versatile, vibrant, with incredible flowerheads, often evergreen during winter, it is a plant for all seasons. One can use these beautiful plants for energy-saving planting as well as the plainer ones.

The rhododendron family is large, with over 2,000 listed varieties and hybrids that include both rhododendrons and azaleas. They grow in every temperate country in the world, from Lapland to Australia, with twenty-seven species in North America alone. The ones we mostly grow in our gardens have come mainly from the Orient; some were probably cultivated in Chinese gardens centuries ago.

In many parts of the world, rhododendrons are hard to grow, and so, in that perverse human way, are more prized. They can be made to grow in most of the United States, except for hot regions that have no cool winter. The East Coast and the Pacific Northwest are blessed with just the right soil and climate, which makes them easy to grow.

In other regions they often need protection, and special microenvironments have to be created for their survival. Some winters may be too cold for most varieties. Wind protection is usually necessary. The summers may be too hot, so that open shade may have to be established. It is important that specific varieties be chosen for each region. Special soil may have to be created. In areas with hard alkaline ground water, acid rainwater may have to be used.

If it gets too complicated, it is not worth the effort to try to get them to grow outdoors, because they are easy to grow as potted plants, in special soil, especially azaleas. In places with naturally acid soil, adequate rainfall and humidity, and temperate climate where they will happily thrive, however, rhododendrons are a most glorious shrub.

## *Rhododendron Requirements*

Rhododendrons must have *acid soil*, 4.5 to 6.5 pH. It must also be friable and soft, so the very fine roots, which grow quite near to the surface, can push through it. A heavy clay soil can be improved with large quantities of acid peat moss, bog soil, rotted oak leaves, pine needles, or acid woodland soil. Or a new bed about 2 feet deep may be excavated and proper soil brought in.

To keep it acid, don't add lime, gypsum, wood ashes, bone meal, or calcium carbonate to the soil. Also beware of new concrete and rain that splashes calcium off stucco or cement onto them because these are alkaline.

Most rhododendrons prefer a *dappled shade*, but they will grow in sun, as long as they have *enough water*. If the shade is too heavy, they will not flower well. Some varieties can stand more sun than others, but for all rhododendrons, water is essential. The shallow roots easily dry out, which is why a *mulch* is always recommended.

It is essential to water new plants with 5 gallons of water once a week for the first year, spring, summer, and early fall. Rainwater does not sufficiently moisten the soil. The second and third year they are still fragile and so must continue to be watched carefully and given supplemental water, because it takes at least that long for the roots to become established. You can tell when they are dry, for the leaves droop like limp hands.

Once established, rhododendrons need little care, except for occasional soakings between June and September in dry years. Interestingly, a good deep soaking in August makes them more winter hardy, but too much water after mid-September promotes winter damage. The plants need to get good water in late summer, to make as much carbohydrate as possible, and then to have time to harden off before winter.

Although rhododendrons need a moist root run, they will rot and die if they sit in standing water. For this reason, it's a good idea to plant the crown an inch or so above the ground level and slope the soil into a saucer to hold the 5 gallons of water for the first year.

The best mulch is 1 to 2 inches of oak leaves, for it keeps the soil acid yet doesn't mat down to form a mushy mess. (Maple leaves are not good.) Pine needles, peat moss, and pine bark mulch also work well. The mulch should never be more than a few inches deep and should not touch the bark but it should begin a little bit away from the stems. If it's too deep, it encourages rot, and if it is piled around the bark, it can interfere with the transport of sap and nutrients.

The best practice is to leave the mulch until it rots, just adding a little more on top as needed, instead of raking everything up each year and putting on all new mulch. For some reason, most landscapers feel compelled to remove all the fallen leaves and old mulch and then charge for both the unnecessary cleanup and the new mulch. Or they pile on a few more inches each year until it becomes too deep, unhealthy, and smothers the soil.

You can save money by letting nature proceed at its slow pace and adding fresh mulch only for cosmetic reasons or when it all decomposes and is too thin.

*Fertilizing* should be done in spring and finished before the end of June. After that, soft new growth is encouraged, which is susceptible to winterkill. In warm climates, however, late-winter fertilizer may be applied.

A balanced fertilizer is best. Too much nitrogen will promote vegetative growth and fewer flowers. Adequate superphosphate and potash will promote flower bud formation and improve winter hardiness and vigor. One trick the commercial nurseries use to enhance flowering is to apply a light top dressing of superphosphate in early August.

The residual by-products of some fertilizers make the soil alkaline, so check with your nursery before buying. There are special fertilizers formulated for acid-loving plants, the by-products of which are acid; however, overuse can cause problems. Alternating chemical and organic fertilizers is probably best; or you can use mostly organic fertilizers, which will make bigger bushes with fewer flowers.

Once the plants are well established in good soil, if they are not overwatered, if they get enough sun, and if the mulch underneath is left to compost naturally, they will bloom perfectly well without any fertilizer.

*Pruning* is not essential. Once established, the shrubs are best left alone except for removal of broken or dead branches. In case of winterkill, always wait well into June to prune out dead wood, because there are almost always live buds, which will sprout, although very slowly, from the branches. If the brown, winter-killed leaves are offensive, trim the brown edges off with a scissors or cut off the individual leaves. But leave the terminal end of the twig, which will usually leaf out again.

Unpruned rhododendrons flower best and are graceful large shrubs that have a natural, woodsy look. Some grow upright, some are spreading, some grow fast and some slowly. If they get too large or grow over windows or into paths, they can be pruned and clipped back. Pruning gives them an Oriental look and fewer flowers.

Many varieties can get quite large and really outgrow their space, yet one hates to remove such beautiful plants. There are several ways to deal with this problem. One is to remove whole branches at ground level. Most members of this family will sprout new shoots from the sides of big, old branches from trunks that are exposed to light. It may take a couple of years, but usually the sides become green again.

Another way is to prune out all the lower side branches, leaving just exposed tall trunks. This creates a beautiful flowering tree, much like the treasured tree rhododendrons from the Himalayas in the magnificent greenhouses at Kew Gardens outside London. An added bonus if one prunes old shrubs this way is that underneath is created a new shady bed that can be filled with ferns, flowers, small shrubs, or ground cover.

The final way to deal with hopelessly overgrown rhododendrons is to cut back everything to about 6 inches, removing the whole shrub. New shoots will eventually appear about 75 percent of the time. Many nurseries cut large wild rhododendron and mountain laurel back to the ground this way and allow new shoots to grow from the large vigorous root system. After a few years, they dig them up and sell them. You can identify these "cut backs" by the large trunk stubs in the root ball. Cut backs will grow into nice bushes but take several years to flower.

*Hardiness and winterkill* can be a problem with rhododendrons. Not all varieties are winter hardy, but many can stand quite a bit of cold. Most good catalogues and specialized rhododendron lists will include the lowest winter temperature each particular plant will stand; you can then check it against the lowest winter temperature in your area. Because rhododendrons have been so highly bred, each has a different cold tolerance.

If you cannot find this information, check with your local nurseries, the Agricultural Extension Service in your area, or the American Rhododendron Society. An empirical way to find out which varieties are hardy in your area is to check which ones bloom well in your neighborhood.

Even varieties that are hardy and will survive in your area, can still suffer from *winterkill*, which is drying and browning of leaves and buds. Evergreen varieties are most affected. Usually just the outer edges of the leaves turn brown, but sometimes whole leaves or irregular blotches may become discolored.

The important thing is not to assume the twigs are dead and prune off stems or tips too soon. New shoots usually appear, although they may be a month later than new shoots elsewhere on the plant. It is best to wait until late June in northern areas, before pruning for winterkill.

The reason for winterkill is lack of water. Evergreen leaves transpire even in winter. When the weather warms up, or when winter sun reflects off a wall and warms the leaves, the breathing holes (stomata) open up, and the sap begins to run. But if the ground is frozen, the roots can't take up any replacement water. This lack of water in the leaf cells causes them to turn brown.

Another weather event that causes browning is repeated warm and cold temperature fluctuations, especially in early spring. It can happen on several days, or it can be just the difference between the warmth of the late afternoon sun (around 65 degrees) and a sudden drop at sunset (often below freezing). These changes confuse and stress the leaf tissue, causing cell death, which appears as brown leaf edges.

Winter wind is very damaging, because it also dries and desiccates the leaves and twigs. Although hardy rhododendrons don't need protection from low temperatures per se, they may not survive if there is winter wind blowing over them.

There are so many varieties of rhododendrons that it boggles the mind. There are deciduous, semi-evergreen, and evergreen varieties. The deciduous ones are generally called azaleas, while the evergreen ones are usually called rhododendrons. Their periods of bloom start with the first warmth in spring (PJM Rhododendrons) and run through the early part of summer (Swamp Azalea) , a span of about three months. Each plant blooms for only one or two weeks, but with a carefully chosen selection a garden can have a succession of blooming azaleas and rhododendrons for a long period.

In each area of the country certain varieties will do better than others. It is always necessary to check your own local conditions before ordering from catalogues, to make sure the varieties you choose will thrive for you.

# SMALL TREES AS SHRUBS

Small trees are the same size as many large shrubs and often can be used for shrub borders and underplantings. Certain varieties of crab apple, cherry, magnolia, dogwood, and amalanchier can easily be kept below 15 or 20 feet tall. They are inclined to have a central trunk, rather than a full, bushy habit. They can be trained, however, to grow as multistemmed shrubs by pruning them at the ground when they are young and allowing many suckers to grow rather than pruning to a single stem.

They can be trained to grow close to the ground by a technique exactly opposite the one used to prune tall shade trees. For a low profile, the highest growing tip is cut out each year. The lower branches are not removed, just cut back (headed back) if they get too long. The lower limbs will absorb more food and increase in size faster. The top will have a tendency to side branch. This technique is practiced in its most sophisticated fashion in espalier fruit trees.

# GROWING WALLS AND ESPALIER PLANTS

Growing walls, or "flower walls," can be as interesting and beautiful as any flat garden. If you wants lots of garden but have too little space, consider growing plants up a wall, up a trellis, up an arbor, even up a fence or post. Vines can be used. Or trees and shrubs can be pruned to grow flat, in two dimensions, as in the famous kitchen garden at Versailles, where espalier fruit trees grow against the walls.

To grow up, plants require support. Short-lived plants such as annual flowers and vegetables can be tied to stakes or simple trellises made of wire. Over time, however, well-designed trellises made of permanent wood, metal, or attractive plastic are more pleasing. How sad it is to grow a magnificent old clematis for ten years and display it on an ugly chain-link fence.

Very elaborate structures are possible, such as pergolas with columns as in ancient Rome or arbors covered with climbing roses intertwined with morning glory or clematis vines. Other vines that grow up are rambler roses, wisteria, and honeysuckle, all of which require yearly pruning. Remember with wisteria that, over time, the main vine will become almost as large as a tree trunk, so train it to the shape you want it to remain. Climbing hydrangea and clematis will tolerate shade.

Many trees and shrubs can be pruned flat into espalier forms. Most of the small fruit trees, particularly dwarf apples, withstand heavy pruning and can be used. Upright yews and juniper also work well. The secret is to start when the plants are young enough to train the way you want them to grow.

Espalier plants are traditionally shaped like a candelabra or other complex geometric designs. They need not be only geometric or classic though for informal clipping can produce a windswept look, or a fan shape.

## Saving Energy

Growing walls and espalier plants are especially useful for energy saving. Plants growing against a south-facing wall will keep it cool. Evergreen plants will provide some protection in winter. Overhead arbors and pergolas are the ancient Roman way to provide cool shade in summer. A vine shading a window air conditioner is highly recommended as it will significantly reduce the energy used for cooling from that unit.

Hit-or-miss planting will not be too successful. Gardening, like agriculture, is complex. Successful growing requires choosing plants that will thrive in each microenvironment. The exposure of the wall should be considered—whether it faces north, south, east, or west, whether it gets lots of wind, and how much sun it receives.

North walls tend to be cool and require plants that can live without sunlight. One could use shade-tolerant trees such as amalanchier and redbud. These might be underplanted with a flower border of spring bulbs, shade-tolerant hosta, ferns, bleeding heart, and lily of the valley, as well as annual impatiens for summer color.

East-facing walls would probably have enough sunlight to add azaleas, rhododendron, coral bells, daylilies, astilbe, flowering cherry, or dogwood.

Sunny south and west walls get very hot and can cook plants. Your choices must be able to tolerate heat to do well on these exposures, and they will require lots of water during hot summer days.

Windy walls also need extra water to compensate for evaporation from the leaves. Keeping this in mind, one would not plant rhododendrons on a south or west wall, but roses and fruit trees would do very well. So would vegetables and most flowers.

Generally, sun-loving plants need at least four hours of sun a day. One can manipulate the light by the use of color. A light-colored wall will be cooler and will reflect more heat than a dark one. To increase the effective sun in a shady spot, hang aluminum foil behind the plants to reflect sunlight back onto the leaves. The more sun, the more these will flower, for sun is the real secret of profuse blooming.

CHAPTER 11

# The Existing Surface
# Materials and What to
# Do with Them

W hat's on the ground? Whatever it is, it is the easiest part of the landscaping to improve or change quickly. It may be plant material such as grass, leaf mulch, wood chips, weeds, ground cover, or low shrubs. It may not be biological, such as bare soil, concrete, paving, or blacktop.

While the energy-saving potential of what's on the ground is less significant than that of the tree cover or shrub borders, the total effect on the appearance of the property is more dramatic.

In hot climates, or during hot summers, a lawn or ground cover is the coolest surface available. Evaporation is the reason. Cooling from any surface can be increased by hosing it down, or by adding a pool and providing for more water to evaporate.

## GRASS

Grass is cooling. It uses up 50 percent of the heat of the sun it receives for evapo-transpiration (evaporating moisture during photosynthesis). Only 5 percent of the sun's heat is absorbed by the ground, so the ground stays cool. With paving or concrete, 50 percent of the sun's heat is absorbed and heats the ground causing the surface to become very hot.

Grass is a very useful plant. One or another kind of grass grows everywhere on Earth, and there are almost infinite varieties, some of which have been specially developed for home lawns. There are grass varieties for sun, for shade, for drought, for moist places, for compacted earth, even for neglecting. (See page 137 for more information about grass varieties.)

A typical suburban lawn may have a million individual grass plants. In the shade, grass is damp and cool and usually not too thick. Shaded areas need to be planted with shade-tolerant grass varieties and heavily fertilized for the grass to be lush. Other varieties are for planting in sun, but they will become brown and hard unless watered during periods of drought. In areas of heavy use such as playing fields, dog runs, and parking areas, the soil becomes packed and hard, the roots can't breathe, and the grass becomes sparse. Nonetheless, even imperfect grass still cools, both physically in absolute temperature and psychologically, because of the effect of its green color and texture.

Grass, however, is a high-maintenance covering, and even less than perfect grass requires maintenance. A lawn must be mowed. It should be watered during dry periods. It needs lime and fertilizer several times a year to have a deep green color. In addition, grass is subject to a host of chewing, crawling, gnawing, and munching animals and insects and a larger assortment of fungi and diseases.

To keep a lawn beautiful, it must have deep loam, feeding, watering, spraying, seeding with improved strains of grass, raking, aerating, dethatching, and continual mowing. When calculated in cost per square foot, a good lawn is costly indeed to maintain. A perfect lawn looks only as beautiful as the proportion of time-consuming and expensive care it gets.

Each person has to decide how beautiful he wants the grass to be and how much time and money he wants to invest. Each one eventually makes his own compromises between appearance and care. A simple area of rough grass is attractive in its own way. And it is as cooling and energy saving as a perfect lawn of putting-green quality.

When planting grass or sod, the soil should be turned or rototilled and then raked smooth and free of stones. It is useful to incorporate fertilizer and lime while rototilling. Grass seed takes about 18 months to become a thick lawn. Sod is an instant thick lawn and often well worth the additional cost. The soil preparation is the same for both.

If funds are limited, a rototiller may be rented with or without someone to operate it. Rototilling a large area is a good day's heavy work. Where the pocketbook is able and the spirit weak, hire a landscape firm to do the work. Fertilizer, lime, and grass seed are spread most easily with a wheeled spreader, which can be rented.

Grasses are actually among the toughest plants known. A meadow with wildflowers is very satisfying and easier to maintain. It may be mowed occasionally, or it may be hayed once a year. It is cooler than bare dirt and provides a home to birds, insects, and butterflies. It is not neat, just romantic. Establishing wildflowers in a meadow is complicated, however. (See page 139 and chapter 13 for more on meadows.)

After decades of trying to make lawns look like living room carpets, the pendulum is finally swinging to the more rational approach of lower-maintenance grasses. And a welcome swing it is.

Using grass is just a question of finding the ones that best fit the need and the ecosystem. Even the lowly crabgrass is useful for summer homes. It grows without care in summer, dies and turns brown with the first frost, then reseeds itself in time for the next summer vacation. The bottom line is that any grass is better than no grass, but there are many more options than just a perfect all-American, high-maintenance lawn.

# GROUND COVERS

Ground covers such as myrtle, ivy, pachysandra, hosta, moss, creeping fig, and mondo grass are cooling and green, too. They require less maintenance than lawns, but are more expensive to establish. They function best in shade.

We tend to think of ground covers as low growing, but they can be any height. A good bed of thickly planted 3-foot-high juniper will provide more cooling in full sun than a paved area and will require very little maintenance. The advantage of a higher ground cover is that it grows taller than most weeds. The initial cost of establishing the plants is high but is still less than paving. A deciduous plant that performs in sun as well as juniper is low-growing cotoneaster. (See List of Ground Covers of Different Heights for Sun or Shade, part III.)

## Flower Beds

Flower beds are another surface treatment, for who can pass a glorious blooming flower border without wishing for one at home? The problem is where to put it. When the planting to save energy is finished, there may not be room for a flower border with all the bushes and trees and areas for shade. A well-landscaped yard or a small lot may also pose problems. If so, then look to the front yard. The two best places that are usually overlooked are on either side of the sidewalk. More and more front yards are blooming with flowers instead of just grass and a boring privet hedge.

One very exciting idea is to use the strip of grass between the sidewalk and the street. These strips actually belong to the city but are left to homeowners to maintain. The grass is hard to take care of and gets weedy. Why not flowers instead? One advantage is that the space is not too large and is nicely contained. Since annuals and perennials require a lot of care, a smaller space is more relaxing.

If old privet hedges exist, cut them down to about 6 inches. This will provide an instant neat border, and, thankfully, they will not need trimming again until the following spring. Next, plan a garden within the new, unobtrusive, low hedge. It may be a single 3-foot strip, or a wider area with stepping-stone paths.

First decide whether you want to look at the flowers or you want passersby to enjoy them most. If they are for you, put the tall flowers along the sidewalk, getting lower in height as they go toward the house. If you want a glorious view from the street (and when you come home each night), put the taller plants nearer the house and the lower ones at the sidewalk. Leave the foundation planting alone.

Don't plan to dig up a whole front lawn in one year—it's too much work. Just begin with the first 3-foot strip. If the bed is narrow, you may just vary all the plant sizes together. As the bed gets wider, you can move them around. The bed will always get wider, because perennials have to be divided every few years to keep them blooming well, and so they increase in number.

It will be necessary to stake many of the flowers, partly because they fall over in the rain and partly because children sometimes vandalize them. Save the twigs and branches when pruning trees and shrubs; they make the best plant stakes.

## Preparing the Bed

To begin the bed preparation, peel off the grass layer, or kill it completely with an herbicide, such as Roundup. (Wear gloves, long sleeves, long pants, and—most important—a respirator mask. Keep children, pregnant women, dogs and cats, and men who are thinking of becoming fathers, away.)

Then improve the existing soil by digging in organic soil amendments, such as compost or old, old manure or peat moss to about one-third its volume. Also incorporate some long-lasting fertilizer, such as Milorganite, and some bone meal. Most likely the soil also needs lime, because most perennials need a pH of about 6.5–7.

Double dig it, to a depth of 12 or 18 inches. This may seem like a real pain, but good, deep, soft soil is the main secret of success with perennials. To double dig, first dig a hole and put the soil aside. Then dig a second hole next to it. Improve that soil and fill the first hole with it. Then dig a third hole. Improve that soil and put it in the second hole. And so on. The advantage is that there is never a huge pile of dirt to deal with. What gets dug from one hole goes immediately into the previous hole. The British invented this micro-managed minuet. They actually dig it twice, to get the subsoil up to the top and the topsoil down to the bottom, but that's an enormous amount of work.

Don't bother digging near maple, eucalyptus, or other trees with greedy, shallow roots. Nothing will grow under them anyway, so just cover the ground with wood chips or try a tough ground cover such as myrtle or ajuga.

Naturally, all the usual details that are needed for good perennials have to be followed. Check the sun–shade ratio and plant accordingly. Fertilize, water, weed, expect things to die, and replace them; plant annuals for summer color and bulbs for spring. Treat the insects and problems as they arise. In freezing weather, use inexpensive 5–10–5 fertilizer on the sidewalk, instead of salt. Ordinary sodium chloride salt is very damaging to plants, while fertilizer salts, which melt ice as well, are not.

If planting near the sidewalk, consider installing a surface drip-irrigation system at planting time. Any homeowner with patience can do it. Drip irrigation will make maintenance much easier, and it conserves water.

Any plant material will cool the air to some degree in summer. In addition to ground covers, grass, and flower borders, shrub beds and vegetable patches are useful to cover the ground surface.

# COLOR, PAVING, AND OTHER MATERIALS

The darker the color, the more heat it will absorb and the hotter it will become. White reflects the most heat and light—it is the coolest to touch. A blacktop driveway may get hot enough to fry eggs. Stone and water absorb heat slowly and stay warm in the evenings. They cool off overnight, and then heat up again slowly in the morning. This principle is important for dry-arid desert areas, where the days are hot but the nights chill rapidly. Warm pavements near the house mitigate the cold evenings. Then they feel cool during the hot mornings. The same principle applies to passive solar-heating systems, which use the retained heat of the day.

When deciding on surface materials near the house, consider which is more important: (1) conservation of warmth, or (2) providing a cooling effect during the day.

If daytime cooling is more important, then lawns, ground covers, or the like are the choice. Sometimes where lawn maintenance is an unwanted burden, people turn to paving. Too often, however, they end up with a hot spot instead of the cool, easy-care area they had bargained for. A house or terrace surrounded with paving or driveways will absorb the heat that reflects from that paving. The area will be much warmer than it was before the paving.

In southern areas, more air conditioning is required to keep a house near paving comfortable. In cold climates, the reflected heat in winter from paving is a cost benefit. In addition a blacktop driveway is always preferred to concrete in the North, because the black absorbs heat during sunny days and also melts ice and snow faster.

Around solar-heated buildings, it is especially important that the ground be as warm and dry as possible, so paving is useful. Even brown or black plastic sheeting can be useful on the ground near buildings that might otherwise be damp and cold. The plastic can be covered with wood chips for a better appearance. These techniques are most useful on the southern sides of buildings, where sun warming can occur in winter. A protective shield of shrubs and trees is still preferred for the north side and any other exposure subject to heavy winter winds.

Paving can be of various materials. There is costly but durable bluestone, brick, or concrete. Crushed stone costs less and is attractive and useful, particularly if laid over a weed-retardant film or fabric. Stepping-stones are useful where passage is needed. If they are set level with a lawn, they can be mowed over without any time-consuming special trimming.

If durable paving materials are used, they should be properly set on a bed of leveled sharp builder's sand or stone dust for permanence and to prevent heaving and settling. The most satisfactory material is bluestone. Slate is good but has a tendency to shale and split off in layers. Stone that splits and shales should not be used near swimming pools or anywhere people go barefoot.

Brick is another excellent material for paving. It is set in sand or stone as above. It has a pleasant texture and color, not too reflective nor too absorbent. Brick is good for temperate and tropical regions where a lighter color surface would be too reflective and a dark one would be too hot.

Preformed concrete paving blocks are attractive and inexpensive compared to bluestone and brick. Color can be added to the concrete mix. Some people actually enjoy making forms and pouring their own blocks. Ready-mix concrete makes this much easier than it used to be. Leaves or other objects can be pressed onto the surface of the moist concrete to make interesting designs.

Pressure-treated wood is useful for decks or walks but needs treatment with a wood preservative or stain every several years. Wood lasts about fifteen years. Wood rounds, or cross-section slices of big tree trunks, make inexpensive paving or stepping "stones," however, they are not permanent. The wood has a tendency to crack and check. Wood preservatives help some. The rounds, which are most attractive and interesting, may last from five to fifteen years. Women wearing high heels may trip in the spaces between the rounds.

Where the absolute lowest cost is a requirement, a load of inexpensive wood chips from a local tree removal company will provide a pleasant surface for outdoor activities. Or when tree work is done on your property, have the wood chips spread around instead of paying for disposal. Being economical, however, can also have its drawbacks. Wood chips are not permanent. Also there is a tendency for the chips to wash away if drainage is not correct, and they can cling to shoes.

A more serious drawback is that wood rounds and chips are flammable. Furthermore they often provide a happy home for termites and carpenter ants and so should be kept away from buildings, where they might cause havoc.

Yet they do provide a rustic, comfortable surface underfoot. If there are cedar, pine, or fir shavings in the chips, the resins will volatize on warm days and give off a most agreeable woodland scent. Dry chips warm up in the sun on chilly days, but because of their porous quality, they never become too hot. In the shade they stay damp and cool. They conserve ground moisture and impart a good spongy texture to the soil beneath. Wood chips are a perfect choice under trees where sitting space is wanted but paving would damage the tree roots.

Bark mulch is similar to wood chips except that it is made of evergreen bark. It looks better. It does not decay as fast as plain wood chips and usually does not bring or harbor insects. It also costs a little more, but, depending on where it's used, it may be worth it.

# CHAPTER 12

# Growing Techniques and Modern Science

We are in the midst of an explosion of scientific discovery. Changes will occur that will dwarf the wisdom of the past centuries. Gene splicing, for example, makes it possible to custom design plants as we now design chemicals. Computers make management and retrieval of vast quantities of information easy. Machines controlled by computers and robots will completely change the way we grow things.

Some of the beginnings are upon us now. These new ideas and the refurbishing of old ideas will create the new syntheses of the future. Considering the current new theories gives us a window to the future and allows us to plan our landscapes so they may adapt and fit into the next century.

An effort to save the planet must be primary. Our soil is eroding away. Our water is being polluted and depleted. Energy is wasted, and its by-products contaminate our air. Our atmosphere may be at risk as well. Uncontrolled deforestation is destroying vast ecosystems. Even in the face of these problems, science will continue in the developed countries with exciting new improvements, new plants, and new products. New techniques will make growing food more efficient and less polluting.

## LEARNING FROM THE FOREST: COMPOST

In the forest, everything is recycled. What grows returns to nourish the trees, as long as Mother Nature is given adequate time and is left alone. We, on the other hand, collect grass clippings, leaves and other biodegradable material and send it to landfills. Ours is a throwaway society.

Twenty-five percent of the garbage that is collected is yard waste, and space for landfills is running out. Yard waste could be recycled and used again, if we just learn from the forest. We love the leaves in autumn, so beautiful, so colorful. In Japan, with intense intellectual scrutiny, they plant so the colored leaves will carpet the ground. Someone into self-awareness classes told of a "wonderful" encounter group where the main lesson was "to stop and watch the leaves float to the ground."

That's fine for refurbishing the soul, but what does one do with them afterwards?

An acre of oak forest drops 2,600 pounds of leaves each year, an acre of pine 3,600 pounds of needles. About 70 percent of their nutrients are recycled back as composted mulch to fertilize the forest soil. Mother Nature is quite frugal, and she doesn't lift a finger.

The practice of raking up every leaf is wasteful. In most areas, they can be left alone under shrubs, or even on top of ground covers such as ivy, pachysandra, and myrtle. If the bushes look too messy in spring, just cover the ground with a thin layer of fresh bark mulch.

Leaves cannot be left on the lawn, however, for they would mat down and smother it. The best way to handle the lawn is to first mow the leaves. This reduces their volume by half. Then collect them with the grass clippings that come along, and pile them in an out of the way spot. In two weeks their volume should reduce itself again by half. This is the raw material for compost.

Raking unmowed leaves produces a huge volume of material. The purpose of mowing first is to reduce the volume to a more manageable quantity both for collection and for the area needed to make compost out of it. Also the smaller the particles, the faster the leaves will turn to compost.

One time-saving trick is to start by mowing a straight line in the center, then keep going around and around, letting the mower throw the clippings to the outside each time around. They get removed this way, and become even smaller and more compact.

Eventually, the mowed leaves and grass all pile up into a big, well-chopped ring for easy raking. If the grass is long or the lawn large, it may be necessary to rake up the clippings whenever they get too thick for the mower to run through them. They may, alternatively, be picked up in the collection bag of the lawn mower.

If you are short of space, consider planting a long row of blueberry bushes about 5 feet inside your back property line. Other bushes or small trees could be used instead. Pile the leaves behind them. Each year just add more. In summer the grass clippings can be spread in thin layers over the top. The blueberries will love it. They will be a verdant screen in summer, produce fruit, and turn scarlet in fall. (Keep the soil acid pH 5.5 for blueberries.) When you need compost, just dig underneath for the nice dark nutritious stuff.

## To Make Compost

If the chopped leaf pile is left alone for six months, the volume will reduce by another half. This material will eventually become good nutritious compost. It can be used, about an inch deep, as a summer mulch on the garden, around trees and shrubs, or in a rustic perennial bed. Or it may be used as a soil amendment, mixed with the top 4 inches of soil in fall. Or it may be dug in about one month before planting in spring. Studies have shown that the more compost the better; several inches is not too much to dig in.

Why compost? Compost renews the soil. It not only adds nutrients and trace elements but also encourages healthy biological soil processes. And it saves the landfills near cities and trips to the dump in other areas.

The best way to make compost is one of those things that true believers argue endlessly about. There are as many recipes for compost as for bread. The basics are approximately the same, however; only the nuances change with the passion involved. If the chopped up leaves and grass clippings are just piled up in an out-of-the-way place, they will turn to compost. The process, however, may be speeded up by more scientific practices.

Such serious composting requires a little understanding of the process. Because heat is necessary for decomposition, composting takes two to three months in summer and five to eight months fall through winter. The warmer the weather, the faster the process. Smaller pieces (that's why one mows the leaves) speed things up.

Essential to the composting process are many soil organisms that break down the raw materials. They are bacteria, fungi, actinomucetes, beetles, sowbugs, slugs, earthworms, centipedes, and millipedes, among others. Their eggs are in the soil or in old compost, so inoculating the mulch pile with them is as easy as throwing in a little dirt.

Also, the more nitrogen, the faster the decomposition. For good composting, a ratio of 30:1, carbon to nitrogen, is ideal. Each plant is made of nitrogen and carbon. Grass has more nitrogen to carbon, per volume. Leaves have less nitrogen and more carbon. Combine different quantities of grass clippings (19:1) and food waste (15:1) with leaves and stalks (60:1) and even sawdust (500:1) to get a good mix of about 30:1. (No meat or grease, or every dog and cat in the neighborhood will be digging around.)

Be sure to cover each layer of raw material with a little dirt to get the necessary organisms. Also, moisten each layer to about the consistency of a squeezed out sponge to provide the proper environment for decomposition. The larger the pile, the warmer it will become inside and the faster the process will go. If the pile is high, it needs to be fluffed up to get air and oxygen inside.

It's not like a recipe for fondue, though. No matter what you do, it will eventually turn to nice dark compost. If it has more carbon, it will go more slowly. If it's too high in nitrogen, or too low in oxygen, it may rot and begin to smell. Most states have excellent free information on how to make compost.

If there is no place for an unsightly pile of leaves and grass clippings on your property, consider using a bin or cannister. There are many very expensive, attractive plastic compost makers on the market. One can save money, however, by making an equally effective one out of a sturdy plastic garbage can with a locking snap top. First drill ¼-inch holes about every 2 inches on the top, sides, and bottom. Put it on rocks or blocks for drainage. Then alternate thin layers of nitrogenous material (grass, fruit, and vegetable peelings) with thicker layers of high-carbon materials (leaves, sawdust). Don't forget to intersperse the layers with soil to supply the decomposing microorganisms. Moisten it at first if necessary. Then fluff it up. This can be done by rolling it a few times. If it starts to smell, fluff it up more, to add more air. The volume shrinks as it composts. (If used for vegetable scraps only, it will take two people about six months to fill a large barrel.)

Another, even simpler, compost maker is to use a large black plastic bag. Poke holes all around. Fill it as above, until half full. Then tie the top. Each week, shake it and turn it a few times to get air inside. The warmer the weather, the sooner it will decompose.

Some public works departments compost their leaves and give it free to citizens. It is an excellent soil conditioner and may be incorporated into the soil to enrich it when planting trees, shrubs, or lawns. It can be rototilled in. Alternatively, about 1 inch of it can be used as a top dressing. Another municipal resource is wood chips. These usually are free at the dump, just for the shoveling.

# MULCHES

Mulches are very useful. They save water, keep roots moist and cool, and keep weeds down. As they decompose, they add organic material to the soil. Good mulches should be about 2 inches deep. If deeper than 4 inches, they cause trouble with fungi, oxygen transfer in the soil and metabolic processes.

It used to be that a good garden was one with the soil bare and cleanly tilled. It was called a "dust mulch," and one kept it that way by using a hoe, with a quick chop-chop-chop. It was neat, it kept the weeds down . . . but it took a lot of work and wasted water. And bare dry topsoil can blow away in the wind.

Fortunately, today there are many mulches available for all tastes and levels of neatness. Slugs live under most of them. Granular fertilizer is always applied *under* the mulch. Liquid fertilizer can go on top if it is watered in enough to reach the soil underneath and the roots.

A two-year California test study showed that organic mulches used alone reduced total weed counts by 50 percent. Underlaying the organic mulch perforated with plastic (polyethylene) or weed-retardant fabric resulted in almost no weeds. (Organic mulches are materials that were once alive.) Pine bark mulch was the most durable and lasted almost twice as long when plastic was laid underneath.

There are neat mulches and messy mulches. Neat mulches are bark mulch, peat moss, and buckwheat hulls. Medium-looking mulches are pine needles, crushed stones, grass clippings, and leaves. Messy mulches are newspaper, exposed plastic sheeting, rough wood chips, and salt marsh hay. It is important to understand each mulch, its strengths and its problems.

BARK MULCH  Made of shredded bark from evergreen trees. It is the most commonly used mulch now and lasts longer than plain wood chips. Pine bark is darker in color than reddish hemlock bark. It keeps light out so weed seeds germinate slowly, and what weeds do grow are easy to pull out. Bark mulch, however, is expensive, and after a while, as it weathers and fades, it begins to look messy. A light top raking neatens it up again, or a thin sprinkling of new chips can be added on top to dress it up.

It is definitely not good to add another 2 inches each year as so many landscapers do. Not only will it encourage unhealthy anaerobic fungus and bacteria, but it wastes money that could be better spent.

PEAT MOSS  Nice and neat but absorbs and holds lots of water, which can deprive the roots unless there is adequate total water. It blows when dry and also mats down.

BUCKWHEAT HULLS  Lovely looking but also blows away. They are not commercial looking. The finest quality gardens use this.

PINE NEEDLES  Attractive but too acid except for acid-loving plants such as strawberries and blueberries.

STONE  Looks nice at first but is hard to keep clean and neat. It must be laid on a weed-proof fabric. Leaves and debris have to be removed from it, and a yard vacuum or blower is useful for this purpose. Stone is nice for paths but a pain in the flower beds. If snow blowers spew stone onto the lawn, it will do a job on the lawnmower.

Stone comes in many colors and sizes. White stone tends to become dirty and stained over time. Lava rock, which is a reddish brown color, stays cleaner and neater. Light-colored stone tends to reflect heat. Darker colors heat up, so don't use them around heat-sensitive plants.

In the wine-growing region around Avignon, France, tan rocks are used to absorb heat during the day and keep the ground warm at night. This keeps the soil temperature from fluctuating and cooling off, which makes the grapes better. Local legend says God made the soil rocky for just this purpose. The concept of a heat-retaining mulch may be useful in areas where warmer soil is desirable.

GRASS CLIPPINGS  Mainly useful as a mulch in beds and borders before the grass goes to seed (late May). After that, the grass seeds will sprout, which may not be a problem in many places. If used as mulch, it should only be spread in a thin layer each time, so it will dry out. If too deep, it gets rank.

Ideally, grass clippings should be mowed with a mulching mower and left to nourish the lawn. Studies have shown that lawns where grass clippings were left in place used half as much fertilizer as ones where they were removed.

LEAVES  Useful under bushes, but are too heavy and may mat down on flower beds.

NEWSPAPER  The easiest, cheapest messy mulch. A thick moist wad keeps the weeds down. It can be covered with bark mulch for a neat appearance. It should not be used in vegetable gardens, because some papers contain low levels of heavy metals and organic chemicals.

PLASTIC FILM  Comes in black, brown, yellow, or red. Be sure there are slits in it, so water can get through. Attach the edges with dirt, rocks, or big plastic staples or wire staples (made from opened up metal hangers). When plastic is covered with mulch and, thus, protected from sunlight, it can last ten or twenty years. The mulch often slips around, however, and exposes portions of plastic. Plastic film is awkward to lay.

WEED-RETARDANT FABRICS  New products are similar to plastic film but are easier to cut and install. They last for several years, particularly if covered with bark mulch. It is easy to cut an X-shaped hole in them for planting new material.

WOOD CHIPS  Chipped wood, with twigs, leaves, and wood bits, make a fine mulch. They may harbor ants, so it is best to use them in areas away from the house. When tree work is done by professionals, they often bring a chipper and make chips right on the site.

SALT MARSH HAY  The old classic. It's not neat, but it carries no weed seeds, and strawberries love it.

COCOA HULLS  They smell delicious but may cause growth irregularities.

SAWDUST  Not good as a mulch because it robs nitrogen from the soil.

COMPOST OR WELL-ROTTED MANURE  The black gold of gardening. A friend with a horse is a friend to treasure. And so is the one who takes the manure, for horse owners always have too much of this good thing. (Fresh manure must be spread by February and allowed to mellow over the winter, or it will burn the plants.) In the South or in very hot areas, manure decomposes more rapidly but should be spread two to three months before planting in spring.

The *real secret* of French and Chinese intensive gardening is a few inches of manure each year, not a transcendental mystique.

# ORGANIC GARDENING

Most soil grows good crops for a few years, then wears out. In early New England, farmers abandoned their tired farms and moved out west, which is why there is so much second-growth forest now. Farmers in primitive countries using destructive slash-and-burn techniques have to move every few years. In Europe, however, they have been using the same soil for centuries, which they keep fertile by adding lots of organic material, mostly manure and annual grasses.

This practice of adding organic materials and compost to the soil enriches it. Many methods are widely touted today. They are variously known as Organic Farming, French Intensive Gardening, The Chinese Method, Thai Terracing, or plain old Raised Beds.

All are variations of the same thing. The technique is simple: Just pile 12 inches of various good organic material on the soil. Best is manure, but also good are grass clippings, chopped-up leaves, fallen apples, clean vegetable peelings, and coffee grounds. For neatness it can be edged with wood ties, rocks, or logs.

In spring this messy heap can easily be dug into the bed. A loose spongy soil, at least 1 foot deep, should result. Plants will grow much faster, taller, and healthier. To correct any chemical imbalances, in spring add lime to bring the pH to 6.5. Also a balanced fertilizer such as 10-10-10 can be added, perhaps laced with extra bone meal or superphosphate. It's the fertilizer, either from the manure or from what's added, that makes these gardens grow so lushly.

# NO-TILL GARDENING

For centuries, farmers have plowed the fields before sowing. And for centuries, the bare topsoil has eroded, blown away and washed away, leaving worn-out fields behind.

In the Midwest it has become an enormous problem as the rich prairie soil has disappeared, floating away as silt down the Mississippi River. The Department of Agriculture has decided that farmers must conserve their soil through better practices in order to get crop-support payments.

No-till farming is not new. It's been around for a half century, but stubbornness has made farmers turn a deaf ear. There is something wonderfully romantic about a freshly plowed furrow. It has been in all bucolic pictures since the Middle Ages. It is our cultural heritage. It's the old comfortable way to go.

In no-till (also called ridge-till, mulch-till, or residue management) finished plants are cut down, and their residue is left to decay into compost right on top of the soil. Sometimes the plants are chopped up, sometimes not. Like the forest floor, the soil self-renews.

No-till fields are rarely plowed. Seeds are drilled or mechanically scratched into the soil. Moisture is conserved. Nutrients are recycled back into the soil. Worms and necessary microbes are conserved. And the soil doesn't wash or blow away. Unfortunately, they require herbicides to keep the weeds down.

For commercial farmers, it's 25 percent cheaper than traditional farming methods. By the year 2000, it is estimated that 80 percent of farmers will be using no-till.

No-till gardening can also be used by home gardeners. It means less work, less weeding, fewer chemicals, and healing the soil. It also means missing the thrill of turning the good brown earth in early spring and enjoying the age-old smell of fresh soil.

Using a permanent mulch is the way to get the benefits of no-till. The mulch may be compost made elsewhere, of leaves, grass clippings, and such. Or the residue may be composted right there on the ground. There are problems with keeping the plant residue right on the soil, however. Eventually there is a buildup of insects and diseases, so vegetable crops must be rotated. It may mean having two or three growing areas and rotating the crops every two or three years.

Naturally, an inch or 2 of well-rotted manure will make everything grow greener and stronger. Bark mulch or wood chips alone won't have the same healing effect as a mixture of green matter and stems and stalks, but bark mulch may be added on top for aesthetics and neatness.

Weeds can be a problem. Commercial farmers use herbicides before seeding and between rows of vegetables later. For home gardeners, hand weeding is most convenient. If mulch is used, there will be fewer weeds, and what weeds there are will come out easily. An alternative is to smother the weeds with a few more inches of new mulch. When using this method, you can make the mulch very thick, up to 10 or 12 inches. Push it back for planting in the spring; then pull it in again when the plants are big enough.

Granular fertilizer has to be applied under the mulch, not on top of it. This can be done by scratching it into the soil when the mulch is pulled back , as for planting. Or use liquid fertilizer on the leaves and stems to be absorbed by the plant.

Because the soil is healthy and the roots cool and moist, the plants are more likely to be vigorous and withstand stresses better.

# GROWING IN A BIOSPHERE— THE GREENHOUSE OF THE FUTURE

The future is now in some places. Plants and food crops are being grown in totally contained greenhouses, without soil, using biological insect controls and liquid fertilizer. The same methods were tested in Russian spaceships to see if food could be grown in space.

At Disney's Epcot Center in Orlando, Florida, the food pavilion has one of these new, space-age greenhouses, where all manner of plants are grown in an enclosed space. Cocoa trees grow beside beans and bananas. Lettuce grows out of holes on a wall, the roots behind, sprayed with a solution of nutrients every few minutes. Wheat grows in a black soil that is the same composition as the dust found on the moon.

In Holland, in a demonstration greenhouse, 12-foot tomato vines, barely three months old, are smothered in red fruit and dark green leathery leaves. They grow not in soil, but from a tiny cube of ground-up volcanic rock wool. Each plant's minuscule root is constantly bathed in a similar nutrient solution. Sun heats the temperature-and-humidity-controlled greenhouse. When nights are too cool, plastic hot-water pipes are lowered to just above the top leaf.

Plants are pollinated by bees that live in cardboard boxes. They cost about the same as human labor for hand pollination, but the bees work twenty-four hours a day. Humans feed them with sugar and water and can tell by how much they drink how efficient they are. Aphids and other insects are controlled with predatory wasps introduced on cardboard squares that look like dirt-smudged price tags.

Life-sustaining water is delivered into the rock wool cube through a black plastic pipe, which also carries the balanced diet of nutrients. The system is totally closed. The runoff water is collected, analyzed, corrected for nutrient balance, and then re-used. Harvesting is done from a hydraulic ladder platform that moves between the rows.

The rock wool eventually gets clogged with fungus, and it is then sent back to a factory where it is chopped up, sterilized, mixed with more ground-up volcanic rock, and packaged for re-use. Even the green plant residue is not wasted. Plant-eating fish, grown in huge tanks, eat the residue vegetation. Then they are harvested, too. No phosphates or pesticides pollute the ground water outside this enclosed, environmentally friendly world.

But no breezes sway the vines, no drop of rain glistens on a limpid leaf. No ray of sun touches a red tomato except through filtering glass. This is not the farm of our fathers. This is the future, and it is now.

# CELL CULTURE AND GENETIC ENGINEERING OF PLANTS

Controlled greenhouses are used by many propagators, flower growers, and plant producers. The plants grown under these conditions have to be modified, because those taken directly from outdoor field farming develop unforeseen problems. So new varieties are developed to fit the new growing systems.

In the past, most new plants were developed by seed, crossing known varieties again and again until the right combination of traits was achieved. But it was slow. And when the desired plant was finally grown, it was very difficult to produce enough of them.

Old production methods were by seed, cuttings, or grafts—all time consuming and problematic. Often the new crosses were sterile and wouldn't produce seeds at all. Or, if they did, the seeds would revert back to undesirable grandparents. Or the plants would root slowly by grafts or cuttings. And it was hard to get enough material to make very many new plants.

Then a new technique known as *cell culture* was developed. A single plant theoretically could yield thousands of identical plants. The growing tip of a plant, called the meristem, contains cells that grow into new leaves or flowers or roots. Some of the meristem could be harvested under a microscope, and each single cell could be planted on a cell culture medium. As each tiny cell divided, it produced a whole plant. These were then transplanted to another growing medium, then another, and finally potted up to be grown on as ordinary small seedlings.

It was found that rotating these plants in a drum made them root better. It has to do with gravity. Who could have imagined that just plain gravity from the center of the earth wasn't as effective? Many commercial strawberry seedlings are started this way because the new plants are reliably free of virus infection.

## Genetic Engineering

Now another more revolutionary system is on the horizon: *genetic engineering*. Bits of DNA that contain the ability to produce a particular enzyme or protein that carries a desired trait can now be put into other plants. For example, if the ability to withstand cold is contained in a small snippet of DNA in a cold-tolerant plant such as lettuce, it can be snipped out. Then it can be inserted into a cell in a tender plant . . . say a strawberry. The strawberry cell could then make the particular protein that confers cold tolerance, and it wouldn't freeze on cold nights.

The possibilities are mind boggling. Currently, research is being done to insert a gene into wheat that would make it resistant to a commonly used herbicide. Also, research is being done to develop wheat's cold hardiness. If wheat were more cold hardy, like rye, the world's breadbasket could be expanded into Canada and Siberia.

In Saudi Arabia research is being done to find food plants that will grow with salt water. In Israel the genetic nature of drought resistance is being studied. It seems that if plants can close their stomata (breathing holes on the underside of the leaves), they can conserve water and become more drought resistant. If the snippet of a gene can make a plant more drought-resistant, it could change the economies of the Middle East.

Other fascinating projects include testing the ability of some plants to produce medicines and useful chemicals. For instance, two genetically engineered plants are bred together to produce seeds, which will grow plants that produce active mammalian immunoglobulins. In another experiment researchers are trying to put a gene into a tobacco plant so it could make interferon. (Immunoglobulins and interferon are useful for human disease control.)

Nongenetic research thrives, too. One project is to use unexploited edible plants, such as quintoa grain from Peru and buckwheat and adzuki beans from India. Of 80,000 edible plants, only fifty are cultivated. And only seven, wheat, rice, corn, potatoes, barley, cassava, and sorghum, make up 75 percent of the world's food supply.

# INSECTS, PESTS, AND BIOLOGICAL CONTROLS

Theoretically, gene splicing can be done with insects and other pests, too. One project has isolated the pesticide-resistant genes from cockroaches, tobacco budworms, aphids, and Colorado potato beetles. They can be used by farmers to see which pesticides certain insects are resistant to and to choose other effective ones for control. Also it opens the possibility that these genes could be put into bacteria, which could then eat toxic pesticide spills and clean up contaminated environments.

The most interesting work at the moment, however, is in biological control. The good news is that an International Organization for Biological Control (IOBC) has been formed, and scientists from all around the globe are cooperating in research projects.

Among the projects being tested are ones in Utah and Oregon, where sheep are being trained to eat weeds, thus saving on herbicide use. Another project is working on controlling a weed called saltcedar (*Tamarix*). Bugs that feed on this troublesome, imported weed pest were collected in their native China to test here for controlling the spread of this weed. Another project is investigating a one-celled microbe that fatally infects destructive Mormon crickets. Nematodes are being tested for Japanese beetle grubs. A fly from African forests may control pine woolly aphid. At the University of Massachusetts, research is being conducted on a predator wasp for euonymus scale.

Plants are also being tested to absorb organic matter from water contaminated with sewage and heavy metals. Some heavy metals are trapped in the leaves, which can then be burned and the metals recaptured to use again.

One fascinating experiment uses poisonous spider toxin. The toxin gene is inserted into a virus that infects a certain insect. Once inside the insect, the virus produces the toxin and kills the bad bug. It sounds like *Star Trek,* but it is the wave of the future.

## *Biopesticides*

Biopesticides are materials that utilize the natural weakness of pests and attack them in more specific ways than do chemicals, which just kill everything. Biopesticides may be predator insects, viruses, or bacteria that attack an unwelcome pest. Their use requires complex information on the life cycles and environmental conditions needed for success. These pesticides have to be applied carefully, at the right time, so the predator insect or virus gets the target pest. Usually a knowledgeable landscape professional is needed to diagnose ills and prescribe these materials. When biopesticides don't provide adequate control, chemicals can still be used.

There is one biopesticide that is commercially useful right now, BT, or *Bacillus thuringiensis*, which kills larvae of many insects. There are different varieties of BT. One is used for gypsy moths; another is used for Japanese beetle grubs, although the method of delivery has yet to be refined to make the soil inoculations permanent. BT is the treatment of choice for cabbage worms, too. Another variety, *BT Israeliensis,* kills the mosquito larvae that spreads fatal, human encephalitis. This variety of BT is also used in Africa to control black flies, which cause blindness. BT is now used extensively in farming, and, unfortunately, this heavy use is causing some insects to develop resistance.

Multiple biopesticides may attack a particluar insect. Although BT is the most commonly used insecticide against gypsy moth, a polyhedral virus also kills them. The virus has been cultured and can be sprayed over infested areas, which illustrates another problem of biopesticides. We really don't know what the secondary effects will be. There is a concern that if the polyhedral virus is widely used, it might mutate into a virus that attacks other desirable insects such as butterflies and bees. To prevent this a genetically modified virus has been made, which lacks an outer coat. An unclothed virus such as this would not be able to survive in the wild, only inside gypsy moths. When the moths die, so will the virus. This method would be safe. Biological pesticides have to be applied very carefully so the predator insect gets the target pest at just the right time without causing other problems.

As our love affair with chemicals wanes, and almost five hundred species of insects have become resistant to some chemicals, enthusiasm grows for biological solutions. Many details have to be ironed out, however, before the theories can become practical realities in the marketplace. Biopesticides are an exciting, though uncharted, territory.

## *Predator Insects*

Simple biological solutions—such as using predator insects to eat bugs that damage plants—are becoming fashionable in home gardens. "Good" predatory wasps lay eggs in and destroy "bad" aphids. The garden catalogues are full of good bugs you can buy. It sounds great. Release a thousand lovely little lady bugs in the garden. (One lady bug per square foot is recommended.) They will eat the bad bugs, and all will be well.

Well, not necessarily. It's not always that simple. To wit, the lady bugs will eat the bad bugs, and if they can't find bad bugs, they will eat each other. Or they will fly to your neighbor's yard, where there are tastier bugs. Or the weather will be wrong when you release them, and they just won't eat anything at all.

Before you buy a thousand lady bugs, you might want to find out more about their life patterns and exactly how to use them for best results. But they certainly won't hurt; they are charming bits of flitting color, and they might surprise you and eat up all the bad bugs.

You will still need to use chemicals when the safer methods fail, but you should start with the less polluting biological controls first.

## *Chemical Pesticides*

Chemical pesticides change very rapidly. Each chemical is licensed by the government for specific uses only, which are listed on the container. These lists are expanded and restricted almost yearly. New chemicals appear to replace those that are restricted. Each state has a Pesticide Board that prepares lists of currently approved pesticides, and usually publishes them in a technical manual. Some can be applied by licensed professionals only, others are for home use. (See Health Hazards in chapter 13 for pesticides lists and safety precautions.)

# INTEGRATED PEST MANAGEMENT (IPM) AND PLANT HEALTH CARE (PHC)

The current best philosophies for growing plants are Integrated Plant Management (IPM) and Plant Health Care (PHC). The idea is to use all the tools available for good plant health and safest pest control. As soon as new research is perfected, it can be immediately incorporated into the management practices. The aim of PHC is to grow healthy plants, while IPM aims to control insects and diseases through the most effective, least-toxic methods.

Instead of just spraying with chemicals, the strategy includes modifying soil and growing conditions for optimal health, since vigorous plants can withstand insect and disease stresses better. Insects and pests are carefully studied to see when they hatch and when they are most vulnerable. Then each plant is monitored to see which pests actually are present and when.

Although multitudes of pests can attack each plant, only one or two are actually around at any one time. Instead of treating all of them, just in case they might come, the new philosophy treats only the ones that are actually found, and only if they are present in large enough numbers to create a problem. When there are just a few insects, their damage might be unimportant and they are left alone. Insecticides are used only when the problem reaches "economic" importance.

This is a radical departure from the agricultural and gardening practices of two decades ago. During the seventies one sprayed everything preventively—for everything that might possibly happen. It was wasteful. It was unnecessary. It poisoned the land. Now one sprays as a last resort, when all else has failed, and only after the target pest is causing serious damage.

It means living with some imperfections. The flower or fruit may not be absolutely perfect, but that is a tradeoff.

IPM and PHC use information creatively. One way is to mesh plant growth cycles and insect life cycles, which can be used to advantage. For instance, the second generation of carrot rust fly comes about the first of September in New England. If the carrots are harvested before that date, they won't be attacked, and no pesticide will be needed. It means the carrots may have to be planted earlier, or a faster-maturing variety must be used.

Cultural conditions may be modified. If the soil around cabbages, broccoli, and cauliflower is kept very alkaline with a high pH, the incurable disease, clubroot, will not occur and infect the soil. Similarly, if potatoes are kept at a very low, acid pH, they will not develop scab disease. Some fungi are kept under control by watering only when the plants will dry quickly and pruning to allow for better air circulation.

## Pheromones

Pheromones, which are insect attractants, are used to monitor the hatch of certain pests, so treatment can take place at exactly the right time. Before these were used, one had to estimate the date of the hatch. Every gardener knows that the weather varies by several weeks from year to year, so estimating the hatch dates involves some guesswork. Sometimes estimated dates caught the insects. Sometimes they missed. With the advent of monitoring and counting to see how the population is growing, it is possible to know exactly when to treat and whether there are enough to even bother.

Pheromones are used in other ways as well. When queen bee pheromone was isolated and sprayed in orchards, there was more fruit set. It seems queen bee scent makes the worker bees work even harder. When pheromones were first isolated, they were used to lower insect population levels. Baited traps caught undesirable insects. But longer experience has shown that these traps don't make much of a difference in the total insect population. With one kind of trap for adult Japanese beetles, for example, the traps actually attracted more beetles than would have been in the yard without them. So now traps are used mainly for monitoring.

## Growing Degree Days (GDD)

A very useful body of information has been amassed about when insects hatch, which can be correlated exactly with the weather. No more seat-of-the-pants old farmer wisdom. Because plants and insects respond to temperature when the spring comes, measuring the cumulative amount of heat they receive allows one to predict when insects will emerge or plants leaf out and flower. This measurement is called Growing Degree Days (GDD).

GDD total the degrees of heat received each day at a particular place. Each day's total is added to the total from the day before, and a running total is kept for the plant-growing season. GDD do not measure an actual number of days, but instead they are a measurement of an amount of heat. The name is confusing.

GDD have been calculated all over the country for several years. For instance, we now know that on GDD 28, the star magnolia blooms. In Boston, GDD 28 is in April. In Washington, D.C., GDD 28 occurs two weeks earlier. On GDD 435, the Kousa dogwood buds are just showing first color, oyster shell scale is in the crawler stage, gypsy moth caterpillars are too big for treatment with BT, and poison ivy is just coming into flower (when it is most susceptible to herbicides). These things happen sooner in the south where GDD 435 occurs earlier than in northern areas. GDD are measured each year in each area by the state agricultural services, and the count is available by telephoning them.

The advances in plant technology are coming at a faster and faster rate. As they do, they are incorporated into IPM and PHC treatment strategies. It is almost impossible for a non-professional to keep abreast of all the new information, modifications, and nuances of old practices. Professional groundskeepers and arborists do keep up on all this information and should be consulted regularly when problems arise, or even before they arise. While their time and expertise costs money, it will save unnecessary expenses and useless treatments.

# CHAPTER 13

# *Maintenance and Common Sense*

Establishing a landscape is only half the battle. The other half is maintaining it. This is what most people forget to take into account when they calculate their energy- and money-saving equations.

Human work energy has a value, especially if it's your own. Water, fertilizer, pesticides, and equipment cost money. Repetitive money. Soil is a limited commodity. Cleaning polluted air is becoming more necessary each year. Maintenance techniques also degrade or preserve the environment as well as one's own health.

In general, trees, shrubs, and many flowers should survive without any special care if they are carefully chosen to fit into your own microenvironment. All gardeners eventually end up loving these survivors the best. The plants that don't make it perhaps shouldn't be there.

Understanding what is really necessary for plant survival helps. While it is nice to know what is desirable for maximum plant health and growth, most plants survive with less-than-optimal care. Some plants are very fussy, however, and the care of a few of those makes a good hobby for the fastidious.

Common sense is the key.

## LAWNS

A lawn is a high-maintenance item. It can be maintained as a beautiful green carpet by weekly mowing, two or three fertilizings a year, seeding of bare spots, liming, aerating, occasional dethatching, and treatment of the inevitable insects and diseases that follow such a coddled ecosystem. Some green carpet worshippers use toxic chemicals in their war to destroy every single intruder weed, which they abhor.

If money is no object, people can be hired to handle the chores. For the less well-heeled, it requires some effort. You can spend a bundle on a lawn service; do it yourself and spend a bundle on mowers, fertilizers, spreaders, seed, and give up your Saturdays; or, have a simple greensward—a casual mowed expanse of green containing grass and weeds and whatnot, instead of a perfect lawn.

A magnificent lawn requires considerable care and is very complex and scientific to maintain. In fact, it's a labor of love, almost to the point of an obsession. You can't have one without the other.

## Mowing

Most people mow about once every week or ten days. The minimum maintenance is mowing when the lawn gets longer than you can stand it. Since grass grows best in cool weather, a more efficient schedule is to mow weekly during spring and fall and mow less during summer, when growth is slower. There are chemicals currently in vogue that restrict elongation of the grass stems, which reduces mowing by about half. Hopefully, grass breeders will perfect a low-growing grass that stops growing at 3 to 4 inches and doesn't need mowing at all.

Lawns in temperate regions should be mowed to a height of 2 to 4 inches to conserve moisture, protect the roots, allow for most green photosynthetic tissue to remain, and discourage weed seeds from germinating. Current research indicates this is the best height, but bear in mind that theories change frequently in the lawn business.

When the lawn clippings resulting from mowing are chopped up and left on the lawn, they add nutrients back into the soil and replace about two fertilizings a year. Mulching mowers are the way of the future, because they chop the grass in small bits that decay fast. If one doesn't have a mulching mower, then one mows in a circle going round and round over each preceding pile of clippings until they are tiny bits. The remaining piled up ring of grass clippings is then collected. If the lawn is mowed frequently, before the grass gets too high, all the clippings will disappear into the grass and none will be left to collect.

## Fertilizing

All fertilizers work the same. They provide certain elements that make plants grow better. The more nitrogen a lawn gets, the greener and faster it grows. Nitrogen gets used up after a period of time, depending on what its chemical formulation was.

Pure chemical fertilizer, such as 5–10–5 is cheapest. It gives a big, fast, green shot, then is used up by six weeks. "Organic" fertilizer such as urea (which may be manufactured chemically) is used up more slowly, over eight to twelve weeks. Its activity is moderated by temperature, and if put on in November, it will not work until spring.

Real pure organic fertilizers (made from once living organisms) often have chicken feathers, tankage, and enzymes as active ingredients. They start working slowly but last a long time.

Theoretically, organic fertilizers improve the health of the soil by adding various important soil bacteria along with the slow-release nitrogen.

In temperate regions, fertilizer is applied just as the lawn starts to grow, which means spring and early fall. If only one application of fertilizer per year is used, then it should be applied at the end of summer, around Labor Day in northern areas. If a second application is used, it should be in spring. Some lawn companies now recommend four treatments a year, but that is extravagant. In hot areas, fertilizing times are dictated by the seasons, type of grass, and irrigation system.

Fertilizer improves the quality, thickness, health, and green color of lawns, but grass will grow without it.

## Lime

Each grass has a preferred pH, or soil acidity. Lime is used to make acid soil areas more hospitable for fine lawn grasses.

Bluegrass and rye grass grow best when the pH is not too acid. Because most fine lawns have bluegrass, it is generally believed that all grasses must have the preferred bluegrass pH of 5.8 to 7.5. Lower-care fescues are happy down to pH 5.5 to 6.8, while sheep fescue, used for wildflower meadows, will grow in quite acid soil, pH 4.5 to 5.8. The pH tolerance of lawn grasses ranges from centipede grass at pH 4.3 to 5.8, to bahai grass at 6.5 to 7.5.

A universal pH that will accommodate almost all grasses is 6.5.

Before liming, have the soil tested. Then correct to the desired pH for the grass mixture to be planted accoding to the instructions on the package. Liming is not usually necessary more than every two or three years.

## Overseeding

A lawn is made up of 500,000 to 1,000,000 individual grass plants at about 850 plants per square foot. It's impossible to keep them all alive forever. The easiest way to have a greener lawn is to grow new grass by planting grass seed. On an established lawn this is called overseeding.

Overseeding is the true secret of low maintenance and lower costs. One simply spreads seed on the bare spots. It must be done at the right time for the seeds to grow best. That time is usually just after the summer heat, when the soil is warm, the weeds and crabgrass are finishing, and the weather will be cool for a few months. In the North, this is about Labor Day. In the South, it is later in the fall season or even in early winter.

First rake the soil lightly. Sprinkle on some seed. Step on it or lightly rake it in to make good contact with the soil. Finally, water it. The more often over several weeks the area is sprinkled and kept moist, the better the success rate for new grass growth.

The second best time to overseed is in early spring. One can even sprinkle seed on the melting snow, which carries it into the moist soil. As the season warms up, the grass sprouts, and Mother Nature takes care of it. In the South, a similar time is toward the end of the rainy wet winter season.

## Grass Varieties

There are many grass species, with hundreds of patented, named varieties. Each does better under certain conditions such as sun, shade, drought, heavy use, poor soil, and low fertilizer. Some varieties are enriched with endophytes, a good fungus, which is poisonous to many insects. Endophytes are bred directly into the grass seeds. (Cattle and horses may get sick if they graze on endophyte-enriched grasses.) It all may seem overwhelmingly confusing when one starts to try to differentiate the various kinds and varieties.

For northern areas the most common grasses are fescue, bluegrass, bent grass, and rye.

*Fescue* stands shade, drought, acid soil, and less fertilizer. Chewings Fescue has very thin leaves; Hard Fescue has wider leaves; Tall Fescue has leaves as wide as bluegrass. Each of these has many improved varieties with special names. New varieties are introduced each year. Hard Fescues or Sheep Fescues are used for wildflower lawns.

*Bluegrass* does best in full or partial shade, on good soil with good care. It is very tough and stands hard wear. Certain varieties will grow well in partial shade, but for problem areas in deep, damp shade, a bright green weed grass called *Poa trivialis*, variety "Saber," will do better.

*Bent grass* is a fine-leafed, very high-maintenance grass used for golf greens and special lawns.

*Rye grass* grows fast and tough. It needs sun and more care but is very easy to reseed whenever quick grass is needed. Annual rye grass (cheap builder's special) dies with the first freeze. Perennial rye grass survives the winter and is the one that should be used. One advantage of rye grass is that it germinates in five days, whereas the others take longer, up to three weeks, to sprout.

Most temperate grass seed is sold as mixtures of several kinds of grass, so that there will be enough varieties to fill each niche of each mini-microenvironment of a yard. These might be shady areas, sunny areas, dry areas, wet and low areas, high-use areas, or irrigated areas. Each yard usually has several different areas. Many varieties have too much cheap annual rye grass and not enough improved perennial varieties. Check the box. What you plant is what you get.

Southern areas are more complicated, depending on whether they are hot-humid or hot-arid, whether they have sprinklers, and what kind of soil they have. There are special grasses for each of these hot climates. They are generally more rough textured than the northern varieties, and most can't be grown easily from seed. Instead they are propagated by plugs of small living plants, and are installed like ground covers. They usually need less mowing than cool-climate grass and may turn brown if not watered and also in winter.

In the south, the grass varieties that are commonly used include Bermuda grass, centipede grass, Bahai grass, St. Augustine grass, and zoysia.

*Bermuda grass* grows rampant with adequate water and fertilizer. Mowing two times a week may be required to keep it neat.

*Centipede grass,* called "lazy man's grass," requires little care under optimal conditions but occasionally dies out in spots. It's slow growing, reaching only 3 or 4 inches without mowing. To keep it at $1\frac{1}{2}$ inches requires mowing only every ten or twenty days. It is dense, relatively weed-free, and of coarser texture than Bermuda or zoysia.

*Bahai grass* is a pasture grass that is seeded into southern lawn mixtures because it is tough, easily maintained, grows on any soil, and withstands drought.

*St. Augustine grass* is a low, creeping variety that prefers a moist climate but is also drought-tolerant and will grow in shade. It is a coarse grass that is mowed to about 2 inches high.

*Zoysia,* a fine-textured grass, makes a fine lawn. Zoysia, however, wears better than Bermuda grass. It turns brown in cool weather, so it is best used where the winters are warm. Slow-growing, it makes a dense, thick carpet, which needs mowing only every ten days or so, normally to a height of between 1 and 2 inches.

In hot climates lawns are very desirable from an energy standpoint. The cooling effect they exert around buildings outweighs the maintenance required. In hot climates, shrubs or thick ground covers sometimes provide a home for undesirable insects, pests, and snakes, so grass may be preferred. Also for fire control, an irrigated bank of lawn around the house is the best protection.

In intermediate areas, such as at the border between the northern and southern parts of the country, heat-resistant types of grass are planted to survive the summers. These have a tendency to brown up when it gets cold, however, particularly zoysia grass. Golf courses in these areas often plant rye grass seed in fall. It germinates quickly and grows during the cool weather to provide green color for the winter. It then dies out in the heat of summer when the tropical grasses green up again.

For weddings or special events, a brown lawn can sometimes be turned green with the application of special high-iron fertilizer. A surer way is to spray green, water-soluble latex paint lightly on the lawn, which survives the beautification perfectly well.

## Insects and Weeds

Since lawns are a man-made creation, they are fragile. Fragile ecosystems can't fend off insects, disease, and weeds as well as tough natural ones.

The traditional practice has been to control these chemically, which is easy to do. But the problems often recur, and repeated treatments are necessary. The chemicals, however, probably have ill effects on the people exposed to them and eventually pollute the ground and water supply. There is no reason that a lawn must look like a weed-free, stain-free green carpet.

Pregnant ladies, men who would like to become fathers, children, and pets should not walk on lawns that use herbicides for weed control. Two common herbicides lower sperm production in healthy men. An overdose of one temporarily stops sperm production. The long-term effects of pesticides are just being documented, so it is better to be safe than sorry. There is serious concern for children that exposure to too many pesticides have a cumulative effect that, over time, is decidedly unhealthful. Lawn pesticides are a major source of exposure. The younger the children, the greater the effect of even small amounts of these poisons.

New theories of Integrated Pest Management and Plant Health Care have formulated strategies for dealing with lawn problems biologically by changing maintenance practices, and timing certain procedures to control particular insects or diseases. This is definitely the way of the future.

Lawns can be simple or fancy, messy or neat, depending on how much care they receive. There is no correct standard of excellence. People have to make their own decisions about how much lawn work to do and how to handle their lawn's problems.

# MEADOWS

It may seem that the way to escape from the lawn care trap is to have a meadow. Meadows are easier than lawns because they don't need so much mowing, and they don't need fertilizing, liming, and watering. They do, however, take a while to get started and brought under control. If a regular lawn is left to go to seed and mowed infrequently, it will usually become a satisfactory meadow. Turning a wild or barren area into a decent meadow requires planting the desired species of grasses and takes a year or two. After the meadow is established, regular mowing will keep it attractive.

If a meadow is never mowed, it will gradually revert to tall weeds, then scrub and brambles, then small trees and thicket, and after a hundred years or so back to forest. That is the natural succession of land. More and more people prefer the informal look of a meadow, although it doesn't fit in every neighborhood. At least not yet.

The secret of having a meadow near a house is to edge it with a neat border that is taller than grass with seed heads, a height of about 2½ feet. The border may be of low-growing shrubs such as *spirea, bulmaldii,* bush roses, tall hosta, or small evergreens. Another technique is to keep a neatly mowed wide strip at the beginning of the meadow and around its edges, particularly along the driveway.

Establishing wildflowers in a meadow is complicated and requires choosing the right grass seed (a noninvasive, clump-type sheep fescue) and flowers for the soil, exposure, and climate. Turning the soil provides a better seed bed, and regular watering or irrigation helps the wildflower seed germinate well. It is not much different from starting a new lawn.

The first year usually has the most flowers. Gradually they get crowded out by the stronger, bigger plants, and invasive grasses overpower the more delicate early flowers. This is especially true if the soil is rich and has barnyard grass seed in it. Most natural wildflower meadows exist because one or a few species do best in that soil, in that exposure. It is hard to approximate the ecosystem niches, but it's worth a try.

Once established, wildflower meadows can be maintained by carefully timing the mowing schedule to favor the desired wildflower varieties. For instance, if spring wildflowers such as violets, Canada mayflower, and ajuga are wanted, the field is not mowed until after they have flowered and gone to seed (about June 15 in the Boston area). If summer flowers such as daisies, black-eyed Susan, coreopsis, and Queen Anne's lace are wanted, then the field is mowed early, before these set flower buds (perhaps some time in May or early June). Then it is mowed again after they have finished flowering and gone to seed. This keeps down the later, taller plants, such as goldenrod and aster, that would otherwise crowd them out.

Micromanagement of wildflower meadows is as yet imperfectly understood. Only experimentation can show which mowing dates favor which wildflowers. But a meadow that's mowed occasionally is definitely less work than a conventional lawn, if you don't mind the rustic look.

# GROUND COVERS

A pleasing green carpet can be achieved with ground covers. They don't need constant care once they're established, and most are almost self-sustaining if decent soil and adequate water are available. All ground covers, however, absolutely require a yearly weeding, usually during late spring, certainly by June. Ground covers also occasionally need water during droughts or when their leaves wilt and drop.

In very dry or cold locations, ground covers should not be raked clean, for the decaying leaves underneath return nutrients to the soil. In moist tropical areas, however, fallen leaves and debris may become rank and unattractive, so occasionally light raking out is beneficial. After raking, the exposed soil and roots are very susceptible to sunburn and drought and should be watered.

Renovation and maintenance of ground covers is usually done in very early spring when hormones that promote vigorous new growth are active. Ground covers benefit from being clipped back, and ivy can actually be mowed with a lawn mower set at the tallest setting (3 to 4 inches). New shoots then grow to thicken the beds.

Ground covers create much lower-maintenance areas than grass or flower beds and are not too difficult for homeowners to plant themselves. The soil should be enriched before planting. It's best to just loosen the soil with a pitchfork, but don't turn it over because that exposes more weed seeds. Before planting, a herbicide should be used to kill everything that's growing, especially grass. Sometimes one waits until a second crop of weed seed sprouts so they can also be killed with herbicide. Then bark mulch is spread, and then, finally, the ground cover plants are planted. (See Figure 57, How to Root Ground Covers from Existing Plants, and Ground Covers in chapter 11 for further information.)

# SHRUBS

Shrubs are very self-sufficient. They take little care once established, but if they are neglected entirely, they take lots of effort to restore and renovate. When young, shrubs should be fed every year or two in spring and watered during droughts. When mature, they need little feeding. Fertilizer just makes them grow more, and then they require more pruning, although an occasional feeding with organic fertilizers is beneficial for maintaining good plant health.

As they age, shrubs become susceptible to attacks of insects and fungi. If the leaves look mottled or speckled, it could be scale, whitefly, or sucking insects. It could be fungus. It could be just hunger for some plant food, or herbicide damage. Or the soil could need adjustment, although that's less likely. Consult your local Agricultural Extension Service or local nursery for accurate identification before spending money for a cure.

A light yearly pruning or shaping will keep shrubs looking good for many years and will keep them neat as they grow older. Eventually, many shrubs get too large or overgrown or sparse. Most deciduous shrubs can be cut back severely without harm. Evergreens must be pruned more conservatively, although they will sprout again, albeit slowly, from old wood. Correct pruning is a skill, and each species requires it be done a certain way and at a certain season. (See Shrubs, chapter 10.)

Proper pruning is especially important for food-bearing plants. Find out how before you hack away at them. The library is a good source of information. So is the Agricultural Extension Service.

Don't assume your gardener or grass cutter knows better than you do. Too many so-called landscape gardeners prune everything like a privet hedge. Many a valuable shrub has been ruined by a trusted gardener.

# SHEARED HEDGES

These require the most work, after lawns. There is no doubt that neat, clipped hedges and borders are a joy to behold. Unfortunately, they are not a joy to keep neat. If left unattended, they quickly look messy. Slower-growing plants or ones shaped in a naturalistic way require less shearing less often. (See chapters 10 and 15 for more information.)

With labor costs so high, many people decide to prefer "naturalistic" hedges and shrubs. A light shearing when the spirit moves you will encourage thick growth. Electric hedge clippers have made maintenance easier, but it still takes time and electricity.

# TREES

Established trees need little regular maintenance. If their roots are near or under a lawn, they will receive some fertilizer and extra water. Established trees rarely, if ever, need feeding. Once every several years is adequate if faster growth is wanted. Sometimes, however, trees get diseases, are attacked by insects, or suffer a general decline in health. In these instances, fertilizer is indicated.

Fertilizer may be sprinkled on the surface of the ground. It is not necessary to punch holes in the surface around the trees. Deep root feeding is also unnecessary; studies showed that trees absorbed surface fertilizer at exactly the same rate. Also, since the feeding roots are in the top 6 to 18 inches, a deep root feeding will miss many of them. Sometimes a sickly tree under a thick mat of lawn will benefit from deep root feeding to get the fertilizer under the grass. Most of the time, though, a top dressing of fertilizer will work fine.

Occasionally fertilizer, trace elements, or pesticides are given to trees through injections into the trunks. This is a job only for a professional tree company and is used only in emergencies. For certain trees that have poor root systems or special disease or insect problems, however, this is like chemotherapy. Very small holes are drilled in the bark and the chemicals inserted. For pesticides, it is environmentally safe, since nothing is sprayed in the air or spread on the soil. All the chemicals stay inside the tree. The main problem with trunk injections is that they are a wound and do allow decay fungi to enter the tree. Small areas of decay, however, can be contained and tolerated by the tree. Repeated injections, though, can cause too many wounds and too much decay.

## *Watering*

All trees appreciate a good, very deep, soaking of their roots during droughts. Mature trees may have long deep roots, often 60 feet or more on some varieties. They get water from the deep underground water table during summer and so are less sensitive than younger ones. City trees, however, have very restricted root systems and so have a more difficult time finding water. The building of roads and foundations interferes with the underground water table. When storm water is piped into a sewer, it doesn't recharge the underground streams. The more built up an area is, the more extra summer water the trees need.

Trees that suffer salt damage in the winter need lots of extra water. Flooding with a hose in early spring will wash some of the water out of the soil. In summer, salt damage shows as brown edges on the leaves, especially maples. Again, flushing the soil to leach out the salt, and regular, deep watering are the best treatments.

## Pruning

As trees get older, they occasionally require pruning of overgrown or dangerous branches. A professional tree company should be called. Pruning large trees is expensive, but a branch through the roof is more expensive. Pruning large trees is also dangerous. Anyone who climbs up a tree on your property should have liability insurance and worker's compensation insurance for himself and his employees. Ask to see the certificates. If someone falls, you could be sued.

Always ask for an estimate, or better still get a bid before work begins. Don't be afraid to get several bids. When in doubt, use a certified arborist. Each state has a professional Arborists Association, which you can call for names.

Young trees are different from old trees. Although they will grow without fertilizer, they will grow faster with it. They should be pruned as they grow to improve their shape. You can easily do this work yourself. A mature tree is only the product of its youthful shape and form (See Tree Pruning, chapters 9 and 10.)

## Pests

Eventually, all trees are attacked by insects and fungi. When this problem occurs, check with your local Agricultural Extension Service or certified arborist before buying equipment and chemicals. Make sure you need a spraying company before you hire one. Every little bug is not a crisis. There is no substitute for competent professional appraisal of the problem. Some epidemics are self-limiting and don't permanently damage healthy trees. Money is easily wasted on the wrong spray at the wrong time. Attacked trees benefit from fertilizing and water, to help them recover from the injury.

In general there are two kinds of insects. Those that chew the leaves or shoots, and those that suck out the plant juices. They are treated with different substances. If the problem is sucking insects, they drip a sticky, sugary substance. Ants milk the sucking insects for the sugar, as a farmer cares for his cows. The sugar also can cause black sooty mold to appear. The science of pesticide use now changes so rapidly that one must check anew each year to see which theories and which chemicals or biological controls are recommended.

Most important is to not do preventive pesticide spraying unless it is for a certain insect or disease problem that actually occurred and was identified in a previous year. Then spray only with the right chemical or biological, at exactly the right time for that pest. The blanket preventive spraying of the past is out.

# DUTCH ELM DISEASE AND OTHER EPIDEMICS

Dutch elm disease is a special case. Because so many elms were planted decades ago, and because there is still no cure, control of this disease is a problem. Proper control depends on good sanitation—which means immediate removal of dead and dying trees. It has to be a county-wide effort to slow the spread. The disease, a fungus that plugs up the water transport tubules of the tree, is spread by beetles. Control efforts have been useful in slowing the spread, but not in halting it, once it has hit an area. It was rampant in the East a few decades ago but has abated because most of the elms have died. It is now in the Midwest, and will surely move to most areas that have large concentrations of elm trees.

One American elm that is more resistant to Dutch elm disease has been specially bred and is available from the Elm Research Institute in New England. There are tree injections that inhibit the fungus once it is in the trees, but there is no cure.

The spread of Dutch elm disease and other epidemics shows the danger of planting too many of one kind of tree. These monocultures become very susceptible to rapid spread of disease. Biodiversity is preferred, which means planting several kinds of trees and shrubs, so if one gets a disease, the others will remain.

Species of trees other than elms also suffer from killing, incurable afflictions. It is not clear whether the cause is just the overconcentration of a single species, air pollution, acid rain, or general environmental degradation. It seems to be occurring around the world, however, and is probably the cumulative result of these factors.

Pine trees are an example. A bark beetle lays eggs under the bark, and the larvae eventually so weaken the tree that it dies. The biology is fascinating. If the tree is very healthy and has lots of sap, the larvae drown in the sap and die. But if the tree is old or otherwise stressed, it does not have so much sap. The sickly trees have a certain odor, and adult female beetles can smell it. They choose sick trees so their offspring will survive. The female beetles release a pheromone that attracts the males to these weakened trees, and to the waiting would-be mothers. The sick trees get sicker and more smelly and so attract more beetles. The cycle progresses until the tree dies. The process may take several years depending on the particular tree.

This seems to be happening around the world. In Florence, Italy, the Aleppo pine trees that were pictured in Italian Renaissance paintings are now mostly dying. In Yellowstone Park, dead lodgepole pines fueled the enormous forest fire of several years ago. Pine bark beetles are causing enormous damage in the pine lumber plantations of the South, where all kinds of stratagems are being tried to stop the killing. Wherever pines are stressed, an outbreak of pine bark beetle seems to follow.

The American chestnut is another interesting case. In the last century, this majestic tree was common and loved. Many towns had a street named after it. Then it developed a disease that killed the above-ground parts. Almost every single tree died. A mature chestnut now is as rare in the United States as a gold nugget. But only the tops were killed; the roots remained alive. In places, young shoots still come up repeatedly where the roots have been left alone. The shoots grow for a few years and then succumb to the disease. Efforts are continuing to find a resistant American chestnut that bears edible fruit.

Gypsy moths are spreading in oak forests throughout the United States, despite valiant efforts to contain them. They ravage new forests and then almost disappear. Once established in a region, however, their population explodes on a regular cycle about every ten years, and they proceed to decimate the oaks once again.

As global warming and changes in the earth's ecosystem occur, they will cause other troubling trends affecting trees and all plants, problems that will have to be dealt with.

# FERTILIZERS

Not all fertilizers are the same, but the chemicals they release are. Any fertilizer is useful only if the instructions on the label are followed accurately. It is easy to burn plants with too much fertilizer salt.

Basically, the three numbers on the package stand for nitrogen, phosphorous and potash (or potassium). The classic is 5–10–5, which stands for 5 percent nitrogen, 10 percent phosphorous, and 5 percent potash. All three elements are necessary for good plant growth, and it is essential that they be in the right proportions in relation to each other. The percentages can be manipulated to change the growth pattern of a plant, but too much manipulation causes malformations and growth abnormalities.

Nitrogen mainly promotes leaf growth. Phosphorous makes strong roots and stems and promotes flowering. Potash enhances maturity and ripening of seeds and fruits. In addition, phosphorous and potash give added insect and disease resistance. Nitrogen dissolves easily and moves quickly through the soil, and nitrogen disappears faster as the temperature rises. Phosphorous, on the other hand, dissolves very slowly and moves very slowly. It lasts longer in the soil than nitrogen.

Grass is usually fed with a high-nitrogen compound (10–6–4) to make it greener and faster-growing. Shrubs and trees generally do better with 5–10–5 or 10–10–10. Higher concentrations such as 20–20–20 really push a plant and make it flower. It is used for annuals and occasionally to force blooms on perennial plants. Pushing plants too much, however, makes them more fragile and more dependent on our ever continuing care. And that makes more work and more expense.

There are many formulations, which are confusing to say the least. The basics, however, remain constant: nitrogen, phosphorous, and potash.

## Chemical Fertilizers

Chemical fertilizers are usually "man-made" chemical salts, most of which dissolve quickly in ground water. They give a quick burst of growth for about six weeks. Some chemical formulations, called "organic" (even though they are man-made chemicals), last longer. Other formulations are coated with plastic or other substances to slowly release the chemicals rather than all at one time. Most chemical fertilizer is made from mineral salts and petroleum, which wastes energy dollars for our country.

## Organic Fertilizers

True organic fertilizers are made from substances that were once alive (leaves, manure, chicken feathers, fish residue, bonemeal, cottonseed meal, and substances such as Milorganite made from sewage treatment waste). These release the same chemicals as synthetic fertilizers but at a slow, steady rate over a long period of time. Temperature is important; they do not work in very cold weather. They are generally more expensive than regular chemical fertilizers, but they improve the soil more in the long run and don't run off and pollute the water supply as much.

Most fertilizers are sold as a dry powder. When used, they must be measured carefully, because too much can burn and kill plants. Dry fertilizers are usually spread on the surface of the soil or mixed with it.

Some granular fertilizers dissolve in water quickly and completely. These are meant to be applied as a foliar spray to be absorbed through the leaves or applied to the soil for root absorption. When plants need a quick pick-me-up, these liquid fertilizers benefit plants fastest of all, through leaves, as well as soil. These very soluble fertilizers are used in hydroponics, where plants are grown in water, without soil, and in biosphere greenhouse production. The constant solution of weak fertilizer promotes constant growth.

Sometimes these very soluble fertilizers are given as an injection into the trunks of trees with compromised root systems, usually urban trees surrounded by blacktop or concrete.

## Trace Elements

Soil science is complicated. It involves not only fertilizer but also calcium (which is the main ingredient of lime) and trace elements (metals such as magnesium, manganese, and iron), plus helpful fungi, microscopic organisms and beneficial insects. Rarely do trace elements cause problems in the home garden. These are of more concern to farmers and in hydroponics. One reason for trace element problems is previous overuse of fertilizers, where residual salts upset the balance. Some soluble fertilizers contain trace elements to compensate for this.

More commonly, too much soil acidity or alkalinity causes problems with trace elements. When the soil is near neutral, about pH 6 to pH 7, most trace elements dissolve easily. When it is too acid or too alkaline, they will not dissolve and so are not available to the plants. This can result in deficiencies of certain trace elements, but it can be easily corrected by improving the pH.

## To Keep Soil Neutral

A pH test will tell if the soil is acid (called sour), alkaline (sweet) or neutral (around pH 7). A universal pH that most plants will tolerate is about pH 6. Lime is used to raise the pH, and make soils more alkaline. It keeps the soil from becoming too acid and also actually improves its texture. There are soil-testing kits and meters for pH, or soil can be sent to a testing lab, usually run by the state. Many nurseries will test your soil for acidity or alkalinity and will recommend the needed correction. Be sure to specify what is to be grown in the soil. Grass, lilacs, and roses, for example, prefer it neutral. Most evergreens actually prefer a slightly acid soil, so they should not be limed. (See List of pH Preferences of Some Useful Plants in part III.)

## To Keep Soil Acid

The soil for many plants, including rhododendrons, azaleas, yews, most hollies, blueberries, strawberries, and potatoes should be acid. Most of these plants prefer a pH between 5.3 and 6.0. New soil is made acid or old soil improved by digging in acid peat moss, bog soil, rotted oak leaves, pine needles, or acid woodland soil. An acid-producing mulch, such as oak leaves, pine needles, acid peat moss, or pine bark mulch, should be kept on top. Don't use other leaves or materials that eventually make the soil more neutral or alkaline, such as maple leaves or wood ashes.

One can also acidify soil chemically by adding a carefully calculated amount of aluminum sulfate after taking a pH reading and doing the necessary arithmetic. This is what most people do to keep it corrected to the desired pH for acid-loving plants.

Most fertilizers, over time, tend to raise the pH. One can use fertilizers specially formulated for acid-loving plants, which leave an acid reaction in the soil. Over a period of time, these may cause chemical imbalances, so it's best not to rely solely on them but to use organic fertilizers as well, which will exert a corrective influence. Beware of adding lime, calcium carbonate, gypsum, or bone meal, all of which contain calcium and raise the pH. Also beware of fresh concrete, which is highly alkaline for two years, as well as rain that splashes off stucco or cement, which picks up calcium and carries it into the soil.

# WATERING AND IRRIGATION

All plants need water. They can grow only as fast as they have water for cell growth. Trees in the rain forest grow so fast because of ever-available water and high humidity. In the home garden one deep watering is worth a peck of sprinklings. Most plants require 1 inch of rainfall each week; the sprinkler should deliver 1 inch of water before you turn it off. (See section on Irrigation Systems, page 153.) During times of drought, very hot, dry, or windy weather, this should be increased to two or three times a week, although water costs and conservation regulations may make this impractical.

Water is a valuable resource, not to be wasted. Overwatering doesn't help plants. Excess water just percolates through the soil into the lower levels. Sprays evaporate into the air. Furthermore, plants, especially trees and shrubs, can die from too much water. Roots need air or they smother and rot. A good watering that is allowed to soak through and then dry out is somewhat preferred to frequent light waterings. Only swamp plants like constantly wet feet.

Light sprinklings don't reach the deeper roots. Sprinklings also encourage the plants to put out new roots near the surface of the soil. These roots are shallow, and, so, very susceptible to drying out as the top layer of soil heats up. The lower levels remain quite constant in temperature.

A lot of water stimulates "soft" growth. Lack of water causes plants to "harden." When plants harden, their outer covering becomes tough and leathery. Both leaves and bark are affected.

Water is one of many triggering mechanisms by which the plants know what seasons are coming, especially in tropical regions where temperature variations are less pronounced. When the rains come (usually in the spring), the plants know to begin putting out leaves and flowers. When the rains diminish (usually in late summer or fall), the plants begin to "harden" to conserve moisture and protect their cells from the winter cold to come. Home watering should mimic the seasons. It is wise to water more often in May and June when it is dry, than in September and October. All plants, however, should go into winter with moisture in the soil. One good late-fall soaking is the most desirable way to do this, especially if the weather has been unseasonably dry.

Some good general rules to consider when deciding if watering is needed are: (1) if the soil is dry 6 inches down; (2) if there has not been a good rainfall recently that soaked in and did not run off; (3) if the plant leaves droop, which indicates water stress; (4) if a water moisture meter reads dry.

# XERISCAPING

Xeriscaping is a style of landscaping that incorporates into landscape design the goal of low water use. This is accomplished by replacing thirsty plants with more drought-resistant ones. It almost always means changing the plant mix to less lawn and more ground cover and shrubs but keeping trees for climate amelioration.

Water is one of our most valuable resources, and when it is in short supply, life becomes complicated and very expensive. As the human population increases simultaneously with global warming, many areas will suffer from acute water shortages.

In California in the late 1980s a water shortage occurred following several years of drought. It was estimated that landscaping used 30 to 50 percent of all residential water. To cope with the shortage, many municipal ordinances for water conservation were passed, and programs with monetary incentives were introduced. The city of Mesa offered a $231 rebate if 50 percent of the total landscaped area was covered with inorganic mulch such as decomposed granite. The North Marin Water District offered $50 for each 100 square feet of lawn replaced with drought-resistant plants.

Many areas of the Southwest, particularly desert areas, have had long-standing water problems. Creativity always follows need, and so xeriscaping was born. The term xeriscaping was invented in 1981 in Colorado. As water prices increased and more frequent shortages occurred nationwide, it became a new landscape style.

Essentially, it follows standard criteria for sound landscape design, except that it uses plants that have low water requirements and can stand the rigors of their local climate. It also takes into consideration such things as natural soil conditions, mulching, waste-water use, and more efficient irrigation.

Using plants that can tolerate the climate and microenvironment into which they are placed is just common sense. When the early settlers went across America in their covered wagons, however, they tried to bring with them the familiar landscape they had left behind.

The lush green trees and fields of the East were in their minds, and so they planted trees and lawns, much as the princess of ancient Babylonia who craved the green northern lands of her youth and so inspired the famed hanging gardens of Babylon. But in California and the American Southwest, as in the Mesopotamian desert of old, keeping things lush and green required constant irrigation.

As the population of the American Southwest kept increasing and as ground water was pumped at ever-increasing rates, it became clear that keeping these imported "artificial" landscapes was becoming more and more of a burden on the water resources of the region.

Xeriscaping in every part of the country aims to replace these eastern landscapes and their eastern plants with native ones that are more at home in the local climates. Replacing high-water-use plants with low-use ones adapted to their particular location can save 20 to 43 percent of water use. Furthermore, a landscape designed from scratch for low water use can cut water dependency by 50 to 60 percent. Part III has a list of drought-resistant plants, with their yearly rainfall requirements, that can be used for xeriscaping.

# WHICH PLANTS USE MORE WATER?

At the University of California, researchers found that lawns needed the most water to stay green and attractive, which explains why they are so successful in cool, rainy England. Trees, shrubs, and ground covers used much less water, although trees used more than shrubs and ground cover for the same area. The ratios were: grass, 8 units of water; trees, 5; shrubs and ground covers, 4.

In hot areas, however, trees use much of their water to contribute to cooling and ameliorating the climate through evapotranspiration from their leaves. Thus, the small amount of extra water they use is returned in human comfort and air-conditioning savings.

An interesting fact is that a multilayered canopy of trees over a shaded lawn actually conserves water. It seems that in the shade, the water requirements of a lawn are reduced by 95 percent over its needs in full sun.

# USING DROUGHT-TOLERANT PLANTS

Xeriscaping merely codified and gave a name to a practice that good landscape design has always used. In all landscape design, the choice of plant material should always be scientific. Among the first considerations must be to match the annual rainfall of any area with the water requirements of the plants to be used; otherwise, irrigation must be supplied. It is just common sense.

Unfortunately, many developers, in their quest for exotic appeal, have planted things that need to be coddled and fussed over, at great cost. At one of the fancy hotels in the arid part of California, the geraniums alone cost $40,000 a year. All the plants have to be constantly irrigated and fed with soluble fertilizer to make them green and flowering. The gardens are a veritable wonderland, a make-believe place somewhere between a perennial border of an English garden and an Arab harem garden. Disneyland is the same fantasy land with its constant irrigation, fertilizing, and oft-changing floral displays. Xeriscaping is a response to this type of resource-wasteful excess.

California has done the most research in the area of low-water-use plants, not in small part because of the need to irrigate most of its gardens and farms. Water ownership has been a political problem since the lands were first settled by Europeans. The state also has the most complex and varied natural ecosystems of almost any state in the union. California has seventeen separate climate zones, each with different temperatures, humidity, and rainfall. They are all influenced by the prevailing winds from the Pacific, which do different things as they hit the various mountain ranges on their passage eastward. This complexity makes optimizing plant choice for efficient water use a daunting task.

California Polytechnic University, working with the Water Resources Board of Orange County, prepared a list of all the plants growing in Orange County, then looked up the annual rainfall in their native habitat. The aim was to find which could survive with less irrigation. It is interesting how many varied plants are growing there.

For example, Japanese viburnum comes from an area where the rainfall is 82 inches per year. Podocarpus gets 124 inches of rain in its native Japanese habitat. A different variety of podocarpus is a graceful forest tree that grows happily in the mist-laden rain forest on the slopes of Mt. Kenya. The annual rainfall for deodar cedar is only about 10 inches in its native India, where the fragrant wood is used for incense. Yet all these varied trees have been planted in Orange County, California, despite their different water needs. It is obvious there is much room for improving the use of water by more thoughtful choices of plant material. (See Plant List #18B, Annual Rainfall of Plants in their Native Habitats.)

## Lowering Water Consumption

Desert cities in the Southwest have made enormous strides in their efforts to reduce water consumption in their landscapes. As Tucson's population and farming grew, water was pumped from the underground aquifer at a rate that threatened the future of the whole system. To conserve water, the city replanted its heavily irrigated grass-and-palm-tree highway dividers with cactus, wild grasses, and native trees. Instead of looking like Florida, the highways in Arizona now look like part of the surrounding desert.

Santa Fe, New Mexico, has planted native desert species extensively, making this beautiful city seem like a gentle continuation of the surrounding natural desert. The whole effect of well-done xeriscaping can be quite beautiful and aesthetically satisfying. (See Plant List 18A, Drought-Resistant Plants for Dry Desert Areas and Xeriscaping, in part III.)

The use of native species is now quite in vogue everywhere. It is another part of the environmental sensitivity that is becoming our cultural continuum. The use of native plants is nowhere more sensible than in low-water-use landscapes. Many of the wild plants and flowers are quite beautiful in their own way, although perhaps not so showy as horticultural varieties developed for their large blossoms. Yet the effect with native plants can be very romantic, not in the style of an English Victorian garden, but more like our western open spaces, rustic and unmanicured.

Desert-style landscapes are encouraged by the trend makers, especially since many movie and TV personalities have homes in states that still have wide-open natural vistas, states such as Montana and New Mexico. Homeowners are encouraged, by government agencies, through education, and by the more compelling reason of raising water prices, to adopt the principles of xeriscaping as part of conservation in general.

Areas other than the desert or water-poor states benefit from xeriscaping, too. Water is expensive everywhere, particularly in urban or heavily populated places. Metropolitan areas such as New York have problems delivering enough clean water. In the Hudson River Valley, the same water is used, cleaned, and recycled many times as it passes from community to community until it reaches the ocean.

In areas where water is scarce and expensive, xeriscaping makes sense despite adequate rainfall. On Long Island, New York, the underground water aquifer is rapidly being depleted. In a demonstration xeriscape garden there, some of the plants being tested are artemesia, broom, potentilla, juniper, Russian sage, sedums, hypericum, daisies, and coreopsis, as well as ornamental grasses. Although rainfall is adequate on Long Island and ocean mists humidify the air, there is still a need to conserve water by growing plants that don't require supplemental irrigation.

Even areas such as the mid-Atlantic states, which have generous rainfall, can benefit from using drought-tolerant plants for those times when rainfall is below average.

# HOW TO BEGIN XERISCAPING AT YOUR SITE

Saving water can begin at home. The basic principle is to reduce the total square-foot area of high-water-use plants and increase the area of plants that require less or no supplemental watering. Start by analyzing the square footage of various kinds of plants—lawn, shrubs, ground covers, wild area, trees. As you plan, don't forget the need for saving energy by using the criteria in the first part of this book.

Proceed by looking around at areas where there is no irrigation to see what plants are growing well. Make a list of those that appeal to you. When re-designing, plan for a sequence of bloom so that there are interesting flowers, shapes, greenery, or natural forms at all seasons. Rocks, dried wood, mulches, statues, and furniture all can be elements in a garden, not just the plants. Choose the plants carefully for low water requirements, and think of their architectural shapes as well as their brief flowering periods. You should like them. There is no reason to live with cactus if you hate it!

Finally, analyze how much of your current plant material can be exchanged for lower-water-use plants. Start with the lawn. Can some of the lawn be taken for ground cover and shrubs, or ground cover and trees? You may want to keep some lawn for aesthetics or to use, but do you need all of it? Can you let it go brown during the dry season? (If so, be sure it is mowed short and is not a fire hazard.)

After determining how much labor-intensive, thirsty lawn you really need and want, consider what to do with the water-guzzling varieties of shrubs and trees. A thoughtful analysis will probably show that many of the existing plants will survive well with minimal or no supplemental water. Carefully planned landscapes need supplemental watering only during times of severe drought.

Finally, look at the borders of the property. Identify which of the screen or shade trees require a lot of water. Should you begin to replace them with drought-tolerant species? As the new small plants grow larger, the old ones may be left to decline. It can take a while to accomplish the changeover to low-water-use plantings, often a period of years.

Most people who like to garden are usually not content with only drought-resistant plants. They need flowers and fruits and their old favorites. Consider transplanting your favorite high-water-use trees, shrubs, and flowers to one area where they can be given extra water, instead of having them mixed in with the other more drought-resistant ones. If you can direct the roof runoff water into this special bed, it will maximize the use of your available rainfall and lower the need for supplemental water. (See Figure 27.)

Xeriscaping does not mean that water cannot be used ever. It aims to lower the total water use. Some parts of the garden will use a fair amount of water, while others will be low- or medium-use areas.

## *Conserving Water*

To conserve water, consider using "gray water" drained from your dishwasher or washing machine for irrigation instead of sending it down the sewer. Of course, use roof water from gutters and downspouts, which can be directed into irrigation systems or rain barrels. If water restrictions become severe, a big pan in the kitchen sink will catch any water used, which can then be emptied on a favorite plant bed if it's not too far from the kitchen door.

Another water-saving technique is to put flowers in large pots or planters, rather than in the ground. It takes less water to keep a planter wet than an equal volume of soil in the ground. Peat moss or the synthetic water-grabbing polymers can be used to help the planting mix absorb and hold more water. Then they release it slowly to the plant roots. The more water that's absorbed, the less often the planters have to be watered. Some flowers survive on less water than others, and eventually one gets to know which they are.

"Pillow Planting" is another useful technique. Place a small plastic bag of loose moist peat moss (not a compressed bale) on its side in a planter or big flowerpot. The plastic bag the peat comes in is the easiest to use. Punch some holes in the bottom of the bag, slash Xs in the top of the bag, and saturate the peat moss with water. Into each X hole, place the root ball of a plant. Each planting pillow can have many plants tucked into it.

Because the peat moss absorbs so much water, it doesn't dry out as fast as the plant root ball would in its own pot or in the ground. But peat moss has no nutrients, so regular fertilizer is necessary to keep the plants growing well, as in hydroponics. Liquid fertilizer is easiest and most reliable, and a 20–20–20 formulation gives the most flowers. Organic fertilizer is more environmentally correct, but it has to be applied carefully. If too concentrated in the small planting hole, it can be too strong for the roots.

An economic analysis of the cost savings realized from xeriscaping was done for a house with irrigation in Atlanta, Georgia, an area with good annual rainfall. The existing landscape was renovated to conserve water use. New plants would cost $1,245. During the first year, however, the renovation would save $112 on water and sewer costs, $237 on maintenance expense, and would use 27,000 fewer gallons of water. As the new plantings matured, yearly savings would increase. It was estimated the total outlay of $1,245 would be recouped in three years as a result of these savings.

# IRRIGATION SYSTEMS

Until genetic engineering makes this a brave new world, water is the most limiting factor in plant growth. It is not by accident that the largest production of biomass is in the rain forests. Humid atmospheres such as the Amazon basin, the Pacific Northwest, and certain temperate forests encourage fast, lush growth of plants and giant trees. Desert conditions produce slow, sparse growth.

To increase growth and lessen dependence on unpredictable rainfall, irrigation was invented. In biblical times and in prehistoric America, early irrigation projects were primarily man-made catch basins to contain the rain. Food plants and trees were then grown in the basins. Later water was carried from rivers to the fields, as from the Nile in ancient Egypt.

Today we have efficient irrigation systems of great sophistication. Although developed for farming, the improvements can be used by everyone. When irrigation is used in agriculture, crop needs are first calculated. Then a system is laid out that delivers the exact right amount of water at the right time, all controlled by computer. A soil meter tests soil-water availability and indicates when the plants are dry. A rain gauge, which automatically overrides the irrigation computer when it rains a lot, saves water.

All irrigation systems need maintenance. The pipes have to be cleaned of dirt, debris, and sometimes gelatinous fungus that clog the holes. Tears and ruptures have to be plugged or repaired. Emitters, that spray or drip the water, are fragile, and often need to be adjusted or replaced. In cold climates, the pipes have to be blown free of water in the fall, for freezing would rupture the pipes.

In communities where the sewer rate is tied to the rate of water usage, it is important to have a separate water meter for any irrigation system, or else one is charged for sewer usage even though the water goes into the ground. Without a separate meter, money is wasted.

## Types of Irrigation Systems

*Leaky hose* is the simplest kind. It has many names, but all are based on the same principle. Old rubber is recycled into a permeable hose. Water leaks out all along the length. It is excellent for vegetables and flower gardens. The hose can be laid on the surface, covered with mulch, or buried. It does not suffer much from freezing because it already has holes in it, and most of the water self-drains. It can be used with a simple computer-timer attached to the hose. A filter helps if the water supply is not perfect. The main problems are that the amount of water cannot be controlled easily, and sometimes dirt or fungus plugs the line.

*Spray sprinklers* are the conventional system commonly used. Pipe is laid underground, with emitters that pop up when water is required. They spray the water into the air, where much of it evaporates, which is very wasteful in most places. The exception is in very hot-arid climates, where the evaporation cools the air and humidifies it. These conventional sprinklers are always controlled by a complex computer, which is usually set incorrectly.

These systems are difficult to install and are best done by a professional irrigation company. They almost always need servicing each spring to keep the pipes clean, repair holes, level any part that gets out of line, and fix sprinkler heads. In cold climates, these have to be drained and all the water blown out with compressed air in fall to prevent freezing.

*Drip systems,* or trickle irrigation, are the most sophisticated, efficient, and cost-effective. Professional companies don't like to lay them because they don't make the same profit as with conventional sprinkler systems. Drip systems supply water slowly and directly to the roots through plastic tubing with small holes (emitters) near each plant. They can be buried or laid on top of the soil and may be covered with mulch. Developed in the Israeli desert, they have been used for years in our western desert, California, and Florida. No water is sprayed into the air. Nothing evaporates. Nothing is wasted.

In the old variety holes are punched in thin plastic tubing where water is needed. An emitter, which delivers a calibrated amount of water, is put into the hole. Some emitters deliver one gallon an hour; others, different amounts. Angle brackets make it possible to go around corners. An in-line filter and a pressure regulator are also needed. A computer-timer may be attached.

The problem with drip systems is that they are difficult to calibrate as to how much water should be given to each plant, and punching each hole is time consuming.

A new Israeli tubing called Netafim has been developed, which takes out all the guesswork. It has pre-punched holes, 18 inches apart, each with a pressure-regulated emitter already installed that delivers exactly ½ gallon of water per hour. It is very easy to lay. The only tool needed is a pair of garden shears or a knife to cut the tube where corner angles or T-angles need to be put in. It can be flushed by opening the ends, and because each hole is individually pressure regulated, it can be laid uphill. It is easily repaired by cutting out any tear and putting in a new section of tubing. To date, this is the most cost-effective way to get irrigation. Installation doesn't take too long; it just requires a little forethought.

## Using a Sprinkler Wisely

When one tires of forever dragging heavy hoses through mud and fragile flower beds, thoughts naturally turn to the joys of a sprinkler system. It sounds easy; just set a computer in the basement, and science will take care of the plants.

A sprinkler is certainly a joy, but it's not that simple. An incorrectly set sprinkler is a silent killer. Much damage is done by wrong settings on the timers, which are usually set by the irrigation companies themselves.

Yet sprinklers are a real benefit. When properly set, everything grows better and bigger and with much, much less work. Most sprinkler companies try very hard to do the best for their clients. They are just trained with the wrong information about how plants grow.

Understanding why this happens helps avoid the problem. Sprinker systems were developed for hot, dry climates such as southern California and Israel, which have sandy soil and no frost. The main markets were agriculture and golf courses, which require frequent sprinklings for optimal growth. Their schedules have become the standard for all systems everywhere.

Consider golf course grass. It is heavily fertilized, grown on sand, and treated with fungicides. The grass that develops is shallow rooted and chemical dependent. So more shallow watering is needed, and more fertilizer is added. It becomes a Catch-22; if either is stopped, the grass is not tough enough to survive.

Irrigation suppliers have sent this watering schedule to northern homes where it makes no sense. For example, in New England it rains a lot. The main dry months are July and August, with occasional hot spells in June and September. Except for new grasss seed, sprinklers should be turned off in September or plants won't harden off for the winter.

For New England, the proper watering schedule is to deliver a deep watering once a week from mid-June to early September. It should be 1 inch of water per week. In case of severe drought, a manual override might deliver extra water in July or August.

*How does one calibrate a sprinkler system to know when it has delivered 1 inch of water?* Set out several glasses or cans at various places under the sprinkler area. Mark them in inches with magic marker. Then turn the water on for half an hour. Measure how much water is in each glass or can and average them. That tells how many inches of water the system delivers in a half hour. Some old systems will flood if 1 inch of water is given at once. Such systems have to be set for $1/2$ inch of water twice a week. Systems used in Florida, California, and the southwest also need to be set to compensate for their hot climates.

## TO USE WATER MORE EFFICIENTLY

1. Use trickle or drip irrigation. Overhead sprinklers lose water to evaporation and put water on areas where there are no roots. Drip irrigation uses half as much water as sprinklers.

2. Irrigate in the early morning, when it is cool. There is less evaporation loss. Also fungus is less likely since the plants can dry off during the day.

3. Water infrequently, but deeply. Deep watering allows the roots to go deeper, where they are less susceptible to drought and heat stress.

4. Water slowly. Watering too fast causes wasteful runoff. Also dry ground will not absorb water until the surface is moist.

5. Use a mulch to keep the soil cool and conserve the moisture in the root area.

6. Make sure the water penetrates to the root area, especially if there is a mulch. It must go through and beneath the mulch.

7. Irrigate during a mist or light rain. Less water will be lost to evaporation.

8. Avoid excess nitrogen, which promotes soft growth and increases the need for water.

# HEALTH HAZARDS

Don't forget about personal safety while you concentrate on saving energy, time, and money. Ignoring your health is a false saving, indeed.

Be aware of the health hazards in the landscape. Hazards exist when using machinery, using tools, and using pesticides.

# PESTICIDES

Fertilizer and lime are safe, but the pesticides that control insects, plant diseases, and plant growth should be suspect until proven otherwise. They are very useful in the garden, but as with chemotherapy, they have side effects.

All pesticides must be used correctly and safely. And they should never be used without compelling reason. Having a perfect lawn is not a compelling reason.

Pesticides are absorbed through the skin, particularly when a person is perspiring. They can also be absorbed by eating contaminated food, from unwashed hands, and from the fur of cats and dogs. The largest amounts, however, are absorbed through the lungs from breathing spray or dust.

Acute exposures can cause skin rashes, itching, eye irritation, coughing, stuffed nose, headache, possible pregnancy problems, and irritability. Larger doses can produce sperm reduction, insomnia, neurological symptoms such as tremors, numbness, dizziness, paralysis, and difficulty breathing. One may feel "hyped up" as the body tries to rid itself of the poison by speeding up metabolism and adrenalin.

People who have repeated, small exposures may become sensitized. For instance, while nothing outward happens the first nine times, antibodies will be formed inside the body. With the tenth exposure, one gets sick with symptoms. After that, the smallest dose will trigger the allergic reaction.

When using pesticides, respect them. To use them safely:

- Read the small print on the label. You may need a magnifying glass, but do read what it is and how to use it. Make a card of the dilution rate with a waterproof magic marker, and attach the card to the bottle with elastic. When microscopic instructions get wet, they become illegible.

- Measure accurately. More is not better.

- Dress protectively. Wear disposable gloves, long pants, and long sleeves.

- Use a proper respirator with a disposable or gauze filter when spraying. A cardboard surgeon's mask won't do.

- Always stand downwind. Don't breathe the mist. More is absorbed through the lungs than by any other exposure.

- Shower with warm (not hot) water and use lots of soap. No bath. Hot water might feel good, but it volatizes the chemicals so they can be breathed in more, and as the pores open, the pesticides can go into them, instead of washing off.

- Wash clothes separately, not in the family laundry. Most pesticides are not very water soluble but float in an oily film.

- Storage should always be in the original container. Never mix them in a container that someone might drink, especially children. No soda bottles, please.

---

## IN CASE OF PESTICIDE INGESTION

*In case of overdose* call a hospital poison center immediately. Also always keep the package, so you can read the contents over the phone. Most hospitals have a poison index with antidotes. Each pesticide has a different antidote. Call immediately for advice; then go to the hospital emergency room and take the package. If you can't reach the hospital poison control center, call the fire chief, police chief, or a telephone operator.

---

# THE SAFER INSECTICIDES

Always start with the safer pesticides, which are less toxic to humans. The safest ones are usually biological substances; the more toxic are usually chemical. (See Insects and IPM, chapter 12.) But be respectful of all of them. The following list contains some of the useful safer ones.

*BT,* or *Bacillus thuringiensis,* is an organism that produces a toxic stomach poison in butterfly and moth larvae after consumption. It is safe for humans and beneficial insects. It is the most useful safe pesticide at the moment, because it is so host-specific. Widespread use, however, is causing some insects to become resistant.

*Rotenone*, a tropical root extract, is widely used and is effective against many insects. Humans are rarely poisoned, but it may cause skin and eye irritation. It is very toxic to fish.

*Ryania* comes from roots and stems of a Trinidad plant. It is more persistent than either rotenone or pyrethrum.

*Pyrethrum* is an old Persian remedy for sucking insects. Made from a daisy, it spread worldwide around 1800. It is nontoxic to humans but occasionally causes skin and nasal allergies. Pyrethrum works better at lower temperatures and breaks down rapidly from lime or soap. Synthetic pyrethroids are longer lasting.

*Insecticidal soap sprays* also kill most sucking insects. They do, however, have to hit the crit-ter, and they have no residual action. Inexpensive but equally effective soap sprays can be made of Ivory dishwashing liquid (1 tablespoon per gallon of water).

*Neem* extract from the Indian lilac tree (*Azadirachta idicia*) is sold under many trade names. One is called BioNEEM, another Margosan-O. They work by preventing immature insects from molting and as a repellent. About 170 kinds of insects are affected by various chemicals refined from the extract. They have a short residual and have to be reapplied every ten days or so. Hon-eybees and beneficial adult insects are not harmed.Would-be fathers should stay away from them, because in India they are used as a male spermicidal contraceptive.

*Sabadilla dust,* from the seeds of a lily, is an effective instant insecticide. Although nontoxic to mammals, it may cause violent sneezing. Honeybees are very sensitive to it, so it should be used at night, when the bees are in their hives.

*Predatory insects* such as ladybugs, nonstinging wasps, praying mantis, spiders, dragonflies, and nematodes appear to hold great promise as better techniques for applying them are defined.

*Horticultural oils* are used for sucking insects. Most are used when plants are dormant, for they are often phytotoxic to the leaves, especially young ones. Some of the newer, lighter ones can be safely used on certain plants when in leaf, however. The oils are not toxic as long as they are not breathed in.

# THE LEAST DANGEROUS CHEMICAL INSECTICIDES
## (SOMETIMES NECESSARY)

- *Carbaryl* (Sevin) is a chemical for chewing insects but is toxic to bees. It has a short residual and harms some plants, including ivy.

- *Diazinon* is also useful against many insects.

- *Malathion*, an old standby that kills on contact.

- *Nicotine sulfate* is an old botanical useful for sucking insects, particularly aphids, but is toxic to people.

These four have the shortest residuals and are the safest, but there are many, many other chemical insecticides as well. Sometimes they are necessary.

A concern with all pesticides, and especially these, is the cumulative effect of low expo-sures, especially on babies and children, so do not use these on homegrown fruits and vegetables fed to children. Also, large-scale spraying of trees or lawns or shrubs should be avoided where children live. Termite and ant control in the house is another source of exposure for children, as are pets and rugs treated for fleas.

# FUNGICIDES AND HERBICIDES

Fungicides are complex and very specific as to timing and host. Expert advice is needed to use them correctly; otherwise, they are a waste of money. Their main purpose is to prevent fungus damage. They do not cure the fungus. It is better to keep plants airy, open in areas, and to water only in the morning, so the plants can dry out at night. Some plants, such as roses, do need them, however, no matter how careful the care and sanitation.

Herbicides are for weed control and are primarily growth regulators. They should not be used by homeowners except for very troublesome problems such as poison ivy or other invasive species. They should not be used routinely for crabgrass and dandelions on the lawn, as is the current practice. Who ever said every lawn has to be a weed-free carpet? Herbicides affect children, cause diseases, and there have been serious questions about their connection to cancer. One herbicide has been linked to a particular cancer, and others are known to affect sperm production. While herbicides are very useful, they should not be used without good reason and never where children play or pregnant women will be exposed; not, at least, until much more is known about their effect on human growth.

Chemicals are being regulated more and more. The uses and restrictions change every year. New ones are approved, and old ones are outlawed. Man-made chemicals are much more effective, more useful, and have a longer protective umbrella than botanicals; however, they are also more poisonous. Landscape professionals keep abreast of the changes and can be used as consultants for problems. Also state agricultural and extension services can be relied upon for current advice.

# MACHINERY AND ACCIDENTS

Power saws cause the highest percentage of serious injuries of any equipment. They are not toys. It's important to take an instructional course before using one. Be very careful of kickbacks, which comes from using the tip of the blade to cut and can be fatal. New saws are sold with kickback safety chains and bars. Have old saws upgraded with safety chains or replace the saw. Goggles should always be used. Also wear hard-toed shoes—never use a power saw while wearing sneakers or with bare legs. Ear plugs, leg chaps, hard hats, and other safety devices are used by professionals. Don't take a power saw up a ladder, or saw above your head. Most old loggers have a few fingers missing. . . . You don't want to join them.

Lawnmowers are another source of serious injuries. Newer ones have safety shutoffs. Be careful of slippery wet grass that causes one to lose footing and fall underneath. Safety goggles should always be worn. Many serious eye injuries have resulted from flying debris or bits of stone. Naturally, never leave children near running mowers of any kind, and don't take them on tractor mowers no matter how exciting it may be for them.

# LEAD IN THE SOIL

Lead in the soil is a concern where vegetables grow, where pregnant women live, and where children play. Lead causes mental retardation, especially to fetuses and children. It is most common in urban yards and around older houses. How did it get there? First from paint. Before 1960, all paint contained lead. On the outside of buildings, it peeled, was scraped off, and fell to the ground. It is still there. Lead does not leach away in water as does salt and fertilizer. It just sits there and piles up.

Lead in the soil also comes from automobile exhaust from leaded gasoline. Unleaded gasoline auto fumes can still contaminate soil up to 50 feet from the road. Compost from street leaves may contain lead. Also, where old apple and fruit trees once grew, there usually is lead. The trees may be long gone, but the pesticide used on them, arsenate of lead, is still there. A new source of lead is dust from de-leading old houses and bridges. It seems you just can't win with pollution.

The lead level in your soil can be tested by sending it to the state soil laboratory that handles soil testing. To protect yourself and your family from lead in the soil:

- Don't grow vegetables in contaminated soil. Leaf vegetables absorb the most lead; root vegetables absorb some; and fruits, such as tomatoes, absorb the least. If you have no small children and are not pregnant, growing tomatoes might be all right, but you may want to buy lettuce.

- Children and pregnant women should be regularly tested at the doctor's office for lead in the blood and take corrective medication if the level is high.

- Don't let small children play on bare soil. Hand-to-mouth contamination comes from sucking their fingers or toys. The dust can be inhaled, also. Fence off areas for play that are covered with thick grass. Or cover all exposed soil with some topsoil and grass sod (not seed), plastic sheeting, blacktop, or something that keeps down all the dust.

Current federal guidelines advocate removing the top 6 inches of contaminated soil and replacing it with clean soil. Federal guidelines, however, change frequently. There is a lead poison center in most large cities or hospitals that can give you the most current thinking.

Replacing the soil, or covering it with several inches of new loam is quite expensive. A medical study showed that removing the soil and replacing it with fresh soil did not significantly change the lead levels in the children who lived in old houses. It seems that dust from opening and closing the windows was much more contaminating.

## CHAPTER 14

# Buying New Plants
# and Trees

Practically every homeowner, whether he or she enjoys the outdoors or hates it, eventually ends up buying plants. No matter how callous, how thrifty, or how resourceful one is, the call of the nursery is like the call of the wild. Improving a building's energy-saving potential invariably leads there. Anyone who remodels or builds is also unwittingly ensnared.

## WHAT TO LOOK FOR
## WHEN BUYING PLANTS

The first sight of a nursery can be overwhelming. Rows and rows of plants in all sizes and shapes assault the eye. It's not easy to tell whether the plants are what you really need and want, or even whether they're healthy. Will each grow to the desired size and height, in its own given spot in your backyard? It makes no sense to plan carefully for energy savings and then have the plants fail you.

There are three main reasons for failure: (1) the plant is not in good condition; (2) it is a variety that's not genetically programmed to grow to the necessary size and shape; or (3) it is not cared for adequately, at planting time or after.

# HOW TO DETERMINE IF A PLANT IS IN GOOD CONDITION

Healthy plants have good firm tissues, stiff branches, and a covering of smooth bark with no bruises, cankers, or fungus discolorations.

There should be no signs of drought or water stress, which shows as soft empty buds, wrinkled bark, split wood, and especially wilted, brown leaves. If a plant has suffered a period of serious drought stress, the lower leaves often turn brown. Well-watered plants have plump buds, wood with good turgor (or crispness), and firm leaves without brown edges or tips. Plants may lose moisture from exposure to wind or sun, even if watered, while in the nursery or in transition.

Check the roots for insects as well as diseases. Are things jumping or crawling on the soil. Are there holes or webs on the leaves? Are they distorted? Are portions of the stem or branches wilted or black? Many a pest is imported home from the nursery.

At commercial nurseries, most plants are dug in spring or late fall; buying at those seasons is more likely to provide fresh material. At the end of summer, or at winter's beginning, outdoor plants are sold at bargain prices to move the inventory. These are good times to try to pick up genetically desirable stock for a bargain price. They may be a little shopworn. Such plants will need loving care, but most of them will come back and thrive after an initial slow recovery and adjustment.

At local nurseries, sometimes one can choose plants still growing in the field and then have them dug. This is a real luxury and one to be cherished. Old-time nurseries grow many of their plants and take better care of them. Unfortunately, such places are becoming rare. It is good to patronize local nurseries, rather than malls and cut-rate price outlets. Plants grown on large commercial tree farms and nurseries are production-line items. They are shipped for sale, often long distances, in trucks that may or may not be temperature and humidity controlled.

When choosing plants, look for a pleasing shape with strong stems from the base. A tree or shrub should be "thrifty," which means it should look strong with good, sturdy branches, not tall, weak, and spindly ones. The lower branches should have a good cover of leaves. Evergreen shrubs, particularly rhododendron and mountain laurel, tend to get "leggy" and too tall. They take time to fill out well, especially on the bottom. Some never do.

With trees, the shape of the young tree determines its mature shape. As grows the whip, so grows the tree. Starting with a good scaffold helps. When buying shade trees, look for a single trunk and well-balanced, evenly shaped branches. A double central leader or a V-shaped trunk is weak and likely to split in half eventually. If you must cut off too many of the branches, you'll delay the tree's growth spurt, so it is better to try to find a good one if you can. The bare trunk should be about the height you want the canopy to be.

When you want a high, leafy canopy, there's no use buying a tree with branches down to the ground. If you must remove lower branches, take no more than two each year, or the tree's growth rate will be compromised. Sometimes, these lower branches can be "subordinated" (just cut back by half). Some of the leaves are left to make food for the first year, and then the branches are removed completely after another year or two.

Similarly, if a privacy screen is wanted, a 6-foot trunk will be too bare. It is always wise to choose each plant yourself, if you can, and attach a sold tag with your name on it so the nursery will hold that plant for you.

Check the root ball. It should be firm and well tied or in a pot. If it's soft and broken, avoid it. Don't be afraid to ask when the material was dug, where it was grown, and whether the nursery will guarantee it in any way. (Most won't unless they planted it themselves.)

You'll find differences in prices. Some nurseries may occasionally try to unload over-stocked items (often a good buy), but beware of unexplained bargains, especially at places that don't regularly carry plants. In general, you get what you pay for. Shopping around is sensible, so check prices and health of plants.

Most plants are propagated in containers in a growing mix (not garden loam) and pushed with frequent, large doses of fertilizer to bring them up to selling size. They are clipped to make them bushier, and multiple blossoms are forced with special fertilizers. If a plant has very big, new bright green leaves and huge buds, especially in fall, it has probably been forced. These look very good in the nursery, but they have been pushed too much and have too much soft tissue, which easily winterkills or suffers from drought. Also, such plants have to be gradually weaned from the high-fertilizer diet.

After planting, attention to adequate watering is essential. Winter protection may also be needed. When plants exhibit signs of fertilizer starvation, a weak solution of liquid fertilizer or root-promoting hormones may be needed. (CAUTION: Do not, however, apply fertilizer in late summer or fall, when the plant should be hardening off for winter.) Plants make most of their new roots during the first eight weeks after being planted, so special attention then, especially to adequate watering, will help them get established.

# USING A LANDSCAPE GARDENER

Most landscape firms get shrubs at a significant discount. They sell them to you for the retail price, or what you would pay anyway at the nursery. It's hard to get a discount yourself. If you buy more than $1,000 worth be sure to ask, though, for a big discount. If you do get a discount, there will be no guarantee. Sometimes you can be sent inferior stock and not be able to return it. Be sure to tag all the plants, if you picked them yourself.

When a landscape company offers free designing services or other bonuses, they are usually counting on their profit from the markup on the shrubs. They make little profit on labor. The only caution in dealing with a firm that both designs and sells the plants is to make sure you are not getting more plants than you need, or unnecessarily large ones. Since the markup on plants is a straight percentage, usually between 25 and 30 percent, the more you buy, the more profit they make. Some unscrupulous companies suggest you buy more plants than you really need.

In general, most people in landscape are good, trying to make an honest living in a difficult business. If you work closely with them, it can be a happy relationship, and their expertise and experience can help you avoid many mistakes. After all, the only person who ever kissed Louis XIV of France, the imperious Sun King, was his gardener, LeNôtre.

A landscape designer or architect who doesn't actually contract out the work may be a good investment, too. You will get a totally impartial opinion, unrelated to the cost of the plants. Not only will it be impartial, but the bonus of truly good professional design can't be overrated. The difference between "mundane" and "distinctive" landscaping is in the design. Both cost the same to execute. You can usually get a simple plan for a fee of a few hundred dollars. Since landscaping is so very expensive, this professional advice can save money in the end. Make sure that you are not getting more plants than you need or unnecessarily large ones.

Landscaping *is* expensive! Around a substantial house, it will easily cost in the thousands, sometimes many thousands. A large tract may cost so much that the amount seems mind-boggling at first. There are, however, ways to save money. One is to be patient and go with Mother Nature's flow.

Small plants cost much less. Instant landscaping is expensive, but some people insist on it. Most landscape firms want their work to look good right away and want their customers to be pleased, so they sometimes plant large specimens too close together. As the plants grow, the place becomes overgrown too quickly. Annual pruning chores become a burden. Most customers do not realize that smaller ones may look a bit bare at first but will cost significantly less and will perform equally well in the long run. (See chapter 15 for what to buy first.)

# UNDERSTANDING PLANT VARIETIES

Better nurseries have plant material properly labeled with Latin names. On some popular varieties, the label might also have a picture and growing instructions. Most labels include size and price. Rarely do they tell where the plant was grown or how large it will be at maturity.

Often plants are labeled inadequately or not at all. Common names, which differ from region to region, tell nothing. Only the Latin name and "clone" (genetic strain) tell what a plant is and how it will grow. Latin names are not hard to understand. Often the names are descriptive, such as *japonica* (from Japan), *pseudoplatanus* (with a leaf like a plane tree), *pendula* (weeping), *fastigata* (upright), *horizontalis* (spreading). Each plant has its own particular growth size, shape, and needs. For example, here are a few of the many maples and how they differ one from the other. Only the Latin name differentiates them.

Before you buy, make sure you know exactly what variety a plant is. In addition to mature size, flower colors, when and how long they bloom, as well as fruit are genetically determined.

# WHAT'S IN A LATIN NAME?

| NAME | GENUS | VARIETY & CLONE | WHAT IT TELLS |
|---|---|---|---|
| *Latin Name*<br>Common Name | (*Acer*)<br>Maple | (*campestre*)<br>hedge maple | **Hardy in Zones 5–6**<br>25' max. height, from seed, can be sheared, makes a good screen, dense, dependable, no fall color |
| *Latin Name*<br>Common Name | (*Acer*)<br>Box elder | (*negundo variegatum*)<br>silver-leaf box elder | **Hardy to Zone 2**<br>60' max., only from cuttings to get silver leaf, not strong, breaks easily, drought-resistant, good for Plains States, grows anywhere |
| *Latin Name*<br>Common Name | (*Acer*)<br>Maple | (*saccharum*)<br>Sugar Maple | **Hardy to Zone 3**<br>75–120' max., from seed, majestic, beautiful fall color, makes maple syrup, salt and drought sensitive, sickly in cities |
| *Latin Name*<br><br>Common Name | (*Acer*)<br><br>Maple | (*palmatum atropurpureum*)<br>('Crimson Queen')<br><br>Red Threadleaf<br>Japanese Maple | **Hardy to Zone 6**<br>12' tall, dwarf, only from cuttings, feathery foliage that stays red all summer, specimen tree |

Performance is also determined by genes. If they are poor, no amount of care can make the plant a winner.

Many of the best, improved varieties are called "clones." They have to be propagated asexually to grow true to form. They are reproduced by rooted cuttings, cell culture, or grafting but never by seed. When they are reproduced by seed, they revert to earlier generations and undesirable traits.

This happened with the London plane tree (*Platanus acerifolia* 'Bloodgood'). The London plane is a cross between the Oriental plane tree and the American plane (also called buttonwood or sycamore). The clone Bloodgood's virtue is that it is resistant to the anthracnose. This fungus decimates the leaves of the buttonwood when spring is wet and cold and it happens two or three years out of every five. Although the affected trees don't die, and they do put out new leaves, it is unsightly; the fallen leaves make a mess. Since plane trees grow huge and live for many years, it is worth starting with the resistant Bloodgood clone and avoiding the problem.

Japanese red maples (*Acer palmatum atropurpureum*) are another tree for which the Latin name and clone are important. There are many varieties: some have red leaves all season, some turn green; some have orange fall coloring, while others have brilliant red; some are dwarfs, some grow to 25 feet. The dwarf ones tend to have shredded-looking leaves called threadleaf or dissectum. The larger, faster-growing ones have a five-pointed leaf. There is a variety called "Bloodgood" in this family, too, which indicates that the leaves stay red-maroon all summer and are brilliant scarlet in spring and fall. If its seeds are planted, however, the color of the resulting trees may be less intense, and they may turn muddy green in summer. It is more reliable to propagate these from cuttings, which are costly, but some nurseries grow them from seed for a better profit. When buying, it is worth knowing what you are paying for.

FIGURE 56: **CLONES OF HONEY LOCUST**

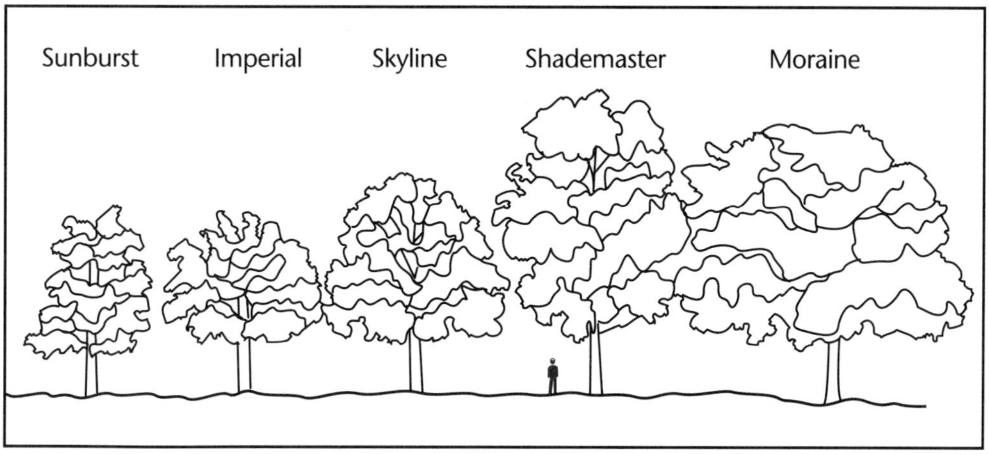

*Each clone has its own shape and growth rate. Sunburst has golden leaves.*

Genes are important, and reputable nurserymen know their stock. Improved varieties are more disease resistant, flower better, grow faster, or are adapted to certain conditions. Fruit trees, particularly, depend on genes for taste and appearance. It is disappointing to buy a particular plant, expect it to be like an arboretum specimen, and end up with an inferior one after years of care and nurturing.

Before you buy, check the plant lists in this book, your local library, and nursery catalogues, especially ones for your particular area.

Mature size is very important in terms of energy planning, maintenance, and beauty. A tree that should be 25 feet but grows to 50 feet can block a solar collector and may need constant pruning. Where a large tree for significant shade is needed, a slow-growing semi-dwarf will just never make it.

# WHAT SIZE TO BUY

Small plants and trees generally transplant better, recover from transplant shock sooner, and grow faster. But sometimes you can't wait, and you want to buy a larger plant for instant effect. The more time a plant has spent growing in the nursery, the more expensive it will be. The decision of what size to buy depends on how much patience you have, and how much money.

The old adage Put a $5 tree in a $10 hole, holds true. (Except that there are no more $5 trees.) Don't skimp on the size of the planting hole or on good loam. (See planting instructions in chapter 9.)

Where screening is wanted, it is wise to start with reasonable-sized plants. If a tall shade tree is needed, a 15-foot tree may be worth the money. It may cost a hundred dollars or more, and you may spend almost as much to have it planted.

Foundation plantings can cost a great deal if one wants instant effect. This is one area where savings are easy. A good thick ground cover, such as pachysandra, with smaller, less expensive rhododendrons, yews, azaleas, and hollies may be used for an effect equal to a plethora of larger expensive shrubs. Plantings of bulbs or flowers among the small bushes will create a distinctive, charming yard while you wait for the bushes to grow. Along the sides and back of the building, smaller shrubs can also be used where it is not so noticeable.

The judicious use of neat ground covers, edged beds of wood chips, borders of flowers, small statues, or interesting rocks can make an otherwise bare area look cared for and complete. Joining all the plantings in a single mulched bed, carefully edged, becomes a unifying factor for the small, widely separated bushes and shrubs. Just messy grass or bare dirt between them will emphasize an unfinished look.

# FOUNDATION PLANTING

Most people start with foundation planting and spend a lot of money. That dear little Colorado blue spruce will soon become a forest-size tree. Proper shrubs and trees that will stay in scale with the building grow slowly and mature gradually. They grow slowly in the nursery, too. Because they take longer to come to marketable size, they are more expensive than baby forest species. Some builders or unknowing gardeners use cheap bushes that will soon grow too tall. In the end, the proper plants are well worth their cost, because they perform well. The only way to save money is to buy them in smaller sizes.

One common mistake is to plant shrubs and trees too close to each other, not leaving enough room for them at mature size. Even a well-planned garden needs to be pruned some after ten years. But if too many plants are put in too close, pruning will become a constant chore much sooner.

It is not necessary to have foundation plantings at all. After all, the castles of Europe don't. Just ground cover is fine. Or stones. Perhaps with ferns or hosta or even daylilies growing through. There may be something special near the door, perhaps a statue. When using this sophisticated approach, however, it should be kept very neat. (See Figure 60 in chapter 15.)

In foundation planting beds, small, low-growing, flowering trees are often used near the door or at the corners. They might even be planted in front of windows to provide summer shade or screen out a bad view. Enough room, however, must be left for them to spread and grow to maturity. The branches may be only three sided (the fourth side against the building can be cut off), but they need room to spread out. Branches can be kep low, almost to the ground, or high with an understory of low-growing shrubs.

# BUYING FLOWERING TREES

Buying flowering trees can be tricky. Many are grown in southern nurseries, even though they are cold-hardy northern varieties. One of the problems is that, while the trees will grow in the North, their blossoms may be genetically sensitive to cold unless the original seed or root stock came from a northern area. This is especially true of dogwoods. Some, from southern stock, will have buds that regularly winterkill, while the exact same variety taken from originally northern seed stock will survive fine. If your dogwood regularly has only two petals instead of four, this may be the problem.

If you are buying flowering trees, try to get them from a local nursery where they have bloomed in your area for at least one winter. In the South, make sure they have survived one summer. Red maple (*acer rubrum*) grows from Florida through Canada; the Canadian trees, however, won't do well in Florida and vice versa. Individual trees, of exactly the same species, will differ in cold and heat tolerance, pollution resistance, and ability to withstand wounding.

Another problem is that young trees often will not bloom until they feel old enough—a relative term. When they break, juvenile growth depends on how each tree reads its microenvironment. High-nitrogen fertilizers, too little light, too much water, or hard shoot-pruning can delay flowering. On the other hand, a side dressing of superphosphate fertilizer, minor root pruning, and a little (but not too much) drought stress can often stimulate flower-bud set. Sometimes one feeding with 20–20–20 fertilizer can start things going.

There are arboriculture tricks that can help. They depend on a plant's response to a high carbohydrate-sugar level in the branches, which encourages flower buds as opposed to leaf buds. The first trick is to tie down the branches, so that the ends are low, below the main part of the branch. A string with a rock on the end works well. This is done just after the normal flowering season, and is left for about six weeks. The sugar manufactured by the leaves stays longer in the branches this way, instead of being stored in the roots.

Another trick to encourage sugar to remain for flower bud formation is to make two or three small, shallow, parallel slashes sideways across the underside of a few branches with a sharp, very clean knife. This will restrict the flow of sap downward until the cuts close. Or tie a string tightly around the branch for a few weeks. *Don't forget to take it off,* or the branch will strangle and die.

Dogwoods, magnolias, and franklinia are particularly difficult to get blooming. Once they start, however, there is no more trouble. When you are buying flowering trees, it's worth getting ones that have already set some flower buds in the nursery.

Unfortunately, some of the most beautiful flowering trees and shrubs are too fragile to be used for windbreaks, except when protected behind tough evergreens or other shelter plants. Fall color and fruit, however, are equally distributed among hardy and delicate varieties. When planning for energy saving, beauty is still one of the requirements and should be a consideration when choosing trees and shrubs for their more utilitarian function.

# BUYING GROUND COVER

Ground cover plants are more expensive to buy than grass, but over time they become cost effective. The long-term maintenance savings are well worth the extra initial expense. When buying ground cover plants, several sizes and prices are available.

The cheapest are rooted cuttings, generally sold in large flat boxes of one hundred plants. If planted in good soil and watered, they will grow fast, particularly in spring when the rooting

FIGURE 57: **HOW TO ROOT GROUND COVERS FROM EXISTING PLANTS**

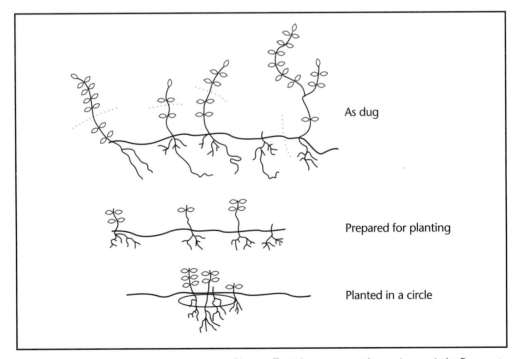

As dug

Prepared for planting

Planted in a circle

*Nip off growing tips back to one or two pairs of leaves. Twist long stems and roots into a circle. Bury roots, but keep some green leaves above ground. Keep moist until plants begin to grow and put out new leaves.*

hormones are highest. When these stringy plants are put in they look very bare, but they fill in within a year or two.

The next larger size are individual plants in small pots, which cost a fair amount. They have larger heads and stronger root systems. They make a better show and grow faster.

It is not always necessary to buy ground covers because they are easy to dig up and move. These transplants take hold faster than the rooted cuttings and eventually look the same. The least expensive plants are free ones given by a friend. Usually they are from good, sturdy stock, or your friend wouldn't have extra. Ultra-fastidious gardeners may want to wash them with water, to try to avoid bringing in insects or disease.

If you have to pay someone to dig them, however, it is more economical to buy flats of plants. Making cuttings from existing plants is too time consuming.

All ground covers need a well-prepared bed. The evergreen ones (ivy, pachysandra, myrtle) appreciate some organic material such as compost worked into the soil. It doesn't have to be dug in deeply, only into the top few inches. Ivy, myrtle, and pachysandra prefer some shade, but pachysandra will stand more sun than the others. In full sun use creeping euonymus, sedum or thyme, creeping fig in southern areas. Do not plant ivy near new concrete, for the ground is too alkaline from the lime or calcium used in cement.

All ground cover plants must be kept moist and faithfully sprinkled until the roots become established. You can tell when this happens because the new growth appears at the top. After that it will take another six months of careful watering. A mulch helps keep the roots cool and moist, and bark mulch is an excellent choice. By the time the bark mulch has decayed, the ground cover will be well established. Don't use grass clippings as a mulch, or anything that will introduce weed seeds. The more closely the plants are spaced, the sooner they will give the desired effect. Six inches apart is the commercial standard.

# CHOOSING PLANTS FOR CLIMATE CONTROL

The trees and shrubs used for climate control should be tough, non-fussy, and long lived. Evergreens, which are so important in the winter landscape, are mostly tough and reliable, so they function well as windbreaks. The best of the shade trees (maple, oak, locust, gum, ash, tulip, beech, lane, and linden) are quite tough and hardy. They leaf out and peak at different times with various colors for the fall foliage parade, and finally lose their leaves each winter.

Many shrubs are also tough. Some even have attractive flowers: lilac, forsythia, spirea in the North and natal plum, hibiscus, and oleander in the South. These, however, grow too big to be used for foundation plants. Vines are very useful for summer shade and cooling, and they're both vigorous and floriferous. Consider the blanket of bloom provided by star jasmine, wisteria, bougainvillea, and trumpet vine.

# SEQUENCE OF BLOOM— CHOOSING FOR DIFFERENT SEASONS OF BLOOM AND COLOR

Beautiful landscapes have plants of interest at all seasons in a continuous changing panorama. We tend to think mostly of spring-blooming flowers, but in fact many trees and shrubs provide color, flowers, berries, or foliage interest all year. Genes, not seasons, determine flower color, when and how long they bloom, fruit, fall color as well as size.

There is a magical day in spring, usually, April or May, when gardens explode with flowering trees and shrubs, but that should be just the zenith of a long succession of blooms that come tumbling, one after another, from very early spring through late fall. First the shy bulbs peek out from melting snow. Then the welcome flowers that bloom in the early spring. And finally that glorious day in May when the whole world seems to be one large bouquet.

Summer has many kinds of flowers, as well as plants of horticultural interest. In fall, flowers such as chrysanthemums grace the fires of fall foliage and continue the show until late in the season. In winter, the subtle varied greens of foliage, snow, ice, bare branchs and their attendant shadow tracery, enliven the landscape.

A good succession of bloom and garden interest doesn't just happen, though. It has to be carefully planned.

For instance, the very early spring starts with pale blue jacaranda trees blooming in the deep South. In Boston, witch hazel blooms with tiny yellow flowers in late February. After spring's major show, there are summer blooming trees and shrubs. The Kousa dogwood blooms spectacularly for a long period in June, its white blossoms upturned to the sun. *Albizia julibrisson rosea* (the silk tree) has feathery pink flowers in July, as does *Stewartia* with its camellia-like flowers, and the beautiful southern crepe myrtle. Franklinia blooms in September with 3-inch white camellia-like flowers for those who are patient and lucky. (See Sequence of Bloom List in part III.)

In autumn, ripening fruit provides additional interest and beauty, as does the sequence of fall color. All trees do not color at the same time but follow in sequence one after another for almost two months. It begins with the early flame-colored maples and sumac and ends with yellow birches and scarlet oaks. The colors are most intense where the nights are very cold and the days warm and sunny. New England has one of the best shows because of the preponderance of red and sugar maples. The south-facing slopes of the Rocky Mountains are often pure gold from the quaking aspen that clothe them.

In a proper succession of bloom, each plant has a charm of its own and should be counted as part of the total landscape. It is a sophisticated concept and takes time to develop. When you plant new material, try to plan for a sequence of bloom.

To design your own continuous sequence of bloom, start by keeping a calendar of exactly which days are bare with nothing blooming in your landscape. Then go to your neighbor's houses and see what's blooming there that you love. Make a note of the plant's name on the bare day in your calendar. Then, for future reference, plan where you will put it and add that information on the calendar also. It's impossible to remember in September exactly where you want the narcissus to bloom in May.

Flowering trees and shrubs give the most color for the work. They are more cost effective in terms of total display per purchase price and per human effort. Bulbs and flowers complement these, but the backbone of any garden is well-planted trees and shrubs.

Since the best time to plant is not the same as when the plants bloom, you will have time to study the particular requirements and growing conditions of each plant. Then you can check out the local nurseries and find out when the desired tree, shrub, or flower will be available for planting.

A garden where something happens each month is more interesting than a feast-or-famine yard. The well-designed landscape uses all the valuable qualities of many plants for a garden of ever-changing beauty and excitement.

**FIGURE 58: A WINTER WINDBREAK GARDEN PLANNED FOR A LONG SEASON OF BLOOM**

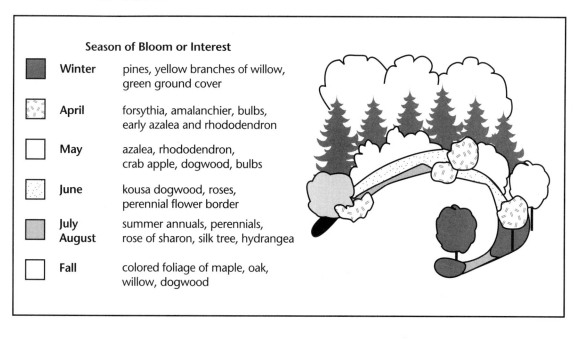

**Season of Bloom or Interest**

| | | |
|---|---|---|
| | **Winter** | pines, yellow branches of willow, green ground cover |
| | **April** | forsythia, amalanchier, bulbs, early azalea and rhododendron |
| | **May** | azalea, rhododendron, crab apple, dogwood, bulbs |
| | **June** | kousa dogwood, roses, perennial flower border |
| | **July August** | summer annuals, perennials, rose of sharon, silk tree, hydrangea |
| | **Fall** | colored foliage of maple, oak, willow, dogwood |

# CHAPTER 15

# Priorities:
# What to Buy First

Buying is expensive. Renovating is expensive. Moving plants around is difficult. No one wants to do it over because it doesn't look good. Calculate your landscape needs for both energy saving and aesthetics, and don't overlook privacy, usability, and ease of maintenance.

## FOR THE EXISTING HOUSE: PRIORITIES

When faced with the prospect of paying for more plants and improvements than one can afford all at once, the question arises of where to begin and how to assign priorities. Prioritizing is the key. Finishing may take several years, even longer. It doesn't matter . . . it's not a race.

The plants needed for design and for energy saving should be planted first. Trees first, for they are the most important. Hedge material, screens, or windbreaks should follow. Usually people don't want to wait too long to renovate the front of the house.

## NEATNESS COUNTS

Overall cleanup should be done very early. Neatness covers many deficiencies in design and plant material. When money is tight, a neat lawn, regularly mowed, with a crisp-cut edge, will compensate for a multitude of sins. The grass does not need to be perfect or lush or weed free. Just green. If things are neat, the yard will look nice.

Future shrub borders can be laid out and planted with ground cover, bulbs, even annuals. Spread with pine needles or wood chips, they will make a good appearance for small cost. Crisp edges and perfect geometric shapes look neat. The front of the house may be treated this way.

# TREES

The most important and most useful plants in any landscape are the trees. They should be the first things bought (after neatening up the property). Since trees take the most time to reach an effective size, correct placement is very important, so a total landscape plan should be worked out before any haphazard planting is done.

To save landscaping money, smaller trees can be bought. If they are carefully planted, regularly watered, and fertilized every spring, they can add several feet of growth each year. And since smaller trees grow faster than big ones, in two or three years, they will be larger than the bigger ones you could afford to buy later.

# HEDGES

Hedges, screens, and windbreak material should be bought next. This is also a good time to put up fences and walls. If there is to be a future patio or paved walks, it is useful to have the sand base put in when walls are built. The paving stones can be laid later, often as a do-it-yourself job. But digging and leveling the ground, as well as moving and spreading several tons of sand, is very hard work, best contracted out.

Where quick growth is wanted, don't skimp on soil preparation. Nothing repays as well as a good planting hole, enriched with compost or manure. There is no substitute for good soil.

Growth can also be speeded up by regular fertilizing in early spring, another dose in June, and plenty of water all summer. Plants that suffer from any bit of water stress stop growing. They start again when moistened, but the lost time is never made up. When fast growth is what you seek, it is also worthwhile to buy varieties and clones known to grow fastest. (See List of Plants for Hedges and Windbreaks, also Fast Growing Trees, in part III.)

Most hedge plants come as tall, skinny, rooted cuttings. If they are allowed to grow without pruning, they will grow upright and be sparse on the bottom. If all the upright shoots are long and unbranched, they will also have a tendency to split apart in winter.

There are times, however, when this upright growth is desirable, when a double- or triple-depth row windbreak may be wanted. (Tough deciduous shrubs or trees on the outside, evergreens next, and flowering shrubs and trees on the inside.) It is advantageous for the outside shrubs to grow as tall as possible; they should be sheared as little as possible.

Windbreaks and hedges should be planted fairly close together to encourage tall growth and multiple twiggy branches and provide an impervious screen at the top. (Recommended distances are in the List of Hedge and Windbreak Plants, part III.)

If you want a thick hedge, the young plants must be specially pruned to make them branch thickly from the bottom up. Obviously, it takes longer for them to reach the desired height. But once a hedge gets both tall and spindly on the bottom, it is a very tricky horticultural job to thicken it up. It may involve cutting the whole thing back to a couple of feet and starting over.

It's better to do correct shearing to thicken it for the first two years to develop the needed mass of short twigs. Eventually, the hedge will reach the same height as it would if you left it unsheared.

### FIGURE 59: **HOW TO SHEAR AND PRUNE FOR A THICK HEDGE FROM YOUNG PLANTS**

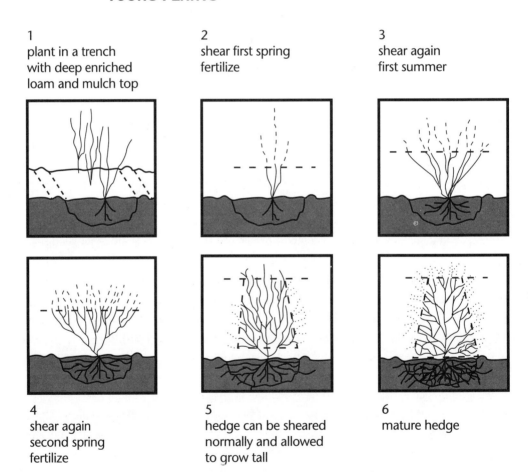

**1**
plant in a trench
with deep enriched
loam and mulch top

**2**
shear first spring
fertilize

**3**
shear again
first summer

**4**
shear again
second spring
fertilize

**5**
hedge can be sheared
normally and allowed
to grow tall

**6**
mature hedge

# THE FRONT YARD

Landscaping the front yard always seems more important than it should be. If it's neat and attractive, it will not be an eyesore or an embarrassment. It is better to spend limited available funds on trees and energy saving. But sometimes a neighbor or relative makes a critical comment, or there can be a compulsion to fix up the front for the unknown strangers who pass by. Landscaping the front is usually expensive because of the landscape styles that are in vogue at any time.

Even in the front, the trees come first. Consider beautiful ones such as magnolias or dogwoods at the corners of the house. Perhaps a weeping cherry or two could be used to frame the entrance. Small flowering trees such as these are excellent for use near buildings, but they should be planted at least 8 feet from the foundation. As they grow, they will easily fill the space. Columnar trees may be planted a bit closer, but even they will have a good spread at maturity.

Flowering trees are the most attractive in the long run, and the scale is right for near a building. Bigger shade trees can be planted along the road and driveway if the front yard is deep enough. Surrounding the base of trees with a bed of ground cover makes a more interesting design and prevents lawnmower damage to the trunk. Also, trees with skirts of ground cover look neat and don't have to be edged.

# FOUNDATION SHRUBS

When the trees are small, they will look like tall bushes. Small, choice shrubs can be added as funds become available. Choose them carefully for bloom sequence, color, and eventual height.

There are two mistakes that are commonly made. One is picking out azaleas and rhododendrons when they are not in bloom. The colors can be beautiful or terrible next to each other. When adding more plants, take a flower to the nursery and see if the colors of new shrubs will complement it.

The other mistake is buying shrubs that normally grow more than 3 to 5 feet at maturity. It breaks your heart to chop off the top of a healthy rhododendron, juniper, or yew because it's blocking the windows. And such a shrub can also break your back, because it will require pruning every year. To save your energy, use varieties in the foundation planting that will stay low and will be the correct size at maturity. (See list of Best Low-Growing Shrubs for Foundation Planting, part III.) Taller ones can be used where there is enough space for them to spread out and up.

Think carefully before adding a traditional row of little round and pointed bushes for foundation planting. It will be a boring, costly, green mustache across the front of the building. Rhododendrons and foundation evergreens are among the most expensive plants to buy. A neat foundation planting of ground cover, bulbs, annuals, a few well-chosen shrubs, and a small flowering tree will give a pleasant, refined look at much less cost.

FIGURE 60: **FOUNDATION PLANTING OF ELEGANT SIMPLICITY**

# ROCKS

I find the currently fashionable practice of planting the entire front yard with small random rocks and varied bushes set in a sea of wood chips to be rather unappealing. It is possible to have shrubs, rocks, ground cover, and wood chips covering large areas, but the effect must be very carefully designed. Rocks are important. To understand a rock's shape, character, and placement is very tricky. It is a most esoteric art form. Just a haphazard scattering of rocks and shrubs will resemble the remains of a glacier that melted, some time ago, on the on the front yard. Carefully planned islands of plants and rocks, alone or set around trees, however, can break the monotony of a sea of lawn.

One of the most durable and satisfying parts of the landscape is stone. It has heat-holding qualities that can be used for climate control and to reduce the fluctuation of soil temperature around plants in areas with hot days and cold nights. In nature, plants grow near rocks because of the shelter given to their roots, keeping them cool or warm and retaining moisture. If you plant informally around rocks and stone walls, the effect will look natural.

All rocks or stone walls should look as though they really belong there. The casual stones should look as though they are part of nature and need to be set in a natural fashion. Rocks should be buried about half their height to look settled and sturdy. The most pleasing face should be visible. Rocks have movement and lines of force like sculpture. Tall rocks carry the eye up. Flat ones are more restful. Before they set a rock, the Japanese spend a great deal of time looking at it. If you do that, too, you can create great beauty with leftovers from building and excavating, although old stones covered with moss and lichens are more prized.

Walls, patios, and rock settings are the most expensive parts of landscape construction and often are delayed. It is possible, however, to set small stones and rocks yourself, as long as they look professionally done. Don't use too many, or make rows of rubble. Think about each stone, as part of the overall plan. Look at it again and again until it looks just right.

# GROUND COVER

It's easy to overplant when you buy small plants such as ground covers. Check the mature spread and allow enough space between plants for them to grow freely. Ground covers take about two years to get established, less if irrigated. A green ground cover will visually pull all the foundation elements together. Evergreens, such as ivy, myrtle, pachysandra, and mondo grass, are the most satisfactory for this purpose. Deciduous ones, such as violets, strawberries, and sedum, are not nearly as neat and are not green in winter. Although deciduous, rows of hosta are very useful and neat in foundation planting around trees and along walks.

Don't use a mulch that introduces weed or grass seeds into ground cover beds. Weeding the first year can be time consuming just from the weed seeds already in the soil. (See Ground Covers in chapter 13 and Mulches in chapter 12.)

# FOR THE NEW HOUSE: PRIORITIES

For a new house, a total plan, before buying anything, is essential for the most economical use of landscape dollars. If the plan is done before the building begins, many valuable trees and shrubs can be protected or moved. Also, loam can be stockpiled where it will be needed.

Terraces and walls can be finished as the house is built. It is worth the money to have this work done and included in the mortgage expenses. There is so much to be finished after moving into a new house that having the backbreaking chores completed is a blessing.

If possible, all loam should be spread before the backhoe leaves, even if the beds won't be planted for several years. Usually the backhoe can be rented by the hour for a modest sum when it is already on the site. Moving soil is hard, heavy work, but for construction machinery, it is nothing. The backhoe can also dig holes for trees and leave the soil piled by the side. That's three-quarters of the work done for you.

If no planting is to be done immediately, the bulldozer can drop small loads of wood chips in convenient locations. It's much easier than pushing them around in a wheelbarrow. Wood chips prevent soil erosion until planting can be done. You can have your own brush chipped on site and use it there. Many tree companies will deliver a load of tree clippings and chippings (chopped leaves and branches) for very little money. But a truckload is a big mound, so coordinate with the bulldozer first.

# PROTECTING EXISTING TREES DURING CONSTRUCTION

If one is fortunate enough to acquire a lot before the bulldozer has leveled it, there will probably be trees on the property. They may look very small. Price their equivalents before heeding the builder's, "Oh, that's a weed tree. You can get another tree better than that." You may even be fortunate enough to have a good large specimen or a grove.

Protecting trees during construction is simple if you understand their growth requirements. Small trees have small root areas. Large ones have enormous root circles that nourish them. The feeding roots' diameter may be a circle twice as wide as the "drip line" (outer edge of the leaves).

Trees breathe and drink through these roots, which are in the top 12 inches of soil. Protect these areas with snow or dog fencing or rope. They are part of your future landscape. Contractors can't be bothered protecting trees—it takes time, and time is money.

The soil under the leaves, as far as the outer drip line, should not be disturbed or packed down. That means no vehicles under the trees, no storage of heavy material, no cutting of roots, and no grade changes over the roots. The construction crew should not eat their daily lunch under the tree. Most important, NO SOIL ADDED OVER THE ROOTS if you want a tree to survive for any length of time. The exception is when new grass or ground cover must be planted.

Trees can tolerate the loss of about one third of their total root area under the drip line through grade change, compaction, or cutting. If they suffer more, their growth will be retarded, but many will survive. Realistically, all construction damages existing trees.

Most tree roots are easily smothered. Some, such as sugar maples and beech, are very sensitive and easily killed. If possible, no soil should be added on top. Ideally, the existing leaf mulch should be left to protect the roots and retain the soil microorganisms necessary for chemical reactions in the roots. Pine, oak, and beech are especially particular about this. The best way to treat the surface under trees is to add 2 inches of bark mulch in a circle or bed.

If grass is to be added, 3 to 5 inches of good loam may be lightly raked on, then seed or sod may be added. Be sure not to use more than 6 inches of soil on top of the roots, as any more than that will throw many trees into decline and kill others. Beech and sugar maple can be killed by more than 3 inches of soil, while Norway maple and apple will stand 6 inches.

Many people buy nice wooded lots, all graded and planted with grass. In a few years, the trees decline and die because their roots were simply smothered with fill or topsoil. You can tell whether a tree has been filled by looking for the root flare at the base. All trees flare, or widen, at the soil level. If the tree looks like a telephone pole and has no root flares, dig down carefully with a trowel and see how much fill has been added. Another way to tell whether the grade was raised is to dig down and see if there is a layer where the color and texture of the soil changes. If so, that was probably the original grade.

If a particular tree is large and very significant, then a large circle around it should be protected. Where the area can't be fenced off, plywood sheets may be placed on top of the soil for machinery to run on. Though not perfect, it's better than nothing.

To protect trees during construction, the rules are simple:

- Don't compress and pack down the soil.

- Don't throw waste paint or light fires over the roots.

- Never add more than 3 to 6 inches of anything over the roots.

- Don't cut away or destroy more than one third the total root run.

Sometimes a building must be constructed close to an existing tree. It can be very close, even 10 feet, if about two thirds of the roots are preserved and protected. When a driveway must be put in, try to design it so the fewest roots will be cut. A driveway doesn't have to be straight. A few boulders from the construction may be set as casual rocks at the bends. These can be planted with flowering shrubs, ground cover, and flowers.

Don't do any pruning at all before construction because there will surely be much damage done by all the people and materials on the job. After construction is finished, prune away the branches that have been damaged, plus dead or unbalanced ones. Use a tree professional who knows what he's doing. The tree will better stand the root loss and will be a safer tree.

If the ground over the roots must be raised or lowered, try to preserve the soil level under the tree. Use retaining walls or a riprap of roughly laid rocks (which are usually left over at the construction site) to contain the area under the tree. When there are different grades, gardens are more interesting. A little landscape planning can often turn these problem areas into assets in a more interesting garden design.

If the area over the roots of important trees must be raised, provide a layer of porous material for water drainage and air exchange. First add a layer of crushed stone, leaving pipe vents to the surface for air. Drainage tiles may be necessary in wet places or if the surface drainage was altered radically. If ground cover or grass is to be planted, top the stones with a soil separator fabric to keep loose dirt from settling and filling in around the rocks. Finally add loam and plant. Don't pile soil next to the trunk, and leave a well, as large as possible, around it.

It is very expensive to raise the grade over an existing tree, which is why it's easier to be creative and design something interesting to protect the tree root zone. The area may be raised into a stone terrace, many inches thick, for tree roots protected by large stones do not smother.

You may want to consider a deck instead. It will give you the same outdoor living space, and the roots underneath will be fine just left alone. Under trees that drip sap, such as pines, it is better, however, to have a crushed stone terrace, because the sticky resin discolors decks.

Carefully protect any area with forest-type undergrowth, such as wild low-bush blueberry, ferns, wildflowers, and small understory trees. The good, rich, litter of forest floor leaf mulch should be carefully preserved as well. The forest floor is the most fragile ecosystem that there is. It takes half a century to become established. When it's disturbed, or even just walked on too often, it does not regenerate and grow back.

Construction workers view this as an area for dumping and piling rubbish and leftovers. Protecting good existing vegetation when building a new house takes a will of iron. Somehow builders view green things as the enemy. Yet, when you go to replant, you will view these things, particularly trees and the forest as cost-saving treasures. It's much more cost-effective to try to save the trees and forest than to pay to replace them.

Mark all trees to be saved with green plastic tape. Put up fences of tape (or something more permanent) over root areas to be protected. If possible, be on the site when the bulldozers do their thing. The builder may hate it, but you're the one who is going to live there.

# WHEN THE WORKERS LEAVE

The once lovely land looks like a battlefield. The easiest thing to do is plant a lawn everywhere to cover up the bare earth. But resist this temptation, except as an interim solution. Instead, make a plan for the long term, for beauty, for succession of bloom, for energy saving, and for future economy.

To hold the land until you can execute the whole design, seed the bare earth with perennial rye grass and fescue, which will give a quick, low-maintenance lawn-meadow. Where you want a very good lawn, add 6 inches of loam and also bluegrass seed to the rye and fescue. On areas that will be planted with ground cover, just spread wood chips. They will protect the soil until you are ready to plant.

# THE SEARCH FOR PERFECTION AND JOY

Planning a garden is a work of joy. It is never done. The garden is always there to fill the empty moments or wash away sadness from the soul. There is always a challenge. A new plant. A new variety. The endless search for perfection. And always discovery.

When sleep won't come at night, instead of counting sheep, you can plan every tiny detail, every nuance, at leisure, in peace and quiet. Thinking through all the possibilities for saving energy, saving time, and saving money is complex, and it takes time to make them grow to maturity. Beautiful energy-saving gardens don't spring up overnight. They are creations of the mind and products of the pleasant passage of time.

# Part III

# PLANT LISTS

## FOR SPECIAL PURPOSES

**PLANT LIST 1**

# HEIGHTS OF MATURE TREES

| LARGE TREES (over 50 feet) | Size | Rate of Growth | Zone | Description |
|---|---|---|---|---|
| *Abies concolor*<br>White fir | 100'+ | moderate | 4–9 | evergreen; bluish needles |
| *Acer platanoides*<br>Norway maple | 90' | moderate | 3–9 | gives dense shade; reliable; yellow fall color |
| *Acer rubrum*<br>Red maple | 100' | fast | 3–9 | good fall color; moist soil |
| *Acer sacchrum*<br>Sugar maple | 100'+ | moderate | 3–8 | good fall color; salt sensitive; not for cities; sap gives maple sugar |
| *Acer saccharinum*<br>Silver or cut-leaf maple | 80' | very fast | 3–8 | not near pipes or buildings; weak-wooded |
| *Aesculus carnea*<br>Red horse chestnut | 75' | slow | 3–6 and CA | pink flowers; horse chestnuts |
| *Aesculus hippocastanum*<br>*"Baumanni"*<br>Baumann horse chestnut | 75' | slow | 3–6 | white flowers; no nuts; no summer drought |
| *Ailanthus altissima*<br>Tree of heaven | 60' | very fast | 4–9 | grows anywhere; female tree only; weedy tree; from *A Tree Grows in Brooklyn* |
| *Araucaria* varieties<br>Norfolk pine, Monkey puzzle, Bunya-bunya | 90' | moderate | 10 | evergreen; unusual shapes |
| †*Betula papyrifera*<br>Canoe birch | 90' | moderate | 2–4 | needs cold winters; beautiful white bark; good foliage; hard to move |
| †*Betula nigra*<br>Black birch | 80' | moderate | 4–9 | short lived in North; wet locations |
| *Carpinus betulus*<br>European hornbeam | 60' | slow | 5–9 | many shapes available; can be sheared |
| *Casaurina equisetifolia*<br>She-oak, Horsetail, Beefwood | 70' | fast | 9–10 | salt and wind resistant; tolerates sand; evergreen; crowds other trees |
| *Catalpa speciosa*<br>Northern catalpa | 90' | moderate | 4–7 | large, coarse tree; flowers; stands drought and heat |
| *Cedrus atlantica*<br>Atlas cedar | 100'+ | slow | 6–10 | evergreen; silvery color |
| *Cedrus libani*<br>Cedar of Lebanon | 80' | slow | 5–10 | evergreen; wide-spreading when old |

† Spring planting only, hard to move.

| LARGE TREES (over 50 feet) | Size | Rate of Growth | Zone | Description |
|---|---|---|---|---|
| *Celtis australis* European hackberry | 50–75' | moderate | 6–10 | withstands drought |
| †*Cercidiphyllum japonicum* Katsura tree | 60' | moderate | 4–8 | wide-spreading tree; pest free; hard to move; attractive leaves |
| *Chamaecyparis obtusa* Hinoki false cypress | 100'+ | slow | 4–8 | evergreen; moist air |
| *Cocos nucifera* Coconut palm | 80' | slow | 10 | Florida palm tree; slow starting; subject to new diseases |
| †*Cornus nuttalli* Pacific dogwood | 75' | moderate | 7–9 | evergreen; most beautiful tree; flowers; moist air; West Coast tree |
| *Corylus colurna* Turkish filbert | 75' | moderate | 4–8 | tolerates dry soil; nice shape |
| *Cryptomeria japonica* Cryptomeria | 100'+ | moderate | 5–8 | evergreen; attractive; soft foliage |
| *Cupressus macrocarpa* Monterey cypress | 75' | fast | 7–9 | evergreen; withstands salt spray and wind; old trees develop interesting shapes |
| *Eucalyptus* varieties Red, white, or silver- | 100'+ | fastest | 9–10 | big, tall trees; Do not use blue gum variety, except for rural reforestation dollar gum tree |
| †*Fagus sylvatica* European beech | 90' | slow | 4–8 | beautiful tree; wide, low, shallow roots; moist soil |
| *Fraxinus pennsylvanica* 'Marshall's Seedless' Marshall seedless ash (green ash) | 60' | fast | 3–9 | good shade tree; seedless variety |
| †*Gingko biloba* gingko | to 100'+ | slow | 4–10 | each clone has a different shape; slow starting; use only male trees; pest free |
| *Gleditsia triacanthos inermis* Thornless honey locust (see Figure 56, page 167) Moraine, Majestic, Skyline, Shademaster | 70' | fast | 4–10 | light shade; lawn will grow under it; city- and drought-tolerant; reliable; different clones have different shapes; leafs out in late spring; drops leaves early in fall |
| †*Liquidambar styraciflua* Sweet gum | 100' | moderate | 5–10 | attractive shade tree; good fall color |
| †*Liriodendron tulipfera* Tulip tree | 100' | fast | 4–9 | grows broad and large; green flowers |

† Spring planting only, hard to move

| LARGE TREES (over 50 feet) | Size | Rate of Growth | Zone | Description |
| --- | --- | --- | --- | --- |
| *Magnolia grandiflora* <br> Southern magnolia | 90' | moderate | 7–9 | evergreen; big flowers; attractive tree in South; shrubby in North |
| *Metasequoia glypto-stroboides* <br> Dawn redwood (recently brought from China) | 100' | fast | 5–9 | deciduous needles; bright green; attractive, upright shape |
| †*Nyssa sylvatica* <br> Tupelo or black gum | 90' | slow | 4–9 | swampy places; good fall color |
| *Picea* varieties <br> Spruce | 75–100' | moderate | 2–5 | evergreen; many useful varieties; good at high altitudes |
| *Pinus* varieties <br> Pine | 50–100' | fast | 2–10 | evergreen; useful for dry soils |
| *Pittosporum rhombifolium* <br> Diamond leaf pittosporum | 80' | moderate | 10 | evergreen |
| *Platanus acerifolia* "Bloodgood" <br> Bloodgood London plane | 100' | fast | 5–9 | large tree; good in city; "Bloodgood" clone is anthracnose fungus resistant |
| *Podocarpus macrophyllus* <br> Yew podocarpus | 60' | slow | 7–10 | evergreen; good green; can be clipped |
| †*Prunus sargenti* <br> Sargent cherry | 75' | moderate | 4–8 | flowers; fall color; beautiful tree |
| *Pseudolarix amabilis* <br> Golden larch | 100' | moderate | 5–8 | deciduous; needles; yellow fall color |
| *Pseudotsuga menziesii* <br> Douglas fir | 200' | fast | 4–6 | evergreen; attractive; Pacific coast |
| †*Quercus* varieties <br> Oak | 60–100' | slow | 3–10 | good, large shade tree; sturdy once established; gets insects and fungi but still most useful |
| †*Sophora japonica* <br> Japanese pagoda tree | 75' | moderate | 4–8 | lovely tree; flowers; good in city; insect free |
| *Taxodium distichum* <br> Bald cypress | 150' | moderate | 4–10 | deciduous; needles; swamps and wet places |
| *Thuja occidentalis* <br> can arborvitae | 60' | moderate | 2–5 | evergreen; grows anywhere; Ameri-columnar; not the most beautiful, but reliable |
| *Tilia cordata* <br> Little leaf linden, European linden | 90' | moderate | 3–8 | good, neat tree; good in city |

† Spring planting only, hard to move

| LARGE TREES (over 50 feet) | Size | Rate of Growth | Zone | Description |
|---|---|---|---|---|
| *Tilia* varieties American linden, Silver linden | 75–100' | moderate | 2–8 | larger leaves; good, useful trees; fragrant when in bloom |
| *Tsuga canadensis* Canadian hemlock | 90' | moderate | 3–6 | evergreen; most graceful tree in sheltered spot; good foliage |
| *Zelkova serrata* "Village Green" Village Green zelkova | 90' | moderate | 5–10 | excellent tree; wide-spreading; low spreading unless pruned up |

| MEDIUM TREES (30–50 feet) | Size | Rate of Growth | Zone | Description |
|---|---|---|---|---|
| *Acacia decurrens* Silver wattle | 50' | fast | 9–10 | good soil; short-lived; flowers; evergreen |
| *Acer platanoides* "Crimson King" Crimson King Norway maple | 50' | slow | 4–8 | red leaves all summer and fall |
| *Aesculus glabra* Yellow buckeye | 35' | moderate | 3–7 | flowers; good fall color; horse chestnuts |
| *Albizia julibrisson rosea* Silk tree | 40' | fast | 5–10 | pink flowers in summer; dainty leaf; attractive, spreading tree; feathery |
| *Amelanchier canadensis* Shadblow serviceberry | 50' | moderate | 4–8 | grows in shade; very early spring blooms (blooms when the shad run) |
| *Amelanchier*, varieties Serviceberry, Saskatoon | 40' | moderate–fast | 3–8 | varieties for each area of country; flowers |
| †*Betula pendula* (*verrucosa*) European weeping birch | 50' | fast | 2–8 | lovely tree; white bark; short-lived; gets borers and leaf miners |
| *Camellia japonica* Common camellia | 40' | slow | 7–9 | beautiful blooms and foliage; acid soil; evergreen; cool nights |
| *Cassia fistula* Golden shower, senna | 35' | moderate | 10 | beautiful yellow blooms |
| *Circus canadensis* Redbud | 35' | moderate | 4–8 | delicate pink flowers; grows in shade |
| *Cladrastis lutea* American yellow-wood | 50' | moderate | 4–8 | nice tree; flowers; stands heat and cold |
| *Delonix regia* poinciana | 40' | moderate | 10 | outstanding scarlet blooms; Royal spreading |

† Spring planting only, hard to move

| MEDIUM TREES (30–50 feet) | Size | Rate of Growth | Zone | Description |
|---|---|---|---|---|
| *Eucalyptus ficifolia*<br>Red flowering gum | 50' | fast | 10 | vigorous tree; shallow roots steal food from surrounding plants; flowers |
| *Fraxinus velutina*<br>Modesto ash | 50' | fast | 5–10 | grows in dry alkaline soil; especially California and West |
| *Gleditsia triacanthos inermis* "Sunburst"<br>Sunburst honey locust | 40' | fast | 4–10 | new leaves bright yellow; grows in any soil |
| *Jacaranda acutifolia*<br>Jacaranda | 50' | moderate | 10 | blue flowers in early spring; Florida and California |
| *Juniperus scopulorum*<br>Rocky mountain juniper | 35' | slow | 4–8 | evergreen; drought-tolerant; used west of Illinois |
| †*Koelreuteria paniculata*<br>Golden rain tree | 35' | moderate | 5–10 | yellow flowers; irregular shape; drought-resistant; reliable, hard to move |
| †*Magnolia loebneri* "Merrill"<br>Merrill magnolia | 50' | moderate | 4–8 | white flowers, excellent large magnolia for Northern areas |
| †*Magnolia virginiana*<br>Sweet bay | 10–60' | slow | 5–9 | shrub in North, tree in South; moist soil; evergreen |
| *Malus baccata*<br>Siberian crab apple | 50' | moderate | 2–7 | flowers; small fruit; upright |
| *Melia azedarach*<br>China berry | 45' | fast | 7–10 | stands heat and drought; lilac flowers; reliable |
| †*Phellodendron amurense*<br>Amur cork tree | 35' | fast | 3–6 | low branching; good in city; insect free |
| †*Pyrus calleryana* "Bradford"<br>Bradford callery pear | 40' | moderate | 5–10 | good city tree; small flowers; neat shape; good fall color |
| *Sapium sebiferum*<br>Chinese tallow tree | 40' | moderate | 9–10 | good in South; reliable |
| *Schinus terebinthifolius*<br>Brazil pepper tree | 40' | moderate | 9–10 | stands dry soil |
| *Sorbus acuparia*<br>European mountain ash | 45' | fast | 3–6 | flowers; good bright berries in sun; upright; neat; gets borers |
| *Tilia cordata* "Greenspire"<br>Greenspire little leaf linden | 45' | moderate | 3–9 | upright; oval crown; neat tree; transplants easily; good in city |

†Spring planting only, hard to move.

| SMALL TREES (under 30 feet) | Size | Rate of Growth | Zone | Description |
|---|---|---|---|---|
| *Acer circinatum* <br> Vine maple | 25' | slow | 5–7 | partial shade; West Coast tree |
| *Acer ginnala* <br> Amur maple | 20' | slow | 2–7 | hardy; no-care; good screen; beautiful fall color |
| †*Acer palmatum* <br> Japanese maple (red and green leaves) | 20' | slow | 5–8 | choice tree; delicate foliage; good fall color; some red-leaved varieties turn green in summer; best ones stay red |
| *Acer tataricum* <br> Tatarian maple | 30' | slow | 3–7 | hardy; no-care; good screen |
| *Amelanchier grandiflora* <br> Apple serviceberry | 25' | moderate | 4–7 | early flowers; grows in shade |
| *Bauhinia blakeana* <br> Orchid tree | 30' | moderate | 10 | beautiful flowers; long blooming |
| *Chionanthus virginicus* <br> Fringe tree | 30' | moderate | 4–9 | feathery flowers; late leafing; attractive; fruit |
| †*Cornus florida* <br> Flowering dogwood | 30' | moderate | 5–9 | most beautiful tree; acid soil; sun or shade; lovely flowers |
| †*Cornus kousa* <br> Kousa or Korean dogwood | 25' | moderate | 5–9 | late flowering; beautiful; sun |
| *Crataegus lavallei* <br> Lavalle hawthorn | 20' | moderate | 4–7 | flowers; thorns; fruits |
| *Crataegus phaenopyrum* <br> Washington hawthorn | 30' | moderate | 4–7 | dry or alkaline soil; stands wind; flowers; fruits |
| *Elaeagnus angustifolia* <br> Russian olive | 20' | fast | 2–10 | silver leaves; grows anywhere; good screen |
| *Ficus carica* <br> Common fig | 30' | moderate | 6–10 | coarse leaves; spreading |
| †*Franklinia alatamaha* <br> Franklinia | 25' | moderate | 5–9 | fine flowers and fall color; protect in North from cold in spring |
| *Ilex vomitoria* <br> Yaupon | 25' | moderate | 7–9 | evergreen; hedge or tree; may be sheared |
| †*Lagerstroemia indica* <br> Crape-myrtle | 25' | moderate—fast | 7–9 | good flowers; hard to move; plant small size |
| *Laurus nobilis* <br> Laurel or bay tree (used in ancient Greece) | 30' | slow | 6–9 | evergreen; hedge or tree; shears well |

† Spring planting only, hard to move

| SMALL TREES (under 30 feet) | Size | Rate of Growth | Zone | Description |
|---|---|---|---|---|
| *Ligustrum lucidum* Glossy privet | 30' | fast | 7–10 | evergreen; hedge or tree; shears well; reliable; vigorous |
| † *Magnolia soulangana* magnolia | 25' | moderate | 5–8 | beautiful early bloom; hard to Saucer move; good in city |
| *Malus* varieties crab apple | 10–30' | moderate | 2–8 | beautiful blooms; fruit, very reliable; useful |
| *Myrica californica* California bayberry | 30' | moderate | 7–10 | evergreen; shrub or tree |
| *Olea europaea* Common olive | 25' | very slow | 9–10 | dry climate; long-lived, spreading; fruit; evergreen |
| † *Prunus* varieties Cherry | 15–30' | moderate | 5–8 (some 2–7) | lovely flowers; some with edible fruit |
| *Syringa amurensis japonica* Japanese tree lilac | 30' | moderate | 3–8 | good flowers late in summer; reliable; watch for scale and borer |
| *Viburnum sieboldii* Siebold viburnum | 30' | moderate | 4–8 | shrub or tree; flowers; fruit; vigorous |

**PLANT LIST 2**

# COLUMNAR TREES

*(For shade from the summer sun, narrow courtyards, and streets.)*
*NOTE: Also called "fastigate" or "sentry." Always buy a named clone.*

| | Size | Rate of Growth | Zone | Description |
|---|---|---|---|---|
| *Acer platanoides* "Columnare" Columnar Norway maple | 50' | moderate | 3 | transplants easily |
| *Acer rubrum* "Columnare" Columnar red maple | 75' | fast | 3 | good fall color; moist soil |
| *Acer saccharum* "Columnare," "Newton Sentry," or "Monu-mentale" Columnar sugar maple | 60' | moderate | 3 | good fall color; very narrow |
| † *Fagus sylvatica fastigata* Upright European beech | 50' | slow | 4 | beautiful tree; long-lived |
| † *Gingko biloba* "Fastigata" or "Sentry" Sentry gingko | 60' | moderate | 4 | moist soil at first; pollution-resistant; very narrow; beautiful tree; good in city |

† Spring planting only, hard to move

| | Size | Rate of Growth | Zone | Description |
|---|---|---|---|---|
| *Malus* "Van Eseltine" Upright Van Eseltine crab apple | 20' | fast | 4 | beautiful flowers; low branches |
| *Populus alba pyramidalis* Bolleana poplar | 50' | fast | 3 | less susceptible to canker disease; caution—roots get in water and sewer pipes |
| *Populus nigra italica* Lombardy poplar | 80' | fastest | 3 | narrow; VERY susceptible to canker disease; caution—roots get in water and sewer pipes |
| *Prunus sargenti* "Columnaris" Upright sargent cherry | 45' | slow | 4 | beautiful flowers; nice tree; hard to find |
| *Prunus serrula* "Amanogawa" Amanogawa Japanese cherry | 20' | slow | 6 | beautiful flowers; nice tree |
| *Quercus robur fastigiata* Pyramidal English oak | 75' | slow | 5 | beautiful tree; long-lived |
| *Ulmus hollandica Groenveldt* Groenveldt elm | 90' | moderate | 4 | semiresistant to Dutch elm disease; upright, but wider than the other trees on list |

† Spring planting only, hard to move

## PLANT LIST 3

# TREES WITH A WIDE RANGE OF CLIMATE ADAPTABILITY—VIGOROUS AND RELIABLE

| | Size | Rate of Growth | Zone | Description |
|---|---|---|---|---|
| *Albizia julibrisson rosea* Silk tree | 40' | fast | 5–10 | pink flowers; mimosa-type leaves; graceful, spreading shape |
| *Calocedrus decurrens* California incense cedar | 90' | slow | 6–10 | evergreen; moist climate; upright |
| *Cedrus libani* Cedar of Lebanon | 80' | slow | 5–10 | evergreen; spreading when old |
| *Celtis australis* European hackberry | 50–75' | moderate | 6–10 | withstands drought; elm-like leaves; not choice, but useful |
| *Elaeagnus angustifolia* Russian olive | 20' | fast | 2–10 | silvery leaves; grows anywhere; salt- and wind-resistant; good screen |

| | Size | Rate of Growth | Zone | Description |
|---|---|---|---|---|
| *Fraxinus pennsylvanica* "Marshall's Seedless"<br>Marshall seedless ash (green ash) | 60' | fast | 3–9 | good shade tree; seedless |
| *Fraxinus velutina*<br>Modesto ash | 50' | fast | 5–10 | grows in dry, alkaline soil, especially West and California |
| *Gleditsia triacanthos inermis*<br>Thornless honey locust | 35–70' | fast | 4–10 | reliable street tree; light shade; grass will grow under it; not graceful in winter |
| *Juniperus chinensis* varieties<br>Chinese juniper | to 30' | moderate | 5–10 | evergreen, useful |
| *Malus* varieties<br>Crab apple | 10–50' | moderate | 2–8 | beautiful spring flowers; fruit |
| *Pyrus calleryana* "Bradford"<br>Bradford callery pear | 40' | moderate | 5–10 | pollution-resistant; white flowers; leathery leaves; good in city |
| *Zelkova serrata* "Village Green"<br>Village Green zelkova | 60' | fast | 5–10 | good shape; good shade tree; withstands wind, drought, and alkaline soil |

**PLANT LIST 4**

# FAST-GROWING TREES

*Good for windbreaks and screens; too vigorous to grow near buildings; should be planted at edge of property or 60 feet from buildings.*

| | Size | Rate of Growth | Zone | Description |
|---|---|---|---|---|
| *Casaurina equisetifolia*<br>She-oak, Horsetail, Beefwood | 70' | fast | 9–10 | evergreen; shallow-rooted; stands sand, wind, drought, and salt water |
| *Eucalyptus globulus*<br>Blue gum | 200' | fastest | 9–10 | evergreen; coarse tree; drops litter; reliable but large |
| *Grevillea robusta*<br>Silk-oak | 150' | fast | 10 | evergreen; attractive; shallow roots |
| *Phyllostachys bambusoides*<br>Japanese timber bamboo | 70' | fast | 7–10 | evergreen; very invasive; spreads everywhere by underground roots |
| *Populus* varieties<br>Poplar, Cottonwood | 50–100' | fast | 1–9 | attractive tree but roots go into pipes; drops litter |
| *Populus nigra italica*<br>bardy poplar | 90' | fast | 3–8 | beautiful; narrow and tall; gets Lomcanker just as it reaches maturity |

| | Size | Rate of Growth | Zone | Description |
|---|---|---|---|---|
| *Populus tremuloides* Quaking aspen | 90' | fast | 1–7 | picturesque; plant in groves; good fall color |
| *Salix* varieties Willow | 50–75' | fast | 2–10 | beautiful, graceful tree; roots get in water pipes; drops litter |
| *Ulmus* varieties Elm | 50–120' | fast | 2–10 | superb tree but gets incurable disease |

**PLANT LIST 5**

# TREES THAT GROW IN SHADE
## (UNDERSTORY PLANTING)

| | Size | Rate of Growth | Zone | Description |
|---|---|---|---|---|
| *Acer circinatum* Vine maple | 25' | slow | 5–8 | twining trunk; good fall color; West Coast |
| *Acer pennsylvanicum* Striped maple | 35' | moderate | 3–7 | striped bark |
| *Amelanchier* varieties Serviceberry | 30' | moderate | 3–7 | flowers very early; berries; shrubby |
| *Cercis canadensis* Redbud | 35' | fast | 4–9 | acid soil; lovely pink flowers |
| *Cornus florida* Dogwood | 40' | moderate | 5–9 | most beautiful tree; flowers; acid soil |
| *Ilex* varieties Holly | 6–50' | slow | 5–8 | dark foliage; acid soil; some evergreen |
| *Magnolia virginiana* Sweet bay | 10–60' | slow | 5–9 | evergreen; white flowers; tall in South; shrubby in North and not evergreen |
| *Podocarpus* varieties podocarpus | 60' | moderate | 7–10 | evergreen; attractive, yew-like foliage |
| *Prunus pennyslvanica* Pin cherry | 30' | fast | 2–6 | flowers; berries; sparse habit of growth |
| *Thuja occidentalis* American arborvitae | 50' | fast | 2–6 | evergreen; columnar tree; grows in any soil |
| *Tsuga* varieties Hemlock | 75–200' | moderate | 3–7 | evergreen; good soil; moisture; beautiful; can be sheared |

**PLANT LIST 6**

# TREES FOR CITIES

*Useful for sidewalks, courtyards, paved areas. Clones developed especially for or suited to city streets.*

| | Size | Rate of Growth | Zone | Description |
|---|---|---|---|---|
| **THE MAPLES** | | | | |
| *Acer platanoides,* Norway maple | | | | all varieties transplant easily, yellow fall color |
| Emerald Queen | 60' | rapid | 3 | upright; oval head |
| Cleveland | 50' | slower | 3 | upright; oval head |
| Summershade | 60' | rapid | 3 | broad shape; resistant to leaf scorch; good central leader and straight trunk |
| Greenlace | 50' | slower | 3 | cut leaf; upright growth |
| Crimson King | 40' | slow | 4 | wine-red leaves, all season |
| *Acer rubrum,* Red Maple | | | | all varieties require more water than Norway maples, all varieties grow faster than Norway maples, red fall color |
| Armstrong | 35' | rapid | 3 | narrow |
| Autumn Flame | 60' | moderate | 3 | small leaves; colors and defoliates early |
| October Glory | 50' | rapid | 3 | similar to Armstrong; wider shape |
| Gerling | 35' | moderate | 3 | good green leaves; glossy; globe-shaped; good fall color (lately some trees have had a problem with the root graft) |
| Red Sunset | 50' | rapid | 3 | persistent red foliage; pendulous leaves; broad upright shape |
| **THE ASHES** | | | | |
| *Fraxinus americana,* White Ash | | | | good street tree; reliable; tough |
| Autumn Purple | 65' | fast | 3 | purple fall color; seedless |
| Rosehill | 70' | fast | 3 | bronze fall color; seedless, oval shape |
| *Fraxinus pennsylvanica,* Green Ash | | | | good tree; reliable; tough |
| Marshall's Seedless | 55' | fast | 3 | drought-tolerant; yellow fall color |
| Summit | 60' | moderate | 3 | more upright; narrow crown; less vigorous than Marshall |
| **THORNLESS HONEY LOCUSTS** | | | | |
| *Gleditsia triacanthos inermis* | | | | all have feathery foliage, irregular-shaped branches |
| Shademaster | 60' | fast | 4 | upright shape; irregular |

| | Size | Rate of Growth | Zone | Description |
|---|---|---|---|---|
| Sunburst | 35' | fast | 4 | new foliage; bright yellow |
| Imperial (Lo-Gro) | 40' | fast | 4 | spreading; round shape |
| Skyline | 55' | fast | 4 | neat pyramidal crown upright |

## PLANE TREE

| | Size | Rate of Growth | Zone | Description |
|---|---|---|---|---|
| *Platanus acerifolia,* London plane Bloodgood | 100' | fast | 5 | large, broad tree; not for small streets; only anthracnose fungus-resistant strain |

## FRUITLESS PEARS

| | Size | Rate of Growth | Zone | Description |
|---|---|---|---|---|
| *Pyrus calleryana,* Callery pear | | | | excellent street tree; holds leaves late; pollution-resistant |
| Bradford | 40' | moderate | 5 | beautiful oval shape; glossy leaves; fall color |
| Aristocrat | 40' | moderate | 5 | improved fall color and leaf shape |
| Chanticleer | 40' | moderate | 5 | narrower |
| Fauriei | 15' | slow | 5 | dwarf; round head |

## PIN OAK

| | Size | Rate of Growth | Zone | Description |
|---|---|---|---|---|
| *Quercus palustris,* pin oak | | | | only oak that moves well; subject to chlorosos; nice tree |
| Sovereign | 75' | moderate | 4 | only pin oak with upright branches, others are pendulous |

## SOPHORA

| | Size | Rate of Growth | Zone | Description |
|---|---|---|---|---|
| *Sophora japonica,* Sophora Regent | 75' | moderate | 4 | beautiful; useful tree wide branches; small flowers |

## THE LINDENS

| | Size | Rate of Growth | Zone | Description |
|---|---|---|---|---|
| *Tilia cordata,* Little leaf linden | | | | easy to move; attractive; excellent tree; reliable |
| Greenspire | 40' | moderate | 3 | excellent street tree; pyramidal shape |
| Cancellor | 40' | moderate | 3 | narrower; pyramidal shape |
| Rancho | 40' | moderate | 3 | even narrower; upright shape |

## ZELKOVA

| | Size | Rate of Growth | Zone | Description |
|---|---|---|---|---|
| *Zelkova serrata* Village Green | 90' | moderate | 5 | graceful; elm-like leaf; spreading; reliable; train to a high head |

# OTHER TREES FOR DIFFICULT CITY SITUATIONS

| | Size | Rate of Growth | Zone | Description |
|---|---|---|---|---|
| *Acer pseudoplatanus*<br>Sycamore maple | 90' | moderate | 5–9 | withstands salt and wind |
| *Ailanthus altissima*<br>Tree of Heaven | 60' | fast | 4–10 | grows anywhere; female tree only; coarse texture; from *A Tree Grows in Brooklyn* |
| *Albizia julibrisson rosea*<br>Silk tree | 40' | fast | 5–10 | pink flowers; dainty leaf; spreading shape |
| *Cedrela sinensis*<br>Chinese toon | 70' | fast | 5–10 | looks like ailanthus; reliable |
| *Crataegus phaenopyrum* and other varieties<br>Washington hawthorn | 30' | moderate | 4–7 | flowers; berries |
| *Elaeagnus angustifolia*<br>Russian olive | 20' | fast | 2–10 | silver leaves; reliable; shrub-like |
| *Koelreuteria paniculata*<br>Golden rain tree | 35' | moderate | 5–10 | yellow flowers; irregular shape; hard to transplant |
| *Magnolia soulangiana*<br>Saucer magnolia | 25' | moderate | 5–8 | beautiful bloom; hard to transplant |
| *Magnolia grandiflora*<br>Southern magnolia | 90' | moderate | 7–9 | evergreen; large flowers |
| *Malus* species<br>Crab apple | 10–30' | moderate | 2–8 | beautiful flowers; fruit; reliable |
| *Phellodendron amurense*<br>Amur cork | 35' | fast | 3–6 | low branches; disease-free |
| *Quercus* varieties | | | | hard to transplant; slow-starting, but finally good; subject to insect attacks |
| *Quercus borealis*<br>Red Oak | 75' | slow–moderate | 3–8 | good fall color |
| *Quercus coccinea*<br>Scarlet oak | 75' | slow–moderate | 4–8 | good fall color |
| *Quercus phellos*<br>Willow oak | 75' | moderate | 5–9 | fine-textured leaves; easier to transplant |

**PLANT LIST 7**

# TREES THAT ARE HARD TO TRANSPLANT

*Trees that are difficult to transplant and/or have deep tap roots. Move only in spring.*
*Keep well-watered the first year.*

*\*Arbutus menziesii,* Madrone
*Betulus* species, Birch
*\*Caprinus* species, Hornbeam
*\*Carya* species, Hornbeam
*Crataegus* species, Hawthorn
*\*Fagus* species, Beech
*Gingko* species, Gingko; slow-starting
*\*Julgans* species, Walnut; very slow-starting
*\*Kalopanix pictus,* Castoraralia
*Koelreuteria paniculata,* Golden rain tree
*Lagerstroemia indica,* Crape-myrtle

*Liquidambar styraciflua,* Sweet gum
*Lirodendron tulipfera,* Tulip tree
*\*Magnolia* species, Magnolia
*\*Nyassa sylvatica,* Tupelo
*Prunus* species, Cherry
*\*Pyrus* species, Pear; slow-starting, except Callery pear
*\*Quercus* species, Oak, especially white and black oak
*Sophora japonica,* Sophora
*Stewartia* species, Stewartia
*Ulmus* species, Elm
*Zelkova* species, Zelkova

\* Very sensitive

**PLANT LIST 8**

# COMMONLY USED DECIDUOUS SHRUBS

*Different varieties of each species grow to different heights at maturity.*
*Check the mature height of the variety sold by your nursery.*

| | Size | Rate of Growth | Zone | Description |
|---|---|---|---|---|
| *Berberis* varieties Barberry | 3–10' | fast | 3–10 | reliable; tough, thorny; vigorous habit; berries; fall color |
| *Chaenomeles* varieties Flowering quince | 3–6' | moderate | 4–9 | early flowers; many bright colors; watch for scale |
| *Cornus stolinifera* Red osier dogwood | 7' | fast | 2–9 | red or yellow stems in winter; very invasive though; spreads |
| *Cotoneaster* varieties Cotoneaster | 1–16' | moderate | 3–10 | very useful; sun; attractive leaves; berries; fall color |
| *Cytisus* species Broom | 1–9' | slow | 5–10 | sun; dry soil; yellow flowers; interesting winter shape |
| *Euonymus alata* Burning bush, Winged euonymus | 9' | fast | 3–10 | spectacular fall color; berries; reliable; sun; city-tolerant |
| *Forsythia* varieties Forsythia | 9' | fast | 5–8 | early yellow flowers; good screen plant; vigorous; tough; city-tolerant |
| *Fothergilla* varieties Large fothergilla | 9' | fast | 5–9 | early, fuzzy flowers; upright shape; good fall color |

| | Size | Rate of Growth | Zone | Description |
|---|---|---|---|---|
| *Hibiscus rosa-sinensis*<br>Hibiscus, many colors | 30' | fast | 9–10 | most useful shrub; flowers daily; shears well |
| *Hibiscus syriacus*<br>Althea, Rose of Sharon | 15' | moderate | 5–10 | summer-blooming |
| *Hydrangea* varieties<br>Hydrangea | 3–20' | fast | 4–10 | big flowers; coarse leaves; easy to grow anywhere; some varieties very beautiful |
| *Pyracantha coccinea lalandi*<br>Firethorn | 8' | moderate | 6–9 | beautiful berries; small flowers; needs support; flowers on three-year wood |
| *Rosa* varieties<br>Rose | 3–10' | fast | 3–9 | beautiful flowers; sun; good soil; high maintenance, except for old-fashioned bush varieties |
| *Viburnum* varieties<br>Viburnum, many common names | 5–15' | fast | 5–9 | good flowers; very useful shrubs; good foliage |

## DECIDUOUS SHRUBS
### For Use Where More Choice Varieties Will Not Grow

*These shrubs are very vigorous and will grow almost anywhere.*
*They are not as ornamental as the shrubs listed above.*

| | Size | Rate of Growth | Zone | Description |
|---|---|---|---|---|
| *Ligustrum* varieties<br>Privet | to 30' | fast | 3–9 | planted too often for hedges, where low growth is wanted; useful for tall screen |
| *Lonicera* varieties<br>Bush honeysuckle | 6–15' | fast | 2–8 | reliable flowers; berries; round shape |
| *Philadelphius coronarius*<br>Mock orange | 9' | fast | 4–9 | white fragrant flowers; tough; old-fashioned favorite |
| *Potentilla fruticosa*<br>Bush cinquefoil | 4' | fast | 2–9 | yellow flowers; reliable; dry soil; useful plant for low care; exposed situations |
| *Spirea* varieties<br>Bridal wreath, Spirea | 1–10' | fast | 4–9 | charming flowers; twiggy bush; many varieties available |
| *Syringea* varieties<br>Lilac | 6–20' | fast | 3–9 | beautiful flowers; uninteresting for fifty weeks of the year; reliable; city-tolerant; like lime; French hybrid lilacs are better ornamentals with better blooms and smaller bushes, but are less reliable |
| *Vaccinium* varieties<br>Blueberry | 3–12' | moderate | 3–7 | edible fruit; good fall color; attractive when pruned; acid soil |

**PLANT LIST 9**

# COMMONLY USED LOW EVERGREENS

*Different varieties of each species grow to different heights at maturity.*
*Check the mature height of the variety sold in your nursery.*

| | Size | Rate of Growth | Zone | Description |
|---|---|---|---|---|
| *Albelia grandiflora*<br>Albelia | 3–6' | moderate | 6–10 | neat; drought-resistant;<br>blooms all summer |
| *Arbutus unedo*<br>Strawberry tree | 10–30' | slow | 8–10 | acid soil; attractive flowers, fruit,<br>and bark |
| *Azalea* varieties<br>Azalea, many kinds | 3–10' | slow | 5–9 | acid; peaty soil; beautiful flowers;<br>part shade |
| *Buxus* varieties<br>Common box | 4–20' | slow | 5–10 | splendid green shrub; shears well;<br>shade; formal |
| *Camellia japonica*<br>Camellia | 4–30' | slow | 7–10 | beautiful flowers; acid soil; partial<br>shade |
| *Daphne* varieties<br>Daphne | 1½–6' | slow | 4–8 | temperamental; pink flowers;<br>fragrant; charming shrub |
| *Ilex* varieties<br>Holly | 2–25' | slow | 5–9 | attractive shiny foliage; berries;<br>many varieties need acid soil and<br>shade |
| *Juniperus* varieties<br>Low-spreading juniper | 1–10' | moderate | 2–10 | feathery foliage; many shapes; sun |
| *Kalmia latifolia*<br>Mountain laurel | 20' | slow | 5–9 | good foliage; flowers; acid soil;<br>shade |
| *Leucothoe catesbaei*<br>Drooping leucothos | 5' | moderate | 4–9 | graceful mound of green; shade;<br>green; shade; acid soil |
| *Nandia domestica*<br>Heavenly bamboo | 8' | moderate | 7–10 | flowers; colored foliage; long-lasting<br>fruit |
| *Nerium oleander*<br>Oleander | 20' | fast | 8–10 | good flowers; reliable; sun |
| *Pieris* varieties<br>Andromeda | 4–12' | moderate | 4–9 | very attractive foliage; flowers;<br>shade; acid soil |
| *Pinus mugo mughus*<br>Mugo pine | 3–6' | moderate | 2–9 | attractive; dramatic foliage; full sun;<br>tough |
| *Pittosporum tobira*<br>Pittosporum, Japanese | 10' | fast | 8–10 | attractive foliage; fragrant flowers;<br>stands dry soil |
| *Rhododendron* varieties<br>Rhododendron, many kinds | 3–20' | slow | 4–9 | most beautiful shrubs; flowers<br>impressive; shade; acid soil;<br>buy in bloom for best color |

| | Size | Rate of Growth | Zone | Description |
|---|---|---|---|---|
| Rhododendron, Southern varieties | 7–9' | moderate | 5–8 | less hardy |
| *Taxus* varieties Yew | 1–30' | moderate | 5–8 | best foliage for winter; reliable; shade; no lime; shears well |
| Podocarpus | to 80' shear to keep small | moderate | 9–10 | use Podocarpus for similar foliage effect as yew |

**PLANT LIST 10**

# BEST LOW-GROWING SHRUBS
## For Foundation Planting

| EVERGREEN | Size | Rate of Growth | Zone | Description |
|---|---|---|---|---|
| *Azalea obtusum* and *kaempferi* hybrids *Kurume,* named azaleas | 3' | slow | 6–9 5–9 5–9 | shade; acid soil; pick in bloom for best color; *kaempferi* varieties stand more shade; semi-evergreen |
| *Buxus microphylla koreana* Korean box | 2' | slow | 5–10 | neat mound; shade |
| *Daphne cneorum* Rose daphne | 1½' | slow | 4–8 | fragrant pink flowers; temperamental |
| *Erica carnea* Spring heath | 1' | slow | 5–7 | sandy; acid soil; sun; neat choice plant; pink flowers |
| *Gardenia jasminoides* Cape jasmine | 5' | slow | 8–9 | beautiful; fragrant flowers; good foliage; shade; moisture; acid soil |
| *Ilex crenata convexa* Japanese holly | 6' | slow | 5–9 | neat; glossy foliage; shears well; acid soil; semishade |
| *Ilex helleri* Heller holly | 2' | slow | 5–9 | lovely green mound; acid soil; shade |
| *Ilex vomitoria nana* Dwarf yaupon | 2' | moderate | 8–10 | stands heat; dry soil; reliable; gray-green |
| *Juniperus chinensis pfitzerana compacta* Compact pfitzer juniper | 3' | moderate | 3–10 | feathery foliage; very useful; sun |
| *Juniperus chinensis sargentii* Sargent juniper | 1' | moderate | 4–10 | creeping; attractive; sun |
| *Juniperus horizontalis plumosa* Andorra juniper | 1' | moderate | 2–9 | sun; attractive mound; purple in winter |
| *Leucothoe catesbaei* Drooping leucothoe | 5' | moderate | 4–9 | graceful green mound; acid soil; shade |

| EVERGREEN | Size | Rate of Growth | Zone | Description |
|---|---|---|---|---|
| *Mahonia aquifolium*<br>Oregon grape holly | 3' | slow | 5–10 | dry sandy soil, shade; good foliage; spreads |
| *Pieris floribunda*<br>Mountain andromeda | 3' | moderate | 5–8 | attractive; graceful; acid soil; shade |
| *Pinus mugo mughus*<br>Mugo pine | 6' | moderate | 2–9 | crisp foliage; sun; well-drained soil |
| *Pittosporum tobira*<br>Wheeler's dwarf pittosporum | 3' | moderate | 8–10 | attractive folige; fragrant blossoms; stands dry soil |
| *Rhododendron laetivirens wilsonii*<br>Wilson rhododendron | 3' | slow | 5–9 | pink bloom; small leaf; stands deep shade |
| *Rhododendron PJM*<br>PJM rhododendron (Weston Nurseries, Mass.) | 5' | moderate | 5–8 | blooms very early; purple or pink; stands sun and cold; vigorous |
| *Rhododendron catawbiense compactum*<br>Catawbiense low-growing hybrids | 3' | slow | 5–9 | semishade; some sun; big blooms; choose in bloom for best colors; nonhybrids grow 12' tall |
|     Lees Dark Purple | 4' | slow | 5–9 | purple |
|     Boule de Neige | 6' | slow | 5–9 | best white flowers; semishade; reliable |
|     Nova zembla | 6' | slow | 5–9 | red |
|     Cunningham's White | 4' | slow | 5–9 | white |
|     Chionoides | 4' | slow | 5–9 | white with yellow |
| *Taxus baccata repandens*<br>Spreading English yew | 2' | slow | 4–8 | low-spreading; semishade; no lime; best winter color; useful shrub |
| *Taxus media densiformis*<br>Spreading yew densiform | 5' | slow | 4–8 | bushy; vigorous; most useful; no lime; good winter color; shears well |
| *Taxus media Hicksii*<br>Hicks Yew | 8' | slow | 4–8 | upright; good accent plant; shears well; good winter color; berries; makes a good screen |
| *Thuja occidentalis globosa*<br>Globe arborvitae | 4' | slow | 3–9 | holds round, globe-like shape; bright green |
| *Yucca filamentosa*<br>Adams needle | 3' | moderate | 4–10 | sun; dry conditions; stiff, pointed leaves; 3' flower spike |

| DECIDUOUS | Size | Rate of Growth | Zone | Description |
|---|---|---|---|---|
| *Azaleas mollis* varieties | 5' | slow | 5–9 | yellow; orange blooms; bloom late; acid soil; sun or semishade |
| Exbury hybrids, all others | 3–6' | slow | 5–9 | magnificent colors—yellow, orange, white, brown, pink, red; acid soil; semishade; choose in bloom |
| *Berberis thunbergii atropurpurae nana*<br>Crimson pigmy barberry | 2' | fast | 4–9 | neat shrub; red leaves; thorns; sun |

| DECIDUOUS | Size | Rate of Growth | Zone | Description |
|---|---|---|---|---|
| *Cotoneaster microphylla*<br>Small-leafed cotoneaster | 3' | slow | 4–10 | sun; neat, small leaves; semi-evergreen; good fruit |
| *Fothergilla gardeni*<br>Dwarf fothergilla | 3' | moderate | 5–9 | nice; early bloom; sun; good fall color |
| *Viburnum carlesii*<br>Fragrant viburnum carlesii | 5' | slow | 5–9 | lovely; fragrant flowers; round shrubs |

**PLANT LIST 11**

# SHRUBS THAT GROW IN SHADE
## (Understory Planting)

| | Size | Rate of Growth | Zone | Description |
|---|---|---|---|---|
| *Albelia grandiflora*<br>Glossy albelia | 6' | fast | 5 | good foliage; small flowers |
| *Acanthopanaxa sieboldianus*<br>Acanthopanax | 9' | fast | 4 | good foliage; grows in city |
| *Aronia arbutofolia*<br>Choke cherry | 10' | fast | 4 | dependable; open shape |
| *Azalea kaempferi*<br>Torch azalea | 12' | moderate | 5 | beautiful red-orange flowers; withstands full shade; acid soil |
| *Azalea* varieties<br>Azalea | 3–15' | moderate | 5 | semishade for best bloom; acid soil |
| *Berberis thunbergi*<br>Japanese barberry | 7' | fast | 5 | thorns; dependable; does not carry wheat rust disease |
| *Buxus sempervirens*<br>Common box | 20' | slow | 6 | evergreen; shears well |
| *Calycanthus floridus*<br>Carolina all spice | 9' | moderate | 4 | any soil; fragrant flowers; aromatic leaves |
| *Camellia japonica*<br>Camellia | 40' | slow | 7 | evergreen; beautiful blooms; acid soil |
| *Clethra alnifolia*<br>Summersweet | 9' | fast | 3 | fragrant bloom; moist soil |
| *Daphne mezereum*<br>February daphne | 3' | slow | 4 | flowers; hard to grow; very fragrant |
| *Ilex* varieties<br>Holly | 3–30' | slow | 3–6 | evergreen; attractive; many kinds; acid soil |
| *Hydrangea arborescens*<br>Hills of Snow | 3' | fast | 4 | big; white flowers |

| | Size | Rate of Growth | Zone | Description |
|---|---|---|---|---|
| *Hamemelis* varieties Chinese witch hazel Vernal witch hazel | 10–30' | fast | 5 4 | big bushes; yellow, fragrant flowers fall blooming blooms in February |
| *Kalmia latifolia* Mountain laurel | 15' | slow | 5 | evergreen; flowers; attractive foliage; acid soil |
| *Leucothoe catesbaei* Drooping leucothoe | 6' | moderate | 6 | evergreen; graceful |
| *Mahonia aquifolium* Oregon holly-grape | 3' | moderate | 5 | semi-evergreen; excellent plant; dry sandy soil |
| *Myrica pennsylvanica* Bayberry | 6' | moderate | 2 | semi-evergreen; aromatic berries; sexes separate; sandy soil |
| *Pieris* varieties Andromeda | 3–6' | moderate | 4–7 | evergreen; tolerates heavy shade; acid soil |
| *Rhamnus, frangula* Alder, buckthorn | 12' | fast | 2 | any soil; berries |
| *Rhododendron maximum* Rosebay rhododendron | 35' | moderate | 4 | evergreen; stands heavy shade; good blooms; good foliage which curls at 32° F. |
| *Rhododendron* varieties Rhododendron | 3–15' | moderate | 5–7 | evergreen; variety of flower colors and shapes; acid soil |
| *Symphoricarpos* species Snowberry, Coralberry | 3–6' | moderate | 2 | dull shrubs; reliable; nice berries |
| *Taxus* varieties Yew | 3–50' | slow | 4–7 | evergreen; attractive foliage; good green winter color |
| *Vaccinium corymbosum* Blueberry | 12' | moderate | 3 | good fall color; edible fruit; acid soil |
| *Viburnum sieboldi* Siebold viburnum | 30' | moderate | 4 | attractive foliage; flowers; fruit; useful; vigorous; evergreen |

## PLANT LIST 12

# BEST GROUND COVERS FOR SUN

| EVERGREEN | Size | Planting distance, Spacing | Zone | Description |
|---|---|---|---|---|
| *Ameria maritima* Thrift | 6" | 8" apart | 5–9 | sandy soil; pink flowers |
| *Arctostaphylos uva-ursi* Bearberry | 6" | 2' | 2–9 | sandy; acid soil; red berries; hard to transplant; also grows in semishade |

| EVERGREEN | Size | Planting distance, Spacing | Zone | Description |
|---|---|---|---|---|
| *Cotoneaster apiculata* Cranberry cotoneaster | 3' | 3' | 4–10 | semi-evergreen; red berries; well-drained soil; pink flowers |
| *Cotoneaster adpressa praecox* Early cotoneaster | 1½' | 3' | 5–10 | semi-evergreen; red berries; partial shade in South |
| *Erica carnea* Spring heath | 1' | 1' | 5–7 | sandy; acid soil; neat; rosy blooms |
| *Euonymus fortunei radicans* | 1' | 1½' | 5–9 | attractive foliage; informal in appearance unless sheared; spreads; climbs; very useful; sun or shade |
| *Euonymus fortunei colorata* | 1' | 1½' | 5–9 | same as above but has red-bronze leaves all winter |
| *Gazenia rigens* African daisy | 9" | 9" | 9–10 | charming flowers; well-drained soil |
| *Ice plant* Many Latin names | 1' | 8" | 10 | flowers during day; succulent; sandy soil; spreads; useful for sunny sea coast |
| *Juniperus* low-grading varieties | | | | most maintenance free; neat ground cover for sun; well-drained soil |
| *Juniperus chinensis sargentii* Sargent juniper | 1' | 2' | 4–10 | green; creeping |
| *Juniperus horizontalis plumosa* Andorra juniper | 1' | 2' | 2–9 | purple in winter; low mound |
| *Juniperus horizontalis wiltoni* Blue rug juniper | 1' | 2' | 3–10 | blue color; creeping |
| *Juniperus chinensis pfitzerans compacta* Compact Pfitzer juniper | 3' | 3' | 3–10 | blue-green color; high enough to hide weeds |
| *Juniperus chinensis pfitzerana* Pfitzer juniper | 5' | 4' | 2–10 | gray-green; more vigorous |
| *Juniperus chinensis hetzi glauca* Hetz blue juniper | 6' | 5' | 4–10 | blue-green; very vigorous and spreading |
| *Phlox sublata* Moss pink, Ground phlox | 6" | 1' | 4–10 | creeping; mass of spring bloom; well-drained soil |

| DECIDUOUS | Size | Planting distance, Spacing | Zone | Description |
|---|---|---|---|---|
| *Cerastium tomentosum* Snow-in-Summer | 6" | 1' apart | 4–10 | silvery leaves; white flowers; spreads rapidly; crowds less vigorous flowers |
| *Coronilla varia* Crown vetch | 2' | 2' | 3–9 | pink flowers; good for steep banks; doesn't like acid soil |

| DECIDUOUS | Size | Planting distance, Spacing | Zone | Description |
|---|---|---|---|---|
| *Cotoneaster horizontalis* Rock cotoneaster | 3' | 4' | 5–10 | good fall color; berries; pink flowers; well-drained soil; semishade in South |
| *Cytilsus praecox* Warminster broom | 6' | 3' | 5–10 | upright shrubs; dry sandy soil; early yellow blooms; green twigs in winter |
| *Cytisus hybrids,* Broom 'California,' 'Pomona,' 'San Francisco,' 'Stanford' | 3–6' | 3' | 7–10 | beautiful colors; very good in California; upright |
| *Cytisus nigricans* Spike broom | 3' | 3' | 5–10 | most reliable; yellow flowers; dry black pods; upright; informal appearance |
| *Dicksonia punctilobula* Hay-scented fern | 1¼' | 1' | 6–9 | spreads; tough; feathery; sun or shade |
| *Sedum acre, spurium* and others Stone crop, Sedum | 4" | 8" | 4–10 | semi-evergreen succulents; dense; low mats of foliage; blooms; useful plants; well-drained soil |
| *Thymus serpyllum* Creeping thyme | 4" | 8" | 5–10 | flowers; scented foliage; well-drained soil; attractive mat of foliage; tiny leaves |

**PLANT LIST 13**

# BEST GROUND COVERS FOR SHADE

| EVERGREEN | Size | Planting distance, Spacing | Zone | Description |
|---|---|---|---|---|
| *Ajuga reptans* Bugle weed | 4" | 8" apart | 5–9 | purple flowers; spreads well |
| *Asarum europaeum* Wild ginger | 5" | 8" | 5–8 | glossy, round leaves; woodland soil |
| *Hedera helix baltica* Baltic ivy | 8" | 1' | 5–9 | very neat; attractive foliage; reliable; spreads; formal appearance; no lime |
| *Ophiopogon japonicus* Mondo grass | 8" | 9" | 7–10 | attractive; grasslike foliage; clumps of green; spreads; lilac flower; sun or shade |
| *Pachysandra terminalis* Japanese spurge | 6" | 9" | 5–8 | very neat; attractive; reliable; good soil; spreads vigorously |
| *Vinca minor* periwinkle | 6" | 9" | 5–10 | most attractive leaf; dainty; graceful; spreads; blue flower; well-drained; good soil |

| DECIDUOUS | Size | Planting distance, Spacing | Zone | Description |
|---|---|---|---|---|
| *Convallaria major* Lily-of-the-valley | 10" | 1' | 4–9 | tough; reliable; spreads slowly; most fragrant bloom |
| *Hemerocallis* Day lily | 3' | 1½' | 3–10 | reliable; summer flowers; sun or shade |
| *Hosta* varieties Plantain lily, Funkia | 1½' | 1' | 4–10 | tough; reliable; good soil; will grow under trees where few things will survive; tall summer blooms |

**PLANT LIST 14**

# FAST-GROWING VINES FOR TRELLISES AND FENCES

*NOTE: All vigorous vines MUST be pruned back each spring ot they get out of control and become pests.*

| | Hardy to Zone | Growth in one year | | Description |
|---|---|---|---|---|
| *Actinidia arguta* Bower actinidia | 4 | 15–20' | twining | |
| *Actinidia chinensis* *Chinese actinidia | 7 | 25' | twining | vigorous; will cover 30 x 30 square feet |
| *Bignonia capreolata* Cross vine | 6 | 15' | tendrils | semi-evergreen; flowers |
| *Campensis grandiflora* Chinese trumpet vine | 7 | 5–10' | tendrils | dry soil |
| *Campensis radicans* "Mme. Galens" Trumpet vine | 4 | 10' | tendrils | Both: big flowers; coarse leaves; need tying for support |
| *Clematis paniculata* Sweet autumn clematis | 5 | 15' | twining | fragrant flowers; vigorous; *one of the best* |
| *Clematis vitabella* Traveller's joy | 4 | 20' | twining | fragrant flowers; vigorous |
| *Lonicera japonica* *Fragrant honeysuckle | 4 | 20' | twining | can become a pest if out of control; roots where it touches ground |
| *Lonicera Tellmaniana* Tellmann honeysuckle | 6 | 10' | twining | needs cool roots; better flowers |
| *Lonicera sempervirens* Trumpet honeysuckle | 4 | 10' | twining | big flowers; dry soil; gets aphids |
| *Passiflora* species Passion flowers | 7 | 6–15' | tendrils | fruits edible; flowers; not dense |

| | Hardy to Zone | Growth in one year | | Description |
|---|---|---|---|---|
| *Pueraria Thumbergiana* *Kudzu vine | 6 | 30–50' | twining | fastest grower; can get 75'; coarse leaves; dry soil |
| *Viti coignetiae* *Glory vine | 5 | 40' | tendrils | very rapid grower |
| *Vitis labrusca* "Concord" Concord grape | 3 | 20' | tendrils | good fruit |
| *Wisteria* species *Wisteria | 4–5 | 7' | twining | should be grown on metal pipes— will break wood, gutters, drain- pipes; flowers |

*Vines that *must* be controlled.

PLANT LIST 15

# EVERGREEN VINES FOR THE SOUTH

*For use to provide year-round shade.*

| | Zone | Growth in one year | | Description |
|---|---|---|---|---|
| *Boussingaultia baselloides* *Madeira vine | 9–10 | 4–20' | tendrils | can get out of control |
| *Cobaea scandens* Cup and saucer vine | 9–10 | 6–10' | tendrils | vigorous; can grow to 40' long |
| *Doxantha unguis-cati* *Cat-claw vine | 8–10 | 20' | tendrils with thorns | clings to hot stone or wood |
| *Euonymus fortunei* species Winter creeper | 5–9 | 5' | clinging | |
| *Ficus pumila* Creeping fig | 9–10 | 7' | clinging | figs inedible |
| *Hedera canariensis* Algerian ivy | 7–10 | | clinging | |
| *Smilaw megalantha* Coral greenbriar | 7–10 | | twining | needs male and female plants for fruit |

* Vines that *must* be controlled.

# WINDBREAK PLANTS FOR WIND CONTROL AND SHELTERBELTS ON THE GREAT PLAINS

Shelterbelts should be broadside to the winter wind and long enough to give good protection. Deciduous material grows fastest. For best protection, there should be two or three rows, staggered. One should be tall, fast-growing, deciduous material; the second, evergreen; the third, shrubs and small trees. If small trees are planted inside the shelter belt, protected by the other two, the shelterbelt can be choice flowering material from other lists.

Most of the trees recommended here are not suitable near buildings and should be between 20 to 60 feet from them. The closer the trees are to the buildings, however, the more effective they will be. The trees recommended here will grow quickly, withstand cold, heat, drought, and wind. Many are soft-wooded and may lose branches in storms. In general, the faster a tree grows, the more likely it will be to have soft wood that can break easily in storms. On the Great Plains, where conditions are harsh, shelterbelts give wind protection, privacy, and relief from the boundless open space of the prairies.

*Spacing.* For effective windbreaks, close spacing of plants is necessary. It may be 2, 4, or 6 feet, depending on the species. The aim is a wall of leaves or needles. All plants can be thickened by correct shearing. Closely spaced plants compete for water and nutrients, whose availability limits growth. If the soil is improved at planting time with peat moss, old manure, and fertilizer, the growth rate will be more satisfactory.

| | Size | Spacing | Growth Rate | Zone | Description |
|---|---|---|---|---|---|
| *Acer ginnala* Amur maple | 20' | 4' apart | slow | 2–9 | no care, good fall color |
| *Acer negundo* Box-elder | 60' | 6' | fast | 2–9 | weak-wooded but reliable; can be removed when better trees grow |
| *Amelanchier alnifolia* Saskatoon | 20' | 4' | moderate | 2–7 | good shrub; edible berries; spreads by suckers (gets fire blight and cedar-apple rust) |
| *Caragana arborescens* Siberian pea tree | 18' | 4' | moderate | 2–7 | very hard shrub; drought-resistant |
| *Eleagnus angustifolia* Russian olive | 20' | 6' | fast | 2–10 | silvery leaves; reliable |
| *Fraxinus pennsylvanica* Green ash | 60' | 6' | fast | 2–9 | good shade tree |
| *Juniperus communis* Common juniper | 3–30' | 2' | moderate | 2–6 | evergreen; buy the upright-growing variety |
| *Lonerica tatarica* Tatarian honeysuckle | 9' | 3' | fast | 3–6 | dependable; little flowers |
| *Maclura pomifera* Osage-orange | 60' | 6' | fast | 5–9 | very spreading; thorns; rough |
| *Picea glauca* White spruce | 90' | 6' | slow | 2–5 | evergreen; best evergreen for wind-screen |
| *Picea pungens* Colorado blue spruce | 100' | 6' | moderate | 2–6 | evergreen; best evergreen for windscreen; blue color |
| *Pinus banksiana* Jack pine | 75' | 4' | moderate | 2–8 | evergreen; dry soil; useful where others fail |

|  | Size | Spacing | Growth Rate | Zone | Description |
|---|---|---|---|---|---|
| *Pinus sylvestris*<br>Scotch pine | 70' | 6' | moderate | 2–7 | evergreen; good, wide |
| *Populus* varieties<br>Poplar, cottonwood | 50–100' | 4' | fastest | 2–9 | most versatile; useful tree |
| *Prunus virginiana*<br>Choke cherry | 30' | 4' | fast | 2–9 | birds like the fruit |
| *Quercus macrocarpa*<br>Bur oak | 75' | 12' | slow | 2–9 | broad, hardy tree |
| *Salix alba*<br>White willow, upright | 75' | 6' | fast | 2–7 | prefers moist soil |
| *Shepherdia argentea*<br>Buffalo berry | 18' | 3' | moderate | 2–7 | shrub; tolerant of alkaline soil;<br>likes cool roots |
| *Ulmus pumila*<br>Dwarf elm | 75' | 6' | fast | 2–8 | less susceptible to Dutch elm<br>disease |

**PLANT LIST 17**

# WINDBREAK PLANTS FOR NORMAL SOILS

*Note: All the plants listed under list 16 may also be used.*

|  | Size | Spacing | Growth Rate | Zone | Description |
|---|---|---|---|---|---|
| *Acer* species<br>Maple species | 25–90' | 4' apart | moderate | 2–9 | good trees |
| *Carpinus betulus*<br>European hornbeam | 60' | 4' | slow | 5–9 | neat, attractive tree; shears well |
| *Cornus mas*<br>Cronelian cherry | 24' | 4' | moderate | 4–8 | pest-free; attractive; small flowers;<br>fruit |
| *Crataegus phaenopyrum*<br>Washington hawthorn | 30' | 4' | moderate | 4–7 | flowers; berries |
| *Eucalyptus* species<br>Red, white, or silver<br>dollar gum | 100'+ | 6' | fastest | 9–10 | big trees; effective; not near<br>buildings |
| *Forsythia intermidia*<br>Border forsythia | 9' | 4' | fast | 4–8 | flowers; withstands some shade |
| *Ligustrum amurense*<br>Amur privet | 15' | 2' | fast | 3–6 | shears well; do not use common<br>privet |
| *Ligustrum japonicum*<br>Japanese privet | 6–18' | 3' | fast | 7–9 | evergreen; useful; stands shade |
| *Philadelphus coronaris*<br>Sweet mock-orange | 9' | 3' | fast | 4–9 | fragrant flowers; stands dry soil;<br>stands some shade |

| | Size | Spacing | Growth Rate | Zone | Description |
|---|---|---|---|---|---|
| *Picea abies* Norway spruce | 100' | 6' | fast | 2–6 | excellent evergreen |
| *Pinus nigra* Austrian pine | 90' | 6' | moderate | 4–7 | evergreen; stands alkaline soil, city conditions |
| *Pinus strobus* White pine | 100' | 6' | fast | 3–7 | evergreen; moist, sandy soil; beautiful tree |
| *Quercus imbricaria* Shingle oak | 75' | 12' | slow | 5–8 | holds some dry leaves in winter; shears well |
| *Rhamnus frangula columnaris* Tall hedge buckthorn | 12' | 2' | fast | 2–8 | narrow; upright; vigorous shrub; makes a tight hedge with little shearing; stays 12' high |
| *Syringa amurensis* Japanese lilac tree | 30' | 4' | fast | 4–7 | good flowers; attractive |
| *Syringa vulgaris* Common lilac | 20' | 2' | fast | 3–7 | hardy; reliable; fragrant blooms |
| *Tilia cordata* "Greenspire" Greenspire little leaf linden | 40' | 4' | moderate | 3–7 | good shape; nice foliage; upright; buy low-branched specimens for windbreaks |
| *Viburnum prunifolium* Blackhaw | 15' | 3' | fast | 3–7 | flowers; berries |
| *Viburnum sieboldi* Siebold viburnum | 30' | 4' | fast | 4–8 | vigorous; attractive; modest flowers; berries |

**PLANT LIST 18A - FOR DRY DESERT AREAS AND XERISCAPING**

# DROUGHT-RESISTANT PLANTS

**Plants for the Southwest Desert**

| Alkaline soil-resistant | Hardy to Zone |
|---|---|
| Agave | 7 |
| Boojam tree | 7 |
| Brittlebush | 7 |
| Cacti | 6 |
| Catclaw (acacia) | 7 |
| Creosote bush | 7 |
| Hackberry, spiny | 6 |
| Jojoba | 7 |
| Mesquite | 6 |
| Ocotillo | 7 |
| Paloverde | 7 |
| Sotol | 7 |
| Tesota | 7 |
| Yucca | 5 |

**Plants for Areas with Less Than 10" of Rainfall**

| Alkaline soil-resistant | Hardy to Zone |
|---|---|
| One-seed juniper | 4 |
| Rocky mountain juniper | 3 |
| Apache plume | 4 |
| Bitterbush, Antelope | 4 |
| Desert willow | 6 |
| Fontanesia, Fortune | 6 |
| Forestiera, New Mexican | 4 |
| Golden rain tree | 5 |
| Leadplant | 4 |
| Rabbitbrush | 3 |
| Sagebrush | 4 |
| Saltbrush | 4 |
| Tamarix, Athel | 8 |

## Drought-Resistant Plants

| Withstand dry soil | **Hardy to Zone** |
|---|---|
| **TREES–BROADLEAFED** | |
| Acacia, gossamer Sydney | 10 |
| Ailanthus (tree of heaven) | 4 |
| Albizia, silk tree (mimosa) | 6* |
| Angelica tree (aralia) | 2 |
| Ash, green, European mountain | 4* |
| velvet | 7 |
| Australian tea tree | 9 |
| Bauhinia | 10 |
| Birch, cutleaf weeping | 4* |
| grey | 5 |
| Box-elder | 2 |
| Bottle-tree (brachychiton) | 10 |
| Buckeye | 4* |
| Carob | 10 |
| Chinaberry (melia) | 7 |
| Cottonwood | 3* |
| Crab apple, flowering | 3* |
| Elm, Siberian (stands alkaline soil) | 2* |
| most resistant to Dutch elm disease | |
| Eucalyptus | 9 |
| Fig (*ficus* species) | 6–10 |
| Golden rain tree | 5* |
| Grevillea | 10 |
| Hackberry | 3* |
| Honey locust, thornless | 4* |
| Jerusalem thorn (parkinsonia) | 9 |
| Jujube | 5* |
| Linden | 4 |
| Locust, black | 5* |
| Maple, amur, silver | 3* |
| Manchurian, tatarian | 4* |
| Norway | 4 |
| Melaleuca (cajeput) | 10 |
| Mesquite | 8* |
| Mulberry | 6* |
| Oak, California black, live | 7* |
| chestnut | 4* |
| pin | 4 |
| red | 3 |
| burr | 2* |
| Olive | 9* |
| Osage orange (maclura) | 5 |
| Pecan | 6 |
| Pepper tree (schinus) | 9* |
| Poplar, white | 3 |
| Redbud, eastern | 5 |
| Russian olive (tolerates alkaline soil) | 3* |
| Sophora | 4 |
| Sycamore | 5* |
| Walnut, black | 4* |
| **SHRUBS** | |
| Almond, Russian, prairie | 3* |
| Autumn sage | 7 |
| Beauty bush | 7* |

## Drought-Resistant Plants

| Withstand dry soil | **Hardy to Zone** |
|---|---|
| Barberry, Japanese, Mentor | 5 |
| Broom (Acid soil) | 6 |
| Bayberry (Acid Soil) | 2 |
| Bottlebrush, lemon | 9 |
| Buckthorn, common, rock, Duhurian | 2* |
| Buffalo-berry, Canada russet | 2* |
| (stands alkaline soil) | |
| Butcher's broom (ruscus) | 7 |
| Butterfly bush, fountain | 5* |
| Ceanothus, inland | 4** |
| Chaste-tree, cut-leafed | 5* |
| Cherry, western, sand | 3 |
| Dogwood, Siberian | 3* |
| gray | 4 |
| Elderberry, blueberry | 5* |
| Euphorbia, milkbush | 10** |
| Firethorn, laland | 5* |
| Forsythia | 5* |
| Greasewood | 4* |
| Hawthorn, cockspur, downey, English | 4* |
| Hebe, species | 7 |
| Honeysuckle, tatarian, Zabel | 3* |
| amur | 4* |
| winter | 5* |
| Lilac, late (villosa) | 2* |
| common | 3* |
| Japanese tree | 4* |
| Persian | 5* |
| Mock-orange, virginal, sweet | 5* |
| Mountain mahogany | 4** |
| Ninebark | 2 |
| Oleander | 7 |
| Peach, pigmy, globe Russian, Siberian | 5* |
| Pea shrub (pea tree), Siberian, maximowicz | 2* |
| little leaf, pygmaea | 3* |
| Pittosporum | 8 |
| Plum, flowering, Newport, beach | 3* |
| Privet | 3* |
| Quince, flowering, Japanese | 5* |
| Rose, Austrian copper, Harrison's yellow | 3* |
| Rosemary | 6 |
| Rosewood, Arizona | 6** |
| Serviceberry, shadblow, saskatoon | 3* |
| Smoke tree | 5* |
| Snowberry | 4** |
| Sophora, vetch | 5 |
| Spirea, Nippon, Vanhoutte | 4* |
| Sumac | 2* |
| Tamarix, five stamen | 2 |
| parvifolio, Odessa | 4* |
| kasgar | 6** |
| Viburnum, nannyberry, cranberry bush | 2* |
| Manchurian | 2* |
| snowball | 4 |
| Wayfaring tree (*lantana rugosum*) | 3* |
| Yucca | 4** |

* 10 to 20 inches rainfall     ** less than 10 inches rainfall

`LIST 18B`

# ANNUAL RAINFALL OF PLANTS
# IN THEIR NATIVE HABITAT[†]

| Vegetation Class* | Tree species and genus | Annual precipitation (inches) | Vegetation Class* | Tree species and genus | Annual precipitation (inches) |
|---|---|---|---|---|---|
| T | Carpobrotus chilensis | 10.2 | T | Jacaranda mimosifolia | 20.4 |
| T | Carpobrotus edulis | 20.0 | T | Koelreuteria bipinnata (elegans) | 19.3 |
| T | Casuarina cunninghamiana | 23.0 | T | Koelreuteria paniculata | 43.1 |
| T | Casuarina equisetifolia | 41.0 | T | Lagunaria patersonii | 52.4 |
| T | Casuarina stricta | 23.0 | T | Leptosperman laevigatum | 46.5 |
| T | Cedrus deodora | 9.7 | T | Ligustrum japonicum | 46.3 |
| T | Ceratonia siliqua | 25.7 | T | Liquidambar styraciflua | 52.0 |
| T | Chorisa specios | 65.8 | T | Magnolia grandiflora | 50.8 |
| T | Cinnamomum camphora | 52.6 | T | Melaleuca linariifolia | 46.5 |
| T | Cupaniopsis anacardiopsis | 44.7 | T | Melaleuca quinquenervia | 44.7 |
| T | Eriobotrya deflexa | 84.8 | T | Olea europaea | 23.3 |
| T | Erythrina caffra | 8.9 | T | Photinia serrulata | 43.1 |
| T | Eucalyptus camaldulensis | 21.1 | T | Pinus canariensis | 3.9 |
| T | Eucalyptus citriodora | 39.6 | T | Pinus halepensis | 25.4 |
| T | Eucalyptus cladocalyx | 9.4 | T | Pinus Pinea | 35.6 |
| T | Eucalyptus ficifolia | 39.7 | T | Pittosporum phillyraeoides | 9.7 |
| T | Eucalyptus globulus | 24.0 | T | Pittosporum viridiflorum | 30.9 |
| T | Eucalyptus grandis | 44.7 | T | Platanus acerifolia | 19.2 |
| T | Eucalyptus lahmannii | 22.4 | T | Platanus racemosa | 14.1 |
| T | Eucalyptus leucoxylon | 17.7 | T | Podocarpus gracilior | 38.2 |
| T | Eucalyptus maculata | 37.2 | T | Podocarpus macrophyllus | 124.8 |
| T | Eucalyptus nicholii | 36.5 | GC | Delosperma "Alba" | 31.8 |
| T | Eucalyptus polyanthemos | 23.0 | GC | Hedera canariensis | 15.9 |
| T | Eucalyptus robusta | 59.3 | GC | Hedera helix | 25.7 |
| T | Eucalyptus rudis | 10.1 | GC | Vinca major | 25.7 |
| T | Eucalyptus sideroxylon | 21.8 | S | Acacila cyclops | 9.9 |
| T | Eucalyptus viminalis | 26.4 | S | Albelia grandiflora | 43.1 |
| T | Ficus benjamina | 63.0 | S | Arctostaphylos densiflora | 15.8 |
| T | Ficus macrophylla | 40.0 | S | Arctostaphylos hookeri | 29.8 |
| T | Ficus rubiginosa | 21.8 | S | Baccharis pilularis "Twin Peaks" | 39.6 |
| T | Fraxinus uhdei | 39.5 | S | Baccharis pilularis "Pigeon Point" | 39.6 |
| T | Fraxinus velutina | 21.9 | S | Carissa grandiflora | 39.7 |
| T | Geijera parviflora | 19.2 | S | Ceanothus "Concha" | 14.2 |
| T | Ginkgo biloba | 44.7 | S | Ceanothus "Joyce Coulter" | 14.3 |
| T | Gleditsia triacanthos | 49.1 | S | Ceanothus cyaneus | 9.5 |
| T | Grevillea robusta | 46.5 | S | Ceanothus griseus horizontalis | 12.3 |

| Vegetation Class* | Tree species and genus | Annual precipitation (inches) | Vegetation Class* | Tree species and genus | Annual precipitation (inches) |
|---|---|---|---|---|---|
| S | Cistus crispus | 25.4 | T | Tristania conferta | 41.0 |
| S | Cistus ladanifer | 16.5 | T | Ulmus parvifolia | 15.9 |
| S | Cistus pupureus | 16.5 | T | Viburnum tinus | 25.4 |
| S | Coprosma baueris (C. repens) | 60.5 | T(P) | Archontophoenix cunninghamiana | 66.5 |
| S | Dodonaea viscosa | 24.0 | T(P) | Butia capitata | 40.1 |
| S | Echium fastuosum | 21.5 | T(P) | Chamaerops humilis | 15.4 |
| S | Elaegnus pungens | 42.5 | T(P) | Phoenix reclinata | 35.1 |
| S | Encelia californica | 12.3 | T(P) | Washingtonia filifera | 3.3 |
| S | Escallonia rubra | 14.1 | T(P) | Washingtonia robusta | 8.4 |
| S | Grevillia lanigera | 26.8 | T(P) | Callistemon citrinus | 44.7 |
| S | Heteromeles arbutifolia | 43.3 | T,S | Callistemon viminalis | 41.0 |
| S | Jasminum humile | 9.1 | T,S | Feijoa sellowiana | 65.8 |
| S | Lantana camarar | 71.3 | T,S | Hakea suaveolens | 11.4 |
| S | Leptospermum scoparium | 36.9 | T,S | Laurus nobilis | 16.5 |
| S | Myrtus communis | 20.0 | T,S | Melaleuca armillaris | 29.5 |
| S | Pittosporum tobira | 44.7 | T,S | Melaleuca nesophylla | 26.4 |
| S | Plumbago auriculata | 36.8 | T,S | Metrosideros excelsus | 49.1 |
| S | Psidium littorale | 53.1 | T,S | Myoporum laetum | 35.1 |
| S | Rhamnus califqrnica "Eve Case" | 14.2 | T,S | Nerium oleander | 23.2 |
| S | Rhus intergrifolia | 15.6 | T,S | Pittosporum crassifolium | 35.1 |
| S | Ribes viburnifolium | 15.6 | T,S | Pittosporum undulatum | 46.5 |
| S | Rosmarinus officinalis | 23.2 | T,S | Prunus caroliniana | 52.0 |
| S | Syzygium paniculatum | 44.7 | T,S | Prunus ilicifolia | 14.2 |
| S | Tecomaria capensis | 8.9 | T,S | Prunus lusitanica | 32.3 |
| S | Viburnum japonicum | 82.8 | T,S | Prunus lyonii | 31.2 |
| T | Acacia baileyana | 23.0 | T,S | Psidium guajava | 53.1 |
| T | Acacia melanoxylon | 55.3 | T,S | Schinus terebinthifolius | 54.5 |
| T | Acacia pendula | 23.0 | T,S | Xylosma congestum | 42.2 |
| T | Agonis flexuosa | 38.9 | T | Acacia "Pecoffverde" | 10.2 |
| T | Albizia julibrisson | 46.4 | T | Acacia rosmarinifolia | 9.1 |
| T | Alnus rhombifolia | 42.6 | V | Bougainvillea glabra | 53.1 |
| T | Araucaria bidwillii | 69.8 | V | Bougainvillea spectabilis | 53.1 |
| T | Arbutus unedo | 23.3 | V | Cissus antarctica | 46.5 |
| T | Brachychition acerifolius | 26.1 | V | Lonicera japonica "Halliana" | 43.1 |
| T | Brachychition populneum | 23.0 | V | Parthenocissus tricuspidata | 52.6 |
| T | Pyrus calleryana | 36.8 | V | Wisteria sinensis | 27.3 |
| T | Quercus agrifolia | 12.3 | | | |
| T | Quercus ilex | 25.4 | | Average of all plants | 32.96 |
| T | Quercus suber | 23.2 | | Max | 124.80 |
| T | Schinus molle | 28.2 | | Min | 3.34 |

+All of these plants are growing in Orange County, California. Some are frost hardy, most are not.

*Vegetation Classes: GC = groundcover, S = shrub, T = tree, T(P) = Palm, V = vine

**PLANT LIST 19**

# SEQUENCE OF BLOOM—SHRUBS AND TREES

*Indicated blooming dates are the approximate ones for Plant Hardiness Zone 5.*
*For more northerly areas, add about one week per zone; subtract for more southerly zones.*

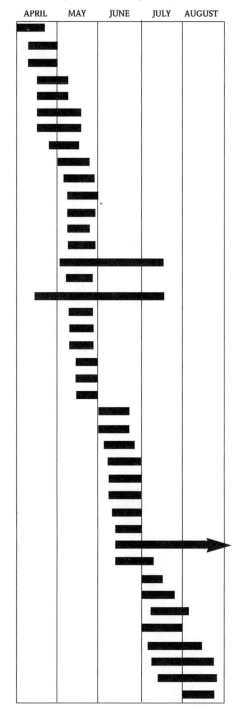

| | APRIL | MAY | JUNE | JULY | AUGUST |
|---|---|---|---|---|---|

Andromeda (*Pieris japonica, P. floribunda*), white
*Shadblow, Serviceberry (*Amalanchier canadensis*), white
*Star magnolia (*Magnolia stellata*), white
Forsythia (*Forsythia* species)
Korean azalea (*Rhodendron macronultaum*)
*Saucer magnolia (*Magnolia soulangeana*), white pink
*Weeping cherry (*Prunus subhirtella*), pink
*Beach plum (*Prunus maritami*), white
Quince (*Chaenomeles lagenaria*), orange, pink, white
*Crab apple (*Malus species*), white, pink
*Dogwood (*Carnus florida*), white, pink
*Kwansan cherry (*Prunus serrulata "Kwansan"*), pink
*English hawthorn (*Crataegus oxycantha*), pink, white
*Redbud (*Circus canadensis*), pink
Azalea (varieties), all colors
Bridal wreath (*Spirea prunifolia plena*), white
Rhododendron (varieties), all colors
Lilac (*Syringa* vulgaris), purple, white
Mayflower (*Viburnum* carlesii), white
Warminster broom (*Cytisus praecox*), white
*Golden chain tree (*Laburnum watereri*), yellow
*Mountain silverbell (*Halesia monticola*), white
*Horse chestnut (*Aesculus hippocastanum, A. carnea*), white, red
*Fringe tree (*Chionanthus virginicus*), white
*Yellow-wood (*Cladrastis lutea*), yellow-white
Mountain laurel (*Kalmia latifolia*), white, pink
*Japanese dogwood (*Cornus kousa*), white
*Japanese lilac tree (*Syringa amurensis*), white
*Washington hawthorn (*Crataegus*), white, pink
*American smoke tree (*Cotinus americanus*), purple, bronze
Mock-orange (*Philadelphus* varieties), white
Rose (*Rosa* varieties), all colors
*Catalpa (*Catalpa speciosa*), white
Hills of Snow hydrangea (*H. arborescens grandiflora*), white
*Golden rain tree (*Koelreuteria paniculata*), yellow
French or house hydrangea (*H. macrophylla*), blue
*Japanese stewartia (*Stewartia psuedocamellia*), white
*Japanese pagoda tree, Sophora (*S. japonica*), whitish
*Silk tree (*Albizia julibrisson rosea*), pink
Althea (*hibiscus syriacus*), pink, white, red
Peegge hydrangea (*H. grandiflora*), white-pink

*Trees

# GROWTH RATE COMPARISON
# OF SELECTED TREES

**Height in ten years**

| | |
|---|---|
| eucalyptus | 40 feet |
| plane | 36 feet |
| willow | 35 feet |
| silver maple | 30 feet |
| thornless honey locust | 30 feet |
| tulip tree | 27 feet |
| green ash | 28 feet |
| linden | 25 feet |
| sugar maple | 25 feet |
| Norway maple | 18 feet |
| sweet gum | 21 feet |
| hawthorn and dogwood | 20 feet |

**Height in ten years**

| | |
|---|---|
| callery pear | 20 feet |
| pin oak | 25 feet |
| red oak | 20 feet |
| live oak | 15 feet |
| horse chestnut | 15 feet |
| amur cork | 17 feet |
| white pine | 25 feet |
| Norway spruce | 25 feet |
| blue spruce | 20 feet |
| hemlock | 17 feet |
| casaurina | 35 feet |

# SALT SENSITIVITY

*Salt is a problem both on winter roads and from ocean spray at the seashore.*

| Salt Sensitive | Salt Tolerant |
|---|---|
| hemlock | white spruce |
| white pine | Austrian pine |
| sugar, red maple | Japanese black pine |
| pin oak | sycamore maple |
| American linden | red oak, black oak |
| ironwood | willow |
| | birch |
| | black cherry |
| | Russian olive |
| | sophora |

## PLANT LIST 22

# pH PREFERENCES OF SOME USEFUL PLANTS

These are the limits between which these plants grow best. When a plant is growing outside of its preferred pH, uptake of certain trace elements (minerals) may be limited, resulting in slower growth. Trace element deficiency symptoms, such as stunted growth, abnormal leaf colorations, and brown tips, among others, can be improved by correcting the pH. Some plants are more sensitive than others to their pH. For instance, pin oak and citrus develop yellow leaves (chlorosis) if the soil rises much above pH 7, and a variety of hydrangea flowers pink in alkaline soil but blue in acidic soil.

| | | | | | |
|---|---|---|---|---|---|
| Acacia | Acacia species | 6–8 | Coneflower | Rudbeckia, many species | 6–8 |
| Alyssum | Alyssum species | 6–8 | Coreopsis | Coreopsis, many species | 5.5–6.5 |
| Amaryllis | Amaryllis | 5–6 | Cotoneaster | Cotoneaster, species | 6–8 |
| American Plum | Prunus americana | 6–8 | Cranesbill | Geranium, many species | 6–8 |
| Apple | Malus species | 5.5–6.5 | Cucumber | Cucumis sativus | 6–8 |
| Aralia | Aralia, most species | 6–8 | Cypress | Chamaecyparis | 5–6 |
| Arborvitae | Thuja, many species | 6–8 | Daffodil | Daffodil species | 6–6.5 |
| Arrow Bamboo | Arundinaria japonica | 6–8 | Dahlia | Dahlia species | 6–8 |
| Ash | Fraxinus, many species | 6–8 | Dahoon | Ilex cassine | 5–6 |
| Asparagus | Asparagus species | 6–7 | Daylily | Hemerocallis, species | 6–8 |
| Aster | Aster species | 5–8 | Dogwood, Flowering | Cornus florida | 6–7 |
| Avocado | Persea americana | 6–8 | Douglas fir | Pseudotsuga douglasi | 6–7 |
| Azalea | Azalea | 5–6 | Eggplant, Common | Salanum melongena | 6–7 |
| Barberry | Berberis species | 6–8 | Elm | Ulmus species | 6–8 |
| Bayberry | Myrica | 5–6 | Eucalyptus | Eucalyptus species | 6–8 |
| Bean | Phaseolus | 5.5–7.5 | Euonymus | Euonymus species | 6–8 |
| Beech | Fagus | 6–7 | Everlasting, Pearl | Anaphalis margaritacea | 5–6 |
| Beet | Beta vulgaris | 5.8–7 | Fern, Asparagus | | 6–8 |
| Begonia | Begonia species | 6–8 | Ferns | Each species is different | 4–8 |
| Bellflower | Campanula, many species | 6–8 | Fir | Abies species | 5–6 |
| Birch, Sweet | Betula lenta | 5–6 | Forget-me-not | Myosotis, many species | 6–8 |
| Bleeding Heart, Fringed | Dicentra eximia | 5–6 | Forsythia | Forsythia species | 6–8 |
| Blueberry | Vaccinium | 5–6 | Foxglove | Digitalis species | 6–8 |
| Box, Common | Buxus sempervirens | 6–8 | Gaillardia | Gaillardia species | 6–8 |
| Broccoli, Cabbage | Brassica oleracea | 6–7 | Gardenia | Gardenia | 5.5–6.5 |
| Broom, Scotch | Cytisus scoparius | 5–6 | Geranium | Pelargonium | 6–8 |
| Buckeye | Aesculus species | 6–8 | Gingko | Gingko biloba | 6–7 |
| Buttercup | Ranunculus, many species | 6–8 | Ginseng, American | Panax quinquefolium | 6–8 |
| Butterflybush | Buddleia species | 6–8 | Gladiolus | Gladiolus, many species | 6–8 |
| Camellia | Camellia, many species | 4–5.5 | Goldenrod | Solidago, many species | 6–8 |
| Candytuft | Iberis sempervirens | 6–7 | Grape | Vitis, some species | 6–8 |
| Canna | Canna species | 6–8 | Groundcedar, | Lycopodium | 5–6 |
| Carnation | Dianthus caryophyllus | 6–8 | Groundpine | | |
| Carrot | Daucus carota | 5.5–6.5 | Gypsophila | Gypsophila species | 6–8 |
| Cherry | Prunus species | 6–8 | Hawthorn | Crataegus, many species | 6–8 |
| Chive | Allium schoenoprasum | 6–7 | Heath | Erica | 5–6 |
| Chrysanthemum | Chrysanthemum species | 6–8 | Heather | Calluna vulgaris | 5–6 |
| Cinquefoil | Potentilla, many species | 6–8 | Hemlock | Tsuga | 5–6 |
| Cinquefoil, Wineleaf | Potentilla tridenta | 4–5 | Holly, Inkberry | Ilex glabra | 4–5 |
| Clematis | Clematis, many species | 6–8 | Holly, American | Ilex opaca | 5–6 |
| Clethra | Clethra | 5–6 | Honeylocust | Gleditsia, most species | 6–8 |
| Clover | Trifolium, many species | 6–7 | Honeysuckle | Lonicera, many species | 6–8 |
| Columbine | Aquilegia, many species | 6–7 | Hydrangea | Hydrangea species | 6–8 |

| | | | | | | |
|---|---|---|---|---|---|---|
| Hydrangea, Blue | acid soil makes the flower blue | 5–6 | Petunia | Petunia hybrida | 6–8 |
| Iris | Iris, many species | 6–8 | Phlox, Garden | Phlox paniculata | 6–8 |
| Iris, Japanese | Iris kaempferi | 5–6 | Phlox, Creeping | Phlox stolonifera | 5–6 |
| Iris, Blueflag | Iris carolina | 5–6 | Pine | Pinus, most species | 5–6 |
| Jack-in-the-pulpit | Arisaema stewardsoni | 5–6 | Planetree | Platanus species | 6–8 |
| Jersey tea | Ceanothus americanus | 5–6 | Plum | Prunus species | 6–8 |
| Juniper | Juniperus, many species | 5–7 | Poinsettia | Euphorbia pulcherrima | 6–8 |
| Kalmia, Bog | Kalmia polifolia | 4–5 | Poplar | Populus species | 6–8 |
| Kerria | Kerria, many species | 6–8 | Potato | Solanum tuberosum | 4.8–6.5 |
| Laburnum | Laburnum, many species | 6–8 | Privet | Ligustrum species | 6–8 |
| Lambkill | Kalmia angustifolia | 5–6 | Radish | Raphanus sativus | 6–8 |
| Larch | Larix, many species | 5.5–6.5 | Raspberry | Rubus idaeus | 5–6 |
| Larkspur | Delphinium, many species | 6–8 | Redbud | Cercis species | 6–8 |
| Lemon | Citrus limonia | 5.5–6.5 | Redcedar | Juniperus virginiana | 6–7 |
| Lettuce | Lactuca sativa | 6–7 | Rhododendron | Rhododendron | 5–6 |
| Leucothoe | Leucothoe | 5–6 | Rose | Rosa, many species | 6–8 |
| Lilac | Syringa species | 6–8 | Rosemallow | Hibiscus | 6–8 |
| Lily | Lilium, many | 5–6 | Sage | Salvia, many species | 6–8 |
| Linden | Tilia species | 6–8 | Shadblow | Amelanchier | 6–7 |
| Lupine | Lupinus hirsutus and perennis | 5–6.5 | Snapdragon | Antirrhinum | 6–7 |
| Lungwort | Pulmonaria species | 6–8 | Sourwood | Oxydendron arboreum | 4–8 |
| Magnolia | Magnolia (except M. glauca) | 5–6 | Spinach, Common | Spinacia oleracea | 6.5–7 |
| Maple | Acer | 5–8 | Spirea | Spirea, many species | 6–8 |
| Marjoram | Origanum species | 6–8 | Springbeauty | Claytonia caroliniana | 5–6 |
| Mint | Mentha, many species | 6–8 | Spruce | Picea | 5–6 |
| Mountain-ash American | Sorbus americana | 4–5 | Squash | Curcurbita maxima | 6–8 |
| | | | Stewartia, Mountain | Stewartia pentagyna | 5–6 |
| Mountain-ash European | Sorbus aucuparia | 6–8 | Stonecrop | Sedum, many varieties | 6–8 |
| | | | St. Johnswort | Hypericum, many species | 6–8 |
| Mountain Laurel | Kalmia latifolia | 5–6 | Strawberries | Fragaria, most species | 5–7 |
| Mulberry | Morus, many species | 6–8 | Sundrops | Oenothera glauca | 5–6 |
| Narcissus | Narcissus species | 6–8 | Sunflower | Helianthus | 6–8 |
| Nasturtium | Tropaeolum species | 6–8 | Sweetgum | Liquidambar styraciflua | 6–7 |
| Ninebark | Physocarpus species | 6–8 | Sweetshrub | Calycanthus species | 6–8 |
| Oak, Black | Quercus velutina | 5–7 | Tamarix | Tamarix species | 6–8 |
| Oak, English | Quercus robur | 6–8 | Tomato | Lycopersicum esculentum | 6–7 |
| Oak, Pin | Quercus palustris | 6–7 | Trumpet Vine | Bignonia species | 6–8 |
| Oak, Post | Quercus stellata | 5–6 | Tuliptree | Liriodendron tulipifera | 6–7 |
| Oak, Red | Quercus rubra | 6–7 | Tupelo | Nyssa sylvatica | 6–7 |
| Oak, Scarlet | Quercus coccinea | 6–7 | Verbena | Verbena species | 6–8 |
| Oak, scrub | Quercus ilicifolia | 4–5 | Viburnum | Viburnum species | 6–8 |
| Oak, Southern Red | Quercus falcata | 5–6 | Violet | Viola | 5–8 |
| Oak, White | Quercus alba | 5.5–7 | Walnut | Juglans | 6–8 |
| Oak, Willow | Quercus phellos | 5–6 | Watermelon | Citrillus vulgaris | 6–7 |
| Onion | Allium, many species | 6–7 | Weigela | Weigela species | 6–8 |
| Orange | Citrus sinensis | 5–7 | Wheat | Triticum aestivum | 6–7 |
| Oxalis | Oxalis, many species | 6–8 | Willow | Salix species | 6–8 |
| Pachysandra, Japanese | Pachysandra terminalis | 5–8 | Winter Jasmine | Jasminum nudiflorum | 6–8 |
| Parsley | Petroselinum hortense | 5–7 | Wisteria | Wisteria species | 6–8 |
| Passionflower | Passiflora species | 6–8 | Witch-hazel | Hamamelis species | 6–7 |
| Paulownia | Paulownia tomentosa | 6–8 | Woodbine | Lonicera periclymenum | 6–7 |
| Pea, Common | Pisum sativum | 6–8 | Wormwood | Artemisia species | 6–8 |
| Peach | Amygdalus species | 6–8 | Yew | Taxus, many species | 5.5–7 |
| Peony | Paeonia species | 6–8 | Yucca | Yucca, many species | 6–8 |
| Periwinkle | Vinca species | 6–8 | Zinnia | Zinnia elegans | 6–8 |

# *Appendix*

## RESOURCE FILE FOR FURTHER READING AND RESEARCH

*Cooling Our Communities*, U.S. Environmental Protection Agency, Editors Hashem Akbari et al, January 1992, GPO Document #055-000-00371-8, Superintendent of Documents, P.O. Box 371954, Pittsburgh, PA 15220-7054, ATTN: New Orders. This publication goes into more statistical detail about energy saving stratagems, and is most useful for warm areas. It has a complete reference list of articles, books, and publications on energy saving.

*Urban Forests* and *American Forests*, publications of the American Forestry Association, P.O. Box 2000, Washington, D.C. 20013. These magazines cover issues of energy saving, tree planting and survival, as well as community reforestation programs such as "Global Releaf." *Tree City, USA, Bulletin*, published by The National Arbor Day Foundation, 100 Arbor Avenue, Nebraska City, NE 68410, has a long list of free bulletins that cover most tree maintenance in great detail.

Each state has Department of Agriculture extension agents. These professionals are a veritable treasure house of technical information on all subjects and have numerous useful publications.

Horticultural Societies and Botanical Gardens exist in many states and have excellent programs in gardening. *North American Horticultural*, by Thomas M. Barrett, Macmillan and Company, is a reference guide to all organizations involved in horticulture.

National plant societies exist for many individual species, among them:

National Wildflower Research Center, 2600 FM 973 North, Austin, TX 78725

American Rose Society, P.O. Box 30,000, Shreveport, LA 71130

American Rhododendron Society, P.O. Box 1380 Gloucester, VA 23061

A useful catalogue for hardy rhododendrons and azaleas (Zones 5 and 6) is Weston Nurseries, Box 186, East Main Street, Hopkinton, MA 01748, for whom the PJM rhododendron is named.

A useful manual for pruning plants is *All About Pruning* by Ortho Books.

*Wyman's Gardening Encyclopedia*, by Donald Wyman, Macmillan and Company, is a classic reference.

# *Index*

# Gardening

From lush picture books to no-nonsense practical manuals, here is a variety of beautifully produced titles on many aspects of gardening. Each of the gardening books listed is by an expert in his or her field and will provide hours of gardening enjoyment for expert and novice gardeners. Please check your local bookstore for other fine Globe Pequot Press titles, which include:

Beautiful Easy Gardens, $24.95; paper, $15.95

The Victory Garden Kids' Book, $15.95

Beautiful Easy Lawns and Landscapes, $24.95; paper, $15.95

Efficient Vegetable Gardening, $14.95

The Naturalist's Garden, $15.95

The Wildflower Meadow Book, $16.95

The National Trust Book of Wild Flower Gardening, $25.95

Garden Flower Folklore, $19.95

Wildflower Folklore, $23.95; paper, $14.95

Folklore of Trees and Shrubs, $24.95

Herbs, $19.95

Dahlias, $19.95

Rhododendrons, $19.95

Fuchsias, $19.95

Climbing Roses, $19.95

Modern Garden Roses, $19.95

Azaleas, $19.95

Auriculas, $19.95

Magnolias, $19.95

The Movable Garden, $15.95

Garden Smarts, $12.95

Simple Garden Projects, $19.95

Windowbox Gardening, $22.95

Perennial Gardens, $17.95

To order any of these titles with MasterCard or Visa, call toll-free 1-800-243-0495; in Connecticut call 1-800-962-0973. Free shipping for orders of three or more books. Shipping charge of $3.00 per book for one or two books ordered. Connecticut residents add sales tax. Ask for your free catalogue of Globe Pequot's quality books on recreation, travel, nature, gardening, cooking, crafts, and more. Prices and availability subject to change.